The Catherine Cookson Companion

The novels of Catherine Cookson are the most borrowed books in Britain. The latest novel is usually at the top of the reserves list in any public library.

The Catherine Cookson Companion

Cliff Goodwin

Tyne Bridge Publishing

To
Catherine Cookson

"Spellbinder in person to her friends.
Spellbinder to millions through her books."

&

Tom Cookson

©Cliff Goodwin, 1999

Published by
Tyne Bridge Publishing
City of Newcastle upon Tyne
Education & Libraries Directorate
Newcastle Libraries & Information Service

ISBN: 1 85795 1050

British Library Cataloguing-in-Publication Data: A Catalogue Record for this book is available from the British Library.

Printed by Bailes the Printer, Houghton le Spring.

Cover design by Tim and Anthony Flowers.

Back cover photograph ©North News and Pictures.

The Perceptual Map of Fellburn and other drawings ©Kemi, 1999.

The short story ©The Trustees of the Catherine Cookson Charitable Trusts, 1999.

Printed on Consort Royal Satin manufactured by Donside Paper Company.

Also by Cliff Goodwin:

Working for the Civil Service
To Be A Lady: The Story of Catherine Cookson
Sid James: A Biography
When the Wind Changed: The Life and Death of Tony Hancock

Contents

South Shields Market around the turn of the century, from an old picture postcard.

Acknowledgments

THIS BOOK could not have been written without the help of a great many people. It is impossible to measure their contributions.

I must, above all, express my sincere thanks to Her Majesty Queen Elizabeth, The Queen Mother, for her interest and words of encouragement during the writing of this book. As a Cookson fan for almost half a century I hope this companion will continue to add to her enjoyment of Catherine Cookson's work.

I am also indebted to Denise Welch, and her father Vin Welch, for generously agreeing to contribute a foreword to this *Catherine Cookson Companion*.

My gratitude goes to the Prime Minister, Tony Blair MP, for his contribution, and also to Mike Neville and Margaret Brown at Tyne Tees Television; Kathleen Jones; Dr James Parker at the Public Lending Right and staff at the BBC Written Archive, Caversham;

This *Companion* would certainly never have been completed without the help of Patrick Conway, director of Durham County Council's Arts, Libraries and Museums Department, and the staff at Consett Library who arranged for all one hundred Cookson novels and children's books to be available during my research.

For help in tracing and granting permission to use photographs and other illustrations my gratitude goes to: Beamish, The North of England Open Air Museum; Tyne & Wear Museums; Little, Brown; North News & Pictures; Random House (UK); The Customs House Theatre, South Shields; the editor and staff of *The Northern Echo;* the editor and staff of *The Journal,* Newcastle; The Tony Hillman Collection; Val Baynton at Royal Doulton (UK) Ltd and the staff at Newcastle Libraries.

There are three people who deserve special and personal thanks. Since its inception, more than five years ago, my agent Jane Judd has never faltered in both her loyalty and enthusiasm for the idea of a *Catherine Cookson Companion*, a dedication equally shared by Anna Flowers at Tyne Bridge Publishing. Lastly my thanks to Sarah Berry, for whose tireless and meticulous research and typing I will always be grateful.

My sincerest thanks, however, must go to Dame Catherine and Tom Cookson who, over a good many years, never failed to answer my questions nor solve my problems and who gave me permission to use family photographs. Sadly, these permissions have now passed to the Cookson Estate, to which I also owe my thanks.

Permission to use the recently rediscovered Cookson short story was granted by the Trustees of the Catherine Cookson Charitable Trusts with Anthony Sheil at Sheil Land Associates Ltd.

Every effort was made to trace and seek permission from those holding copyright to material used in this book. My apologies to anyone I may have inadvertently omitted.

Cliff Goodwin, 1999

Foreword

I FIRST DISCOVERED Catherine Cookson when I was about sixteen. There was an instant attraction and I became a regular reader of her books. At the time I was not set on the path to becoming an actress, so being in a position where I could bring her characters to life was very far from my mind.

Later on I must admit that I would select the character from the book that appealed to me most and would visualise myself in that part. Tilly Trotter was the character which most endeared itself to me. I always wanted to play the young Tilly.

The fact that Catherine Cookson's books sell or are borrowed more than any other author is a great testimony to her writing skills. Evocative and moving, the characters come to life before your eyes. They are a wonderful documentation of times past and a testimony of her passing.

For me the most enjoyable aspect of Catherine's writing was her ability to evoke the atmosphere of the time or period she was writing about. My grandfather was born in Walker and, having started his life in very humble surroundings, used to talk to me about his young days and of the poverty and hardship of the early years of the century. So I knew how believable Catherine's work really was.

My first acting role in one of her works was in *The Gambling Man* at Newcastle Playhouse in 1983. This was the first stage play I had appeared in in the North East since leaving drama school, on my home ground so to speak. It was exciting but quite nerve wracking.

I met Catherine before we opened and she was very charming and excited herself to see her "baby" coming to life on the stage. We talked about the character and she kindly told me how she felt about her and the background to her creation. A few years ago I appeared in *The Glass Virgin* on television, yet another exciting Cookson experience.

Catherine was a lovely, warm, honest person and her relationship with her husband, Tom, was a magic blend of fairy tale and reality. They were both wonderful people.

I sincerely hope this book helps to keep the memory of Catherine Cookson alive for those who love her, read her and for those who have yet to discover her magic.

Denise Welch

Author's Note

THE TELEPHONE was ringing as I walked through the door. I had returned home after three days in London promoting my biography of Catherine Cookson and still had my coat on. The voice was instantly familiar. "Please hold on," Tom said. "Catherine would like a word with you."

We had not spoken since the publication of *To Be A Lady* and I was unsure of Catherine's reaction. "I just wanted to thank you for saying such nice things about me," she began.

"Tom has been reading your book to me and we heard you on the wireless." I thanked her and visualised her speaking from the blue and white bedroom of her Newcastle home where we had once talked.

Catherine, I was sure, would be lying on the left hand side of the bed, propped almost upright on the pillows. Her hair white and thin. On the pink, quilted bedspread beside her is a radio. And beside the bed, within arm's reach, is a trolley with a dictating machine and a push-button telephone with outsized numbers.

The room is lit by a wall-to-wall picture window to the left of the bed. The wallpaper is blue; bold, wide stripes and flowers. There is a framed collection of Catherine's own sketches. And, hanging between them on the wall to the right of the bedroom door, is the framed citation for her OBE.

Catherine no longer wears her glasses, her eyesight registers only light and shade—"I can only see your outline, no detail."

Forty minutes later Catherine asked me what I was working on next. "Another biography," I admitted, "but I do have another idea for a Cookson book."

There was an ominous silence.

"I want to write a Cookson 'companion', listing every character you created," I added.

"Who on earth would want to read that?" she said, slightly shocked.

I explained the idea. "It sounds an awful lot of hard work," said Catherine. "But good luck, anyway."

Two days later the telephone rang once again. By now Tom had finished reading my biography and Catherine—"you know I'm a stickler for accuracy"—disagreed with two things I had said. I defended myself by quoting the archive records. "In that case," Catherine cut in, "we will have to agree to disagree."

There was another silence and I hoped I hadn't offended her. "By the way," she asked enthusiastically. "How is the *Companion* going?"

Cliff Goodwin, 1999

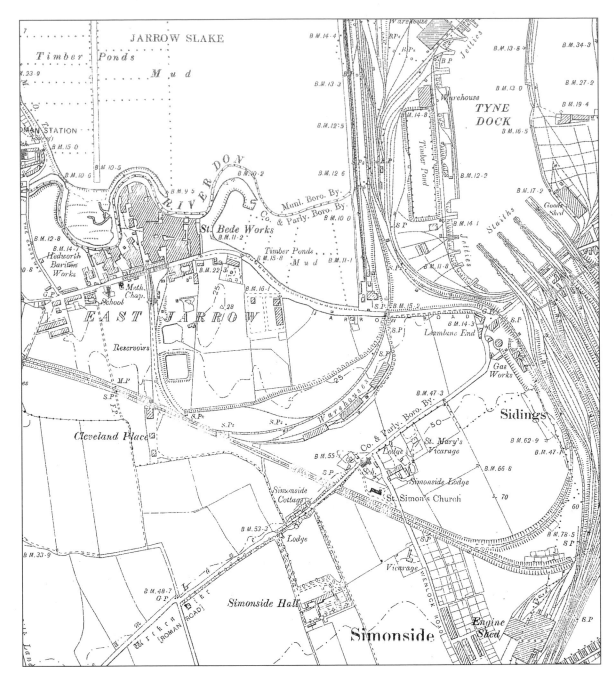

*East Jarrow from the 1898 O.S. map.
The first terrace of the New Buildings—
just to the right of 'East Jarrow'—was
completed two years earlier. In the winter
of 1898 the McMullen family moved to
Number 6 William Black Street.
Leam Lane End—Catherine's 1906
birthplace—can be seen below the Tyne
Dock staiths.*

Cookson on Cookson

I N THE YEARS following the publication of her first novel, *Kate Hannigan*, in 1950, Catherine Cookson gave hundreds of interviews and appeared on scores of radio and television programmes.

Her life, like her stories, was there for the telling. And, like the pieces of a giant jigsaw, she would relive the popular incidents of her childhood or retell the events of her adult life and career. There was seldom time to probe below the surface or complete more than a fraction of the picture.

An intensely private person, international popularity brought with it the double edge of fame and frustration. Details of her personal history, at least those offered for public consumption, were offered in carefully measured doses. The boundary between publicity and privacy remained well guarded.

The imaginary "autobiography" which follows—compiled from almost five decades of interviews—attempts for the first time to present Catherine Cookson in her own words; telling her own story in her own unique way.

Hudson Street, South Shields. At the far end, and next to Tyne Dock railway station, was the Crown cinema to which Catherine escaped each Saturday afternoon.

... on Childhood

I can smell memories of my childhood.

I was born in 1906 in Leam Lane, Tyne Dock, the illegitimate daughter of Kate Fawcett. Kate went back into service, leaving me to be brought up by her mother [Rose McMullen] and step-father, Old John McMullen.

When I was five years old, Kate had to return home to look after her mother—who was dying of dropsy—and my step-granda and her step-brother and the numerous lodgers who flitted in and out of our three-roomed house at Number 10 William Black Street.

My early days are very clear to me. I can remember some incidents from as far back as when I was three, but those that stand out vividly must have occurred after I was seven. When I was sent for the

Tyne Dock—with its twenty-six jetties and wharfs—dominated employment in South Shields. John McMullen would walk the three miles from his Jarrow home for a single ten-hour shift and be paid just 3s 6d (17 $\frac{1}{2}$ pence).

beer in the grey hen, a stone gallon-jar; sent to borrow money; and sent often to gather wood from Jarrow Slake, a kind of floating timber yard on the edge of the River Tyne. This was a job I liked, but it was dangerous and it's a wonder I ever lived to tell the tale.

I was the only child who, as I remember went on the slakes with a sack. If you could get a sackful of wood to keep the fire going and there was a big baking day, that was marvellous. And I think I must have been a natural beachcomber because I always liked scraping, getting stuff for nothing.

As a child I would follow the coke carts. The carts would come from Jarrow into Shields from the gas works. They were very like farm carts, with the sides up. I used to love the horse to shy, or see the cart rumble over the tram lines, because a few nice lumps of coke would fall off and I would pick them up and take them home.

And I was the only child from the New Buildings who was sent to Bob's pawn shop every Monday. Bob Gombertz's pawn shop in Bede Street, Tyne Dock. I hated those weekly visits because they reduced me to shame…

When I was young I wanted most of all "to be a lady and talk proper", and so I used to tell people I had been educated privately at home. And by heck! I was educated at home; being brought up by my stepgranda was an education in itself.

All I craved was a job in a chemist's shop. It was ladylike to work in a chemist's shop. I remember too my first attempt at make-up. I bought a tube of Ponds Vanishing Cream for 6d [2$\frac{1}{2}$p]. It vanished all right, into the rafters of the outside lavatory where Kate wouldn't find it. It wasn't considered proper to wear anything on one's face.

I get cross when I hear people say I was brought up in the slums. East Jarrow wasn't slums. It was a good working-class community with standards. High ones. Proper ones. I believe everybody is a result of their environment and no matter what was in me what is passed on to me—it was the environment that set me and made me what I am today.

When I went into service as a young girl of four-teen I just knew it wasn't for me. There was always a question of who was the mistress and who was the maid—it was clear I was not destined for service.

I may well have the sin of pride, but it was a sustaining pride.

I went into South Shields workhouse as a laundry checker when I was eighteen. My wage was £2 a month, plus four square meals a day and a free uniform. But in those days the main inducement was the promise of six shillings [30p] a week pension after forty years service. Oh, I thought I'd really fallen on my feet there, I felt that the Virgin Mary to whom I was always praying, had taken notice of me at last.

This feeling continued for about three months; then that irritating question began stabbing at me again. Why was I using my hands and not my head? Didn't I want to be a lady? Oh, yes. Yes, I did.

Ellison Street, Jarrow, c.1900. Rose McMullen, Catherine's grandmother had lived in the Tyneside town and married her first husband, William Fawcett, there in 1877.

I always felt I was a bit above laundry work. At home they thought I was stuck up because my mother wouldn't let me go into permanent service. "You're different," she used to say, "you're not made for that life." So I had a false impression of myself.

What I needed was culture. I bought a second-hand fiddle for ten shillings, took ten lessons at a shilling a time, then found there was something wrong with the fiddle—I couldn't play it. I took up French, again a shilling a lesson, only to realise there was something wrong with the teacher. I took up physical culture: I imagined, if I was beautiful some titled bloke—well, at least a gentleman, as I imagined my father had been—would whip me away. It didn't work; I developed in all the wrong places; some of them I haven't been able to push back since.

Inside I am still very much the child that was Katie McMullen of East Jarrow. I am still hurt as she was hurt. I still laugh as she laughed.

... on her Mother

Kate rejected me from when I was born. She went through hell, having to come home and give birth and live in that little two-bedroomed house in Leam Lane where her drunken stepfather and half-brother and mother existed.

For ten years she had to look after her stepfather and the family, work fourteen hours a day inside and outside the house, and never receive a penny from anyone. I was born when she was twenty-four. She was a really beautiful woman in her younger days and she never touched a drink then.

When I was seven I learnt that she wasn't just our Kate, a relation, she was my mother. But she was never a mother to me. She didn't know how to be a mother. For instance, she wouldn't even tell me the facts of life.

When this great, terrifying incident—the onset of menstruation—happened Kate ran up the street to her sister Mary, who had to come down straight away and pacify me and tell me the facts of life. I was thirteen at the time.

Kate was never made to be a mother, and the fact is nor did I want her to be my mother when I realised she drank. I looked upon myself as the poor little orphan of the storm; the one you could really feel sorry for.

During all my early years, from when I was a very small child, the main thought in my mind, the daily wish, the constant desire, was that Kate would give up the drink. But I wish I could have understood then, as I do now when I look back, what her life must have been like from the time when she came home from her place of service when she was thirty. I would have looked on her weakness through different eyes.

When I look back, £10 would have cleared my mother, Kate, of debt. But then, if she'd had £10, at least £5 would have gone on drink. So my happiest times then were when there was no money coming in at all.

One time it was my mother's birthday and I had saved tuppence-halfpenny, I had heard her say she loved a pear so I went to the fruit shop up Stanhope Road, South Shields, and I bought the biggest pear they had.

I took it home and I can still see the pleasure that registered on Kate's face as I gave it to her. She cut it in half and gave one half to me. It was marvellous.

King Street, South Shields in 1910. Early in June, 1919, a neighbour set Catherine free among the shelves of a King Street bookshop. As a thirteenth birthday present she chose the complete Grimm's Fairy Tales.

... on her Father

I felt the isolation. I was different. We all have our own points of suffering but, when you're a child and you're a bastard everything is exaggerated, and my God it hurts.

I always gave my unknown father credit for the artistic side of me. I knew that if I hadn't been a writer I would be a painter because I painted naturally without lessons.

Then I wanted to be different. I wanted to talk proper. Swanky. I wanted to be like me Da. The Da I never knew. Because he must be a gentleman. He had to be that.

I did not know until fifteen or sixteen who or what he was, but something happened in the kitchen at home and I remember saying to my Aunt Mary, who lived up the street, that I did not like what had happened.

She said, "Well, you wouldn't lass, because your Da was a gentleman."

That was the first mention. I said, "How do you know, Aunt Mary?" And she said, "He wore an astrakhan collar and carried a silver-mounted walking stick and he talked lovely. He always came into the best end of the saloon. Kate helped serve in the bar there and they knew each other for two years."

Here, then, was the creator of my being. When I knew I was begat of a gentleman, I knew what I was. I had this feeling that I must be better—I must …

Illegitimates never do think their fathers are navvies or dustmen. They always place them in professions—solicitors, doctors, Sirs, the youngest sons of impoverished families, even Lords. But I didn't know that then.

All through my growing up years I was determined to get away from Number 10 William Black Street, East Jarrow.

I tried to find out something about my father. I even told one fellow I would marry him if he could find my father, thinking of course, that if he did succeed, this father—who I was convinced was a gentleman—would whisk me away to his great mansion, and there I would become a lady.

God help me. I never blamed my father for leaving Kate in the lurch. I used to think who would want to be connected with our family in any way? And yet I loved Kate. I loved them all.

When I was eighteen I wanted above everything else to be a lady. To live graciously.

Because I was born on the wrong side of the blanket. I never knew what was on the other side, but I was convinced it was something grand. Everything I did, all the striving to better myself, was so that I'd be worthy of my father when he came to claim me.

... on Religion

I had never thought of going to heaven. My thoughts never ascended that far. Heaven was a closed shop.

I was either saying prayers to prevent me being thrust into hell or saying prayers to get somebody out of hell and purgatory.

As I knelt in the pew with the other penitents I went over in my mind what I had to do. I had to tell the priest how wicked I was and when my turn came I did just that. The strong hand on my collar thrust me into a black box in which I could see nothing but a glimmer of light above my head, and in it an outline of a profile which had no resemblance to a priest or his master.

I recall one Sunday morning, which was the only time I remember Kate or my granny going to Mass. We walked up the long freezing road to St Bede's in Jarrow, where I had my first communion. I had a coat on. Kate had a coat on. My granny was wearing a bead cape and a bead bonnet. But the worshippers at that seven o'clock Mass were made up of poorly shawled women and thinly clad men, but they were saving their souls and that was all that mattered.

Then there was communion. I hated the taste of God on my tongue. From an early age my imagination went to work. I had a picture of thousands of nuns all over the world and all those bakeries turning out God by the billion.

It was unthinkable that you should eat or drink for hours before God was placed on your tongue. I myself went out every Friday morning, which was the school's day for taking the Eucharist, cold and hungry and thirsty and longing for the time when I could take the lid off a can of tea and gollop my slice of bread and dripping.

To miss this occasion was not only a mortal sin, but to come under the thunder and exposure of the dreaded headmistress. I am angry when I think of the millions of children like myself, who suffered in the same way, not in the last century or in the Dark Ages, but in this century.

But I loved Benediction, I could listen to the Latin for hours on end.

As a teenager I had to pass the Church of St Peter & Paul, Tyne Dock, every time I went home from the Workhouse, about two miles from East Jarrow. At night the church doors would always be open, and inside would be complete darkness except for the red glow of the Sanctuary lamp. I would kneel at Our Lady's alter and pray that Kate would give up the drink.

Catherine with her grand-mother at the door of Number 10 William Black Street.

... on Boyfriends

From when I was about fifteen I was courted, as the word was, by three pit lads—and may I state emphatically they were all gentlemen.

My first lad, a fellow called Micky Moran, was a pit man who spent all his spare time decorating the church, you know these stencils that go round the church—all the crosses, all the way round. Granda used to call him "the spare priest".

Then there was Kit Gannon, he was also a miner. And finally, Todd Lawson who became a Newcastle footballer.

They were all miners from mining families. Although there were very few miners in the New Buildings—they were mostly working in the shipyards or on the trams and things like that—in my teens my friends were from mining families. That is how I know so much about what went on in their homes.

I do wish I'd known more about sex. At that age I still thought that babies came through kissing. I imagined that if you opened your mouth while you were kissing you'd had it, so I must have been the closest-mouthed kisser in the north.

... on moving South

At eighteen the only thing I thought of was getting away from Number 10 William Black Street, East Jarrow, and the daily struggle of life there.

The only thing I knew about the North was work, that was my culture. During my teens I saw the work gradually fading away. In my twenties it vanished. It wasn't the only thing that made me leave the North, it was a number of things, but quite prominent was the feeling of depression.

It was in 1929, when I was twenty-three, that I left the North to take up the position of head laundress in the workhouse at Tendring, Essex. I was stuck there for nine months and I realised that I hated the country. The land was mainly farmland; it was like a different country and I was so lonely.

Suddenly this girl who had come from an industrial area—where even at night you heard the horns of the ships and the background noises of the goods trains—found herself desolated.

I was a foreigner there, I think I only left the place once and that was to go to a fete in the village.

Nine months later I moved to a Hastings Workhouse laundry where as manageress my wage was £3 a week, plus six shillings [30 pence] for dinners. Big money in those days for a young woman.

I did not imagine then that I would live in Hastings for the next forty-six years and that within two years of my arrival I should buy a gentleman's residence, and too, that I should make the mistake of bringing my mother to live with me and by this emotional action create for myself once more a hell through my fear of drink; that I should meet and marry a schoolmaster, that I should lose four babies, have a breakdown when I was thirty-nine and experience the residue of it for the following ten years.

... on Marriage

Tom had what I needed: kindness, a lovely nature, a high sense of moral values and, above all, he had what I wanted most—a mind.

But besides the physical attraction I had a strength of purpose and I was determined to marry this man, Tom Cookson.

Next I went to the priest and asked him to marry us. He said he wouldn't because Tom was not a Catholic. So I said well, it was the register office for us—he married us on Saturday, 1st June, 1940, at the Catholic church in Hastings.

I'd known I was going to be married sometime so I'd made plans to have my dress made at Plummers in Hastings, which was a lovely shop. Well; when I went to see about it in the few days before the wedding, all the dress makers had left or been evacuated or something, and my dress was still at the cutting stage.

So it didn't matter and I wore a blue dress I had had some time and a lovely fur cape Tom gave me for a wedding present. I loved high hats and very high heels and though I always say Tom and I are the same size, I must have looked a good foot taller than him on the day.

It was supposed to be a two o'clock quiet wedding, but quite a few people turned up.

I was given away by George Silverlock, the Hastings workhouse master. He'd always called me his adopted daughter and he wanted to give me away—only the day before the wedding he fell and broke his arm. So he had his arm in a sling.

People said afterwards they had never heard so much laughter in the vestry. I could never understand it. I had this great sadness inside me, not sadness really, more an aloneness, but I always wanted to make people happy and laugh and that's what they remembered on the day.

Then we went back to The Hurst and had some wine and there was a little cake.

I had no flowers, I don't think Tom's ever bought me flowers because he knows how I feel. Oh, it didn't matter. What is all the fuss about a wedding anyway? It's the two people and what they feel about each other that matters. The rest is all show, for other people, I always think.

I didn't even have an engagement ring, though Tom did buy me a ring a few years later. I've got a brooch he bought me, too, but I don't go for jewellery. I only wear my wedding ring. It's never been off my finger. Even when I go into hospital they can't get it off and they have to tape over it.

Buy him a wedding present? Why, no. He had me, didn't he. What more did he want?

We had a one-day honeymoon. We caught the train up to London and stayed in the Charing Cross Hotel.

What spoiled it for me was that on the way the train stopped at Tunbridge Wells. It was during Dunkirk and there was another train stopped at the station full of men from France. The Red Cross were there handing out tea and these men looked so bitter, so angry, so full of despair that I cried all the way from there to London. You could see part of the miracle of Dunkirk on that train and it affected me dreadfully.

On Saturday night Tom and I went to the theatre to see Ibsen's *Ghosts*. There was only about five other people in the audience, I'll always remember it.

... on her Lost Education

As a teenager all I read each week was *T.P. and Cassell's Weekly* and *John O' London's*. I was an utter ignorant.

I was twenty before I went into a library and discovered the writings of Philip Dormer Stanhope, the fourth Earl of Chesterfield. Reading his letters to his illegitimate son, I suppose I saw a parallel. Suddenly my eyes had been opened.

Lord Chesterfield became my mentor, and the public library my university. It was Lord Chesterfield who introduced me to my first history and geography; with him I travelled the world and conversed with the mighty of his day—you never merely talked with Chesterfield.

I can honestly say that from this time my life changed. It was just as though a huge door had been swung back and out there was this marvellous world of reading.

By now I was reading blindly. I wish I had had someone at that stage who could have guided my reading. In the library I asked for Chaucer, and some smart-aleck gave it to me in Old English, and I couldn't understand a word. It was just like Geordie dialect

If only I'd had an education at that age. It was my husband who eventually drummed it into me that I'd educated myself to such an extent that I'd read more than he had at university.

I invented a phrase: "We learn daily by gaining a greater knowledge of our ignorance." Years later, I read Socrates' *Apologia*, and I came across those exact same words and I thought I had invented them. How do you account for that?

Nothing is new, but I do know we are given gifts and we must use them.

... on Children

When I found I couldn't have children, the agony I went through was unbearable. Seeing other women have babies like rabbits ... it affected my mind.

Now I realise that had I had a baby or babies they would have all likely been haemophiliacs because of my hereditary blood disease. And that would have been terrible to have passed on without realising it.

If I had had children then I would have not written a word. I would have spent my time raising them and caring for my family.

... on Depression

I couldn't remember one happy incident that had happened in my life. Nothing. Everything I looked back on was black. There was no humour, there was nothing.

My illegitimacy had created a sense of shame and rejection. All I wanted to do was get away from everybody who knew about the circumstances of my birth—I wanted to get away from the shame.

My breakdown came in 1945. I had a weird feeling that I would never see the end of the war. I had had a long illness while we were living at Hereford and now the business of being illegitimate began to assume mountainous proportions. Despair, shame, bitterness.

I had driven myself. I had wanted education, education, education. I was practising for an arts exam; I was writing, while ill in bed; I had taken up the piano for a second time. Everything was out of proportion.

I went away for voluntary treatment at St Mary's psychiatric hospital at Burghill, near Hereford, and because I imbibe atmosphere—soaked it up—I knew that if I stayed in hospital I would soon be worse than the worst patient there.

My salvation could only come from work. I went back to Hastings and The Hurst. My fifteen-roomed gentleman's residence was in a dreadful state. I had no help and an acre of garden to tend. I wrote out a schedule of work and a hospital chart for myself showing my bad days and my good days.

During the black period of my breakdown I used to sit in the bathroom every morning and say to whatever was there: "Please give me peace of mind, joy of living; the power to make other people happy." It was only after a long time that I realised that of the three, the latter is the most important.

In a breakdown you have to look at your reflection and say: "What now? ... Where am I going?"

And my reflection told me I would not improve a step unless I owned up to my early environment. Until I owned up to being a woman of the North. Until I could say the words "illegitimate" and "bastard"—and not cringe. And say so what? Look what a bastard has done, you know?

I realised then I would never write a word anybody would want to read until I faced up to myself. I had not only run away from the place but I had run away from the person I was—a product of the North.

... on *Suicide*

Some days I was at rock bottom. I felt I could not stand it any longer. I thought I could not bear it any more. Twice I felt I could not go on.

One cannot describe a breakdown. Only people who have endured it can know. With the years it may fade, but the horror comes back in the cold of the night sometimes.

I just couldn't stop thinking how nice it would be to go to sleep and never wake up to drag myself through another day.

I went up on the hill to pick the biggest cliff from which to throw myself and I thought: "When you drop down there it will be all over ... You will not feel anything any more ... But think of the people who will suffer ... Nobody has loved anybody like Tom loves you, now you are going to leave him and he needs you."

And then I thought about Tom and what he'd do without me. He was coming home at weekends from the RAF and he was the only solid thing in my life. The more I thought about him the more I knew I couldn't take my own life.

So I realised in that moment that I should stay alive a little longer and I did—for a few more weeks.

I could never sleep for more than two hours fitfully. And one night I had two big bottles full of sleeping tablets. I was tempted to end my life again. But it was as if some strength came from somewhere saying: "No, by God, you are not going to go without a fight." And I took the bottle and threw the tablets down the lavatory.

I had the most wonderful feeling of release and relief. I thought: I've done it. At last I had done something positive.

I was shouting inside, telling myself I had done something to help myself. At last I'd seen some light in the darkness. It didn't last long, that feeling, but at least I'd experienced it. It was good enough to try to recapture.

What does a soldier do? What does somebody do when they're in battle? They don't turn and run away. The only thing to do is to face your fear and go towards it. So I learned a trick; if I have a fear coming on, I go to the mirror and swear at myself—aloud.

I would shout: "You're bloody well not going to get the better of me this time." People would think I was barmy, but I knew I could conquer it just by going for myself.

... on getting Published

The writer in me made its first appearance when I was ten years old—my first story was called *The Wild Irish Girl*. I continued to write about that girl, in different ways, over many years.

Six years later, when I was sixteen, I sent a 16,000 word short story called *On the Second Floor* to the *Shields Gazette*. They hadn't any sense and sent it back.

So, a few years later, answering an advert by the Regent Institute. I sent them a sample of my work; a play set in a workhouse. Now they had some sense. They returned it and written across the back page in red ink were the words: "Strongly advise author not to take up writing as a career".

I had to start earning my living, but I still kept on writing poetry, sketches and plays and this went on for years.

I had talent but no training. You have to serve your time first and I did. I have always looked upon writing as a trade. I simply apprenticed myself to it until I learned the craft. So I spent the next twenty years educating myself until I was ready and able to write a novel.

I had been doing full-length plays about ladies and gentlemen of course. I knew nothing about ladies and gentlemen so you can imagine what they were like.

Then I realised I knew nothing about these people. But I did know something about the ordinary people in the North-East. I dropped this veneer and started writing things I knew about.

It was 1946 and I was fighting a breakdown when I started to write seriously, hoping to release all my mental anguish. Here I was, forty years old, plunged back into my beginnings by my breakdown, and my early life poured out of me. I had faced up to myself in myself and I was away—I couldn't stop.

I knew I had to face up to myself and if I ever wanted to be read I would have to write about things and people I have lived among and knew about and had knowledge of.

So I wrote my first novel which was *Kate Hannigan,* and I set it in the background of my mother's time, reminiscing right back and it was accepted by the first publisher.

Do you know, when I sent off my first novel to a publisher, he read three pages and then pushed it to the end of his desk, and said to his secretary, "This is no good." That secretary, either by chance or by divine intervention, took the manuscript home and read the book in bed." The next day, she came back to the office and told her boss he was wrong, and that if he had any sense, he would go back to this book and look at it again.

I had by then got myself an agent. *Kate Hannigan* was reviewed by John Betjeman—and that was the beginning. I was away. I was a real writer at last.

You go a little doo-lally-tap. There is nothing quite like it again. You see thousands of books in a library, but you don't really notice them because you only see your own book. Then you come down to earth with a bang.

You wouldn't believe it, but some of my neighbours tried to get *Kate Hannigan* banned because I had dared in the first two or three pages to write about a baby being born—actually coming out of the womb.

It was banned in Ireland. It was too much for the Catholic Church and I was advised to cut down on this sort of thing.

Most of us have a first novel in us, but it is the second; the third; the fourth that take the writing. Things don't get easier, but it is a profession. It is a trade and you have got to do your apprenticeship and keep learning every day.

... on *Rejection*

What I'd done in the past had been practice games. I had embarked on a career and it had to be worked at. There were, I realised, exams to be passed with myself the examiner and myself the critic.

Kate Hannigan had been published in 1950. I was already practically through the sequel, *Annie Hannigan.* This, in my opinion, was even better than *Kate Hannigan.* But I got a letter from my publisher, Murray Thompson, to say that they would take this book but it wasn't as good, in their opinion as the first. They would do what they could with it. That inflamed me, those words—"do what they could".

I know now why there were doubts about it because I was still expressing my feelings about the Catholic Church. What was more, I was also going into the mind of a young man, thinking about his sex life and arising thoughts concerning it. Hearing it now, his thoughts were quite poetic, but Mr Thompson must have thought they were a bit way out. That is the only thing that I can think made him question the book.

Anyway, I remember crying my eyes out and getting on the phone and saying: "I won't have it accepted on those conditions. Send it back."

I think it was one of the bravest things an author has ever done, specially when starting out as ignorant as I was of how difficult it was to get a book published.

It was a hard lesson, but one I had thankfully learnt early. I was merely a trainee in a game which was for real.

Forget about *Roget's Thesaurus* and all the long-winded descriptions. Remember Chesterfield: Stick to plain English; you're not writing a thesis; you are, in your kind of writing, dealing with ordinary human beings, their hates, their loves, their loyalties, their lying. Your experience is packed with fact, turn it into fiction, but make it read like facts.

... on Writing

Writing is not only my work, it is my hobby. They used to say I was a writer who became a business ... and then an industry.

Writing for me is a mania. I have never had difficulty thinking up new ideas. They keep tumbling over each other in my mind. I think in some previous incarnation I must have sat among the cinders in some baronial hall—a bit like the court jester—regaling the guests with my stories.

Once I did try to use a typewriter, but found it too slow for my way of thinking. For fifteen years I wrote my stories down in long-hand. Then I got writer's cramp, and I thought it was the end. It was my husband who urged me to use a tape recorder, huge things with valves in those days. I took to this like a duck to water, for it proved to be my natural medium.

> ## Kate Hannigan
>
> *It's the greatest psychiatrist's treatment in the world because you're your own judge, and I knew that unless I faced up to my early beginnings, unless I could throw this pseudo lady and pseudo gentleman out of my life and admit to my beginnings, admit to these two terrifying words, which upset me even when I read "bastard" or "illegitimate".*
>
> *Unless I could look in the mirror and say, "Well, yes, that's what you are. You're a bastard," I knew I would never get any peace. And I had to have this long session with myself, and I said: "All right, I'll write it down. I'll write the background of my early beginnings."*
>
> *I didn't think I'm going to write a novel, or I'm going to do fiction, or romance, nothing like that. I just wanted to put down the background of my mother and my grandmother, from what I felt in the kitchen, from the surroundings of the New Buildings.*
>
> *And so I wrote this story called Kate Hannigan. And I thought, "That's it!" But it wasn't. The breakdown was still with me.*
>
> ❧ *Catherine Cookson*

I see everything in film form. Primarily, I am a story-teller who sees everything in film form. Talking comes natural to me. I act my characters; I laugh; I cry, fight and sorrow with them.

I know that the basis of my writing stems from my having absorbed information like a sponge from all those people in the side streets of the villages where I lived, between Jarrow and South Shields. Here was the substance of my writing and here were the people, fully-clothed characters. Their lives and hardships inspired my writing.

When I was in service I always kept a pen and paper in my apron pocket while I was peeling potatoes or scrubbing floors. I still use some of the notes I jotted down all those years ago.

I am fortunate that I am able to store a complete story in my mind, even one comprising a trilogy, without making one note, except for dates and names. As long as I get my end first, the rest leads up to it.

I might go on working until eleven; my mind is always very alert. In the black dark at two o'clock in the morning I'm grappling with characters. I always use the same process in my writing—the characters come first, not the plots, ever.

I don't think of plots, never have. I place a character in an environment or an incident or personality and generally the environment guides their behaviour. If you put certain characters in certain settings, the story unfolds itself—what happens is inevitable.

I never take a character from a person I know, but I take bits. Sometimes I see people for the first time in a hotel or restaurant and I recognise them as just someone I have written about.

An incident might occur, which I don't pay much heed to at first, but it sinks into my subconscious mind, which I use a lot, and years later perhaps it pops up and gives me the formation of a story or a character on which to base the story. The ideas never go away even if I were to want them to; they will always be there when I want to draw them up.

I must know the end of a story before I begin. The characters might change here and there, but the main story remains the same.

If I am very tired I might go to bed at half-past-nine, but not to sleep—to work again on my scripts. Even if I am ill and stay in bed I am always working. I've got to be very very ill to stop work altogether. I would go bats if I just laid in bed and did nothing.

Most nights I try to pretend to be asleep but Tom always knows: "Aren't you ever going to sleep?" he says. The next morning I get started on my tapes at about half-past six: I always have them there by the bed.

I know that I overwork. I know I exhaust myself and am sometimes flat out and speechless, but I enjoy working. Some mornings I don't feel any joy, but I have an idea for a story, which is the next best thing.

Years ago a lady in St Leonard's (which nudges Hastings) said: "Couldn't you write about any other place than the North-East? Why not a story about Hastings? So many things happened here." And I thought then: You can come to hate somebody in two minutes dead flat, can't you?

I thought: "I'll show her, I can write anything I set my mind to it. It is only a question of homework." So I went around Hastings' fishing fleet because I was going to write a romantic story. After six months of writing that story I stopped because I knew the only thing in it that had any guts was the fish.

I knew then I was a regional writer. I knew all I wanted was in the North. These were the people I knew. I was part of them. It was my land.

There is romance in my stories but I like to think there is a lot more to them than just romantic tales.

The people who call me a romantic writer have never read me. It's a prejudice. I've written as Catherine Marchant for a woman's magazine because they wanted lighter stories. They could be called romantic, but I wouldn't write them under the name Catherine Cookson. Catherine Cookson is not a romantic writer. If in the process of writing I say something worthwhile, something that might make someone laugh or cry or think—most of all I hope it makes someone think, and often I have letters that tell me that they do.

It is when the rough sheets come back from my secretary that the hard grind of correcting and deleting—very rarely adding—begins. This is another hard lesson I had to learn, cut wherever you can.

Cutting from 30,000 words down to 13,000 words, taking out the padding, is vital when you're telling a story. It is, after all, the story that makes a novel.

I am often asked how I manage to write two books a year. I'll tell you. I have an excellent staff … a marvellous butler, footman, a first class secretary, a very good chauffeur and part-time gardener and a day and night nurse—all embodied in one man—my husband Tom.

Every writer wants to write a great book. I get an idea and I think this is going to be it. And it isn't. Once I stop wanting to do this, I suppose I shall stop writing.

Beginning a story

I take two, four or six characters and place them in a certain environment, and it is the environment that affects their characters.

That started, I then find my end. I always think of the end of the story—the resolution—before I begin it.

So what I do next is to go to the pictures. By this I mean conjure up every scene and every character in it as if I was looking at a film and I act these characters. This is mostly done when I am sleepless. It might take me until two o'clock in the morning.

Do you know, really, I think I am a frustrated actress. Because I act every part. I do every bit of the dialogue and then the following morning I wake up and wonder why I am tired, forgetting that I have lived a number of other people's lives in the night.

I start now and whatever I have thought of last night, I put it down on to tape. It might not be exactly in the same words that I used in the night because my mind at night delivers brilliant answers to questions, but, they are very mundane in the morning when I attempt to put them down.

Catherine Cookson

... on *Our Kate*

I didn't write my autobiography, *Our Kate*, to help anyone but myself, I just wanted to get rid of the great hidden secret and disgrace of being a bastard.

When I read the first draft I felt relieved but I thought I could never publish this. It was full of bitterness. The bitterness came up off the page. I should have thought of all the nice things that did happen, but it didn't come like that. I felt relieved, but I thought I could never publish this.

And so I left it—I was still writing other books—and I thought I mustn't say that about Kate there. I must describe her as I know she was, as I know her beautiful character; the kind character; the humorous character; the loving character. The woman who was working to the ground, I must see her like that.

But in the second draft she didn't come like that. There was still bitterness. I poured it out, all these things that had happened to me. I thought I can't do it. So I did it again and again.

It took me twelve years to write it out of myself: I rewrote it eight times. But even when it was ready to go to the publisher. I wanted to withdraw it, because it was like walking in the street naked. And yet I knew it had to go through.

You see, I was still suffering the fragments of the breakdown and I knew that I would never be any better until I didn't give a damn who knew that I was illegitimate and who knew about my life. I'd hidden it so long, you see, I'd lived this sort of double life inside myself. Outwardly I was Catherine Cookson, a well-known author and schoolmaster's wife, and inwardly I was Katie McMullen, the illegitimate daughter of Kate Fawcett.

But in 1969 it was published and I was free. At last I was me. Of course some of the sediment of the past remains. At times my fears return, but I've acquired strength and a bit of wisdom since I was eighteen and I can dispel them now.

... on *Critics*

I am told that success engenders hostility; well, if this is the case I must consider myself very successful for most of the critics have flayed me.
I am described as an old lady who writes about rape; I may be seventy-three but mentally I am merely thirty-seven.

And all these critics imply they haven't read me. As one Midland journalist said:

"A North country woman who has read Catherine Cookson's books swore I would be hooked. I am not and nothing would induce me to read a page of it."

Every man is entitled to his own opinion, but to my mind the duty, and I mean duty, of a critic is to be, as far as is possible, unbiased, at least he should not be allowed the power of the press to put over his prejudices.

But it isn't only male critics who have plunged their knives into me. Two of the meanest criticisms came from a lady, and in a newspaper which had previously made *The Mallen Streak* the Book of the Month.

When I think of the hundreds of letters I receive from both men and women telling me how my work has helped them through bad times because they are able to identify with the characters and are given an insight into why we act as we do, it is rather distressing to read that I write only for morons. This was the term used.

It is no comfort to be told I am now in the company of Hardy, Lawrence, Joyce, and many others whose lives were torn apart by critics; for one reason I am not big-headed enough to consider myself as being in the same category.

... on returning *North*

I intended to stay in Hastings for twelve months, but I remained here for forty-two years. I confess I never wanted to come back.

Tom persuaded me to return North so I could die among my own folk. I was seventy and we were still working like people in their fifties or even forties. I know now, and he knew then, he was using me as an excuse to get away. He was tired of Hastings, which was changing vastly, especially the school that he had once loved.

We landed in Newcastle and we lived in this very nice house for about a year, but it had no garden, and so when we heard of this house on the outskirts of Corbridge, Northumberland, we went after it.

Well, I hadn't been in Corbridge more than six months or so (which I spent mostly in bed because the cold weather did nothing for me and I ended up with very bad bronchitis) when a lady from the town came to tell me that people weren't very pleased with me living here because I didn't show myself in the town. Why didn't I?

The first time I met her she was living in a glorious house in Langley, Northumberland.

I walked in and she marched over to me and shook my hand. All I could see in her eyes was this little girl from Leam Lane, she had the zest for life of someone much younger.

I believe she is one of only a handful of modern authors whose work will still be read and re-read in a hundred years time.

She had the gift to be able to bring the essence of Tyneside to the printed page, and that was one of her quite remarkable attributes. People all over the country—and the world—could empathise with her for her northerness. It was a unique talent.

But the main thing about her writing was that it had to be honest ... not just the main female character, but every character.

❧ *Piers Dudgeon, biographer*

That was the beginning of the end at Corbridge. When we first took the land next to High Barns we had an anonymous letter telling us that members of the community weren't pleased that we had dug up an ancient patch of ground that went back to the building of the moat around the "town".

There was also a pub on the opposite side of the road, a very old pub, where the visitors to the town used to go, and of course they were told about this Catherine Cookson and so I had people at the door at all hours wanting autographs.

Then Tom was stopped in the street one day by a beaming lady who told him gleefully that she had me on the rota of the sightseeing bus in Durham. Twice before this we'd had a bus load of people unload at the gate. This lack of privacy did not endear Corbridge to us.

After four-and-a-half years we found Bristol Lodge in Langley by the side of a lake—originally dammed to supply water to the one-time smelting works there. Today, it is probably one of the most beautiful areas in Northumberland.

Isn't it strange that from the wider world into which I escaped I have returned, like the eel to the Sargasso Sea.

... on Money

Since the days I put my pennies into the lavatory as a child I was a saver, a planner. I could make a sixpence go as far as a shilling.

The best piece of financial advice I have received came from a woman who lived in Blyth. She said, "Get your first £100, then aim for a thousand." I must have been thirty before I had a clear £100.

I've never written purely for money, but it's come. I was never interested in the money, I simply wanted to write books. If you are a writer, you'll write for writing's sake alone—the money will come automatically later.

Another thing I have found is that the only money worth having in life is what you earn by hard graft. You value it then. You value the things that it can buy, but if it comes easy then it isn't the same, and that is one thing I can say, money has never come easy for me.

... on *Illness*

I'm rotten from the eyebrows downwards, and spend most of my time in bed or in hospital, but as long as my mind is active I'll carry on. My body's rotten. But my mind is still brimming with stories.

Little did I know that the heavy nose bleedings I had been experiencing since I was eighteen were the first stages of my inherited blood trouble telangiectasia and that as time went on I should bleed not only from the nose, but also from the tongue and finger tips, and then internally.

And then I started to lose my sight. The word "blind" screamed in my head. I, Catherine Cookson, the writer, whose life depended upon her writing, was going blind. I was admitted to hospital and diagnosed as having "aging maculopathy", a common ailment in older people which does not cause total blindness but dims the vision.

An inner voice told me, "Go on putting you stories down on tape". I cried back at it, "What's the good? I can't correct them", to which came the answer, "Tom can read them to you and you can dictate the alterations to him; and just as you used to delete and scribble alterations between the lines, he can do the same".

... on *Retiring*

The business of retiring: It's like signing a paper and expecting a sentence of death.

Active: there is the crucial word with regard to old age, and I think being so is the solution. Perhaps not the whole, but in good part, because stagnation of the mind can create boredom, and this becomes the breeding ground of depression, when loss of the will to live can take over.

I don't believe in retiring at sixty or sixty-five unless you are going to take up something else. People are planning for the leisure of the working man and woman. You get tired of leisure and you get bored of leisure. The thing is to go on working right to the end and then you won't know when the end has come.

I would like to finish working. If I am going to peg out, or kick the bucket, or whatever you call it, I'd like to do it while I am still in harness. When I stop writing my readers will know I'm dead.

I'll have on my tombstone: She had the last word.

... on Death

I used to worry about death all the time. In fact I could write a book about it. But I have come to the conclusion that death is one of two things—either the start of a great adventure—if there is something after death—or, if there isn't, one long peaceful sleep.

So that has been my life. A father I never knew. The lonely look of my eyes in those early photographs. The feeling of rejection. The breakdown in later life. And the in-between.

> *The passing of Dame Catherine Cookson has left a void in the literary world.*
>
> *Her fine achievements, despite the hardships she endured during her lifetime should be an inspiring example to all.*
>
> *Tony Blair, Prime Minister*

The Man by her Side

FOR YEARS Tom Cookson guarded his own private thoughts—just as he had physically protected his wife. His need for Catherine—who he referred to as "Kitty"—had grown into a passion. He claimed once he never closed both his eyes when he went to sleep in case Kitty had one of her bleeding fits and needed him.

Catherine McMullen, the manageress of the Hastings Workhouse laundry, first met Tom Cookson in 1937. Her first words to the young maths master boarding with Catherine's mother were: "Do you fence?"

Thomas Henry Cookson had arrived in the Sussex resort six years after Catherine. As staff at Hastings Grammar School reconvened for the start of the 1936 autumn term they were joined by an "inexperienced and timid" twenty-three year old maths master.

Tom Cookson was the son of an Essex verger, Thomas James Cookson. As a boy he soon developed the analytical mind and rational nature which governed his future life. At school he enjoyed mathematics, although he also achieved his Higher School Certificate in French and Latin.

It was a natural and expected progression to win a place at university. His Oxford college was—prophetically—St Catherine's and his three years of study financed by a fund for underprivileged students. In 1935 Tom returned south of the Thames with a respectable second-class honours degree in mathematics and a yearning to teach.

"I was a very quiet person then, very shy," admitted Tom. "To me, Catherine was the exact opposite. To feel that she took notice of me did something for me straight away."

For Tom it was something more than love. When his natural father died in 1915 his mother, a strong-willed and determined woman, married a plumber's mate, a quiet man whose gentleness soon captured his young stepson's devotion. It was a marriage of contrasting—and sometimes conflicting—characters which worked well. Equal, in many ways, to Tom and Catherine's all-consuming relationship.

"Catherine has always said that a man's first love is his mother and I suppose I saw in her the strength and character of my own mother," he admitted many years later. "She has been good for me and although I didn't know it at the start, my sort of personality has been good for her."

They married three years later in June, 1940. Catherine was thirty-three and a Catholic. Tom was six years younger and the son of a Protestant verger .

Through the war years he guided his wife's passion for learning. Together they listed the one hundred books Catherine should read. Ranging from Chaucer to 1920s novels, it took her years to complete.

In the late 1940s, when the loss of four babies plunged Catherine into a black and painful fifteen year nervous breakdown, Tom never lost faith in his wife's ability as a writer—even though his early insistence on correct grammar did spark some tearful clashes.

Following his retirement from teaching and the Cooksons' permanent move north in May, 1976, Tom was never far from his wife's side.

He rarely spoke of their life together but it soon became apparent that Tom Cookson oversaw his wife's success in the same way he managed the pupils who had passed through his classes, with loyalty and faith and continuous encouragement. It is also certain he saved Catherine's life on numerous occasions. Awoken in the night by one of his wife's bleeding attacks he would calmly drive her—very often covered in blood—to hospital in Newcastle.

He was once asked what life would be like without Catherine. His voice broke and he found it difficult to answer. "Life without Kitty would be no life at all," he finally said.

Tom Cookson always refused to discuss his childhood and early life. He couldn't remember much of it. It didn't matter anyway. "My life only began when I met her," he said defensively. "Everything stems from that."

20th June, 1986: Catherine celebrates her 80th birthday with a special lunch at her favourite Corbridge restaurant—and pays tribute to her husband, Tom.

The Journal, Newcastle

In 1983 he broke his self-imposed silence when he spoke for the first time: "People always assume I'm in the background and always have been throughout our marriage, that Kitty was the strong one, pushing me. But deep down I never believed I was inferior.

"I'm proud to stand just behind her shoulder. People say 'Who's that?' when they see me, then 'Oh, he must be her husband.' Well, that doesn't bother me. Not a bit.

"She's the most wonderful person on earth. I always hoped she was meant for me. With her beside me I felt there was nothing I could not do. There was this person who to me exuded such magnetism that I must have craved it all my life.

"She believed in herself and in me and she made me believe in her and me too, by golly she did. If she asked me to swim the Channel for her, you know I would.

"I have learned that if a man is only prepared to let go of his ego and let a woman have the reins where she clearly has the strength, then there's nothing that can't be achieved. She really is an inspiration."

"She was always telling stories, right from when we first met in Hastings," Tom recalled. "I always liked it when she went to the pictures. I didn't have to go. Hearing her tell me about it was always far better than it would have been seeing it myself. She makes everything come alive."

"I used to teach on a Saturday morning and I would tell my boys that if they were good all week, then I read them one of my wife's stories on the Saturday morning. They never misbehaved."

For more than four decades Catherine had rigidly worked a fourteen-hour day. Even before his retirement Tom would search the garden at Loreto in Hastings or High Barns in Corbridge or Bristol Lodge on the Northumberland fells for a fresh flower to accompany his wife's early morning cup of tea. By the time he returned from the kitchen Catherine would be hard at work.

"Her talent you know is quite wonderful," Tom would say. "You should see her. The words just come out of her mouth.

"You tell yourself that you are an agnostic and then you watch this gift materialise. It has to come from somewhere, doesn't it? She makes words of wisdom come out of the mouths of ordinary people. I used to criticise back at the beginning. Now I don't think I can find anything to criticise."

Typically Catherine maintained her husband was always a crucial part of the creative process. Stories, still fluid in her mind, would solidify as they were told to Tom. "As a writer, I am indeed blessed and as a wife, I am doubly blessed," said Catherine. "I could not have achieved all I have done without Tom's constant care and advice."

On 1 June, 1998—just ten days before Catherine's death—they celebrated their fifty-eighth wedding anniversary. "We would be nothing without each other,

Corrections for the 1989 novel The Harrogate Secret. *With Catherine's eyesight failing, Tom Cookson read each manuscript to his wife who dictated final changes to the story.*

Catherine and Tom at work at High Barns, Corbridge. Tom made sure each of the many letters that Catherine received was answered.

Catherine always maintained. "I could never have achieved so much in my profession without him.

"I would never have had the strength and the will to keep going without my Tom. Our minds are linked. I can't imagine what life would be without him. He can't even bring himself to talk about what will happen if he's left behind.

"It's just too painful to think about dying. I wish there was a way we could go together. We talk about everything else, but the subject of death hurts too much."

When his wife died on 11 June in the bedroom at White Lodge Tom was holding her hand. He had not left the Jesmond bungalow for almost three years and had rarely been more than a call away. Life without Catherine would be painful and confusing.

He was taken by a friend to have his hair cut and to order the flowers for his wife's funeral the following Tuesday. "When Tom came to pay he discovered that he had no money," recalls Piers Dudgeon. "Neither he nor Catherine carried any; they had no need to, they never went out. Money simply didn't figure in their lives, except as a happy opportunity to encourage others."

Returning home after the funeral Tom sat in his wife's favourite chair and thanked the friends and relatives who had surrounded him during the solitude of the past six days. As each left the reality "seemed to drain from him" and for the first time in more than four decades Tom prepared to face a night without "Kitty".

A week later, on 23 June, he attended the Royal Victoria Infirmary for a check-up and was persuaded to remain overnight. He never returned to White Lodge. The following Sunday Tom Cookson fell asleep and died of heart failure—seventeen days after Catherine.

Letters of Love

TO HER READERS Catherine Cookson had been endowed with the ability to understand. Despite the sex and violence and jealousy in her books she was seen as entirely moral, gifted with an insight into feelings and human failings that, at times, seemed like second sight.

Writing to Catherine—talking to Catherine—was like finding a long lost member of your family or calling on a favourite aunt.

Some letters read like confessions—as if their authors were seeking a greater power to grant forgiveness. Catherine had assumed the role of agony aunt; mother confessor; friend and confidant all rolled into one. And she took on the responsibility of a thousand other tragedies without complaint.

"If you read the letters I get it would be impossible for you not to answer them," she said. "When people tell you that your work has saved their sanity in some cases, or lifted their loneliness, or that my characters make them cry, get angry or laugh, then you know that you cannot send a typewritten slip to people like that."

But Catherine was never able to bring herself to sign copies of standard letters in reply. Until the 1960s she would answer every letter in longhand. Her painful shoulder—which forced her to talk her stories into a tape recorder—also made her dictate the messages. But she still kept them personal.

Although for many years she employed a part-time secretary to transcribe her tapes and retype her manuscripts, Tom continued to act as her correspondence secretary. He maintained an exhaustive card index of every letter, cross-referenced, and including coded comments. "V W L"—very warm letter. "V N P"—very nice person.

Her days, some stretching as long as fourteen hours, were divided equally between her writing and her fans.

"It takes me only five or ten minutes at the most to eat my breakfast and, even then, I'm looking at my scripts," she would explain. "Then I get up, come down to the study at about ten o'clock and do a half-a-dozen or so telephone calls, mostly business, London probably; then I get started on the mail. Most days I stay in the study until twelve or half-past and get as many letters off as I can.

"If I have been ill, the mail mounts up tremendously and I get very worried about it. My publishers have been at me for ages to get stereotyped letters done. They couldn't believe I received so many letters; some people have been writing for twenty years."

By the early 1980s an average 3,000 letters a year—almost sixty letters a week—were arriving at the Cookson home.

Each week would also bring its share of gifts. American generosity could manifest itself in surprising ways, such as a silver coffee set. Other gifts included a box of flowers from a reader on holiday in Guernsey or beautifully knitted shawls or sweaters. "But the dishcloths I got from one old lady were just as precious," she said.

One woman wrote to Catherine as "Lady Chesterfield-Cookson", a reference to her early mentor. Letters from overseas could arrive addressed to "Catherine Cookson, England."

Some were highly emotional, thanking Catherine for books which had guided a reader through a personal trauma or grief. Others quite openly told her: "You have saved my life."

"People tell me my books have changed their lives," she said. "I am very pleased with the honours but I am more pleased to think I have helped people through my writing.

"If I had to choose as years go by between writing a novel and answering letters I would give my time to my letters first. These are the people that writers must realise make them what they are."

A Brief Affair

WE HAD BEEN talking about the claim in my biography—*To Be A Lady*—that Catherine had learned as early as 1929 that her father had once been employed as a turn-of-the-century footman at Ravensworth Castle.

I had published, for the first time, an account of Catherine's search for her father's identity and a meeting with a member of a village blacksmith's family. She admitted her visit to Lamesley and the meeting but denied she was ever told her father was on the castle staff.

Catherine admitted her pre-war meeting with a member of the village blacksmith's family, but resolutely denied that her father was ever on the castle staff.

"I can tell you my father was not a worker there." It was her way of answering a question with a negative and protecting herself at the same time—simultaneously opening and closing a door.

"So he was a member of the family?" I asked. "Or a guest?"

"He was not a member of the family."

"When did you know the truth?"

"Kate knew," said Catherine. "Oh yes, Kate knew." It was a deliberate and calculated pointer which took me several months to understand.

We parted with my promise that I would not disclose the identity of Catherine's father until after her death. To me, and her millions of fans, Catherine is still very much alive. So is my promise.

The only thing I have omitted from the account which follows is the surname of Kate Fawcett's lover and Catherine Cookson's "gentleman" father.

Cliff Goodwin, 1999

❧

Sometime during the third week of May, 1929, Catherine McMullen caught the train from Tyne Dock to Lamesley. It was a pleasant ride, taking her from the back-to-back grime of South Shields and Jarrow to the open fields beyond Gateshead.

When she called at the Ravensworth Arms, the public house and hotel where her mother once worked, the twenty-two year old was sent next door to the blacksmith's cottages. If anyone knew the identity of Catherine's father it was Bella Thompson.

The blacksmith's wife was one of the few people who still remembered, or cared, about a village scandal more than a quarter of a century earlier. Confronted by Kate Fawcett's daughter, Bella decided the story needed to be buried once and for all. Over a cup of tea in the back kitchen Catherine listened as the woman revealed the secret of her mother's gentleman lover. Her father, Bella told Catherine, had been employed by Lord Ravensworth as a footman. He was dismissed early in 1906 and returned south where he was born.

It was a bland lie which Catherine never willingly accepted. Her father, her gentleman father, could never have been a mere footman—"I could feel it in my bones. He was something special. And I was something special."

The truth, as Catherine was to learn, is as intriguing as any Cookson plot.

Sometime in the early 1900s the teenage Bella had been employed as a domestic servant by the blacksmith's family before marrying one of the sons. During the summer of 1903 she was befriended by one of two sisters employed at the adjacent inn. Mary Fawcett was a snobbish and volatile sixteen year old. Mary's elder sister Kate, Bella soon discovered, possessed a character as soft and charming as her looks. The teenagers were soon close friends, sharing gossip during their off-duty hours.

August, 1903, was unusually wet. One rainy afternoon a stranger entered the saloon bar of the Ravensworth Arms. He was served by nineteen year old Kate McMullen. The man was in his mid-thirties and spoke with an accent Kate had never heard before. His English was good, almost too good, as if he had been taught as a child to choose each word and pronounce each syllable with care.

Between drinks the man studied the attractive teenager tending the bar and clearing the tables. "She had two great azure blue eyes, with dark curving brows. Her hair was brown and abundant" (*Kate Hannigan*). Kate had a good, if not full figure. Her smile was warm and full of good humour, but she looked prettiest when she was serious. Occasionally the man would make little sketches on a pad he had taken from his coat, self consciously closing the cover whenever any one approached. Kate studied the man with equal curiosity. He was dressed in a black top coat, trimmed with an astrakhan collar, and carried a silver-mounted walking stick and black leather gloves. There was no doubt he had class, but what was he doing in the tap room of a County Durham village inn?

By his second or third visit to the Ravensworth Arms, Kate knew she had fallen hopelessly in love with this gentleman who spoke "different … lovely". Very soon they arranged to meet on her afternoon off. He was, Kate sensed, the perfect gentleman. He walked neither too close nor too far from her side. He made no attempt to make physical contact, save for steadying her hand as she climbed a sty or stepped round a puddle. He also appeared genuinely interested in her working-class family. Kate and her companion chatted freely. On their first walk together he told her his name. It was Alex. Kate could never remember, nor pronounce, his French surname.

It is almost certain Alex never told Kate about his family history or background. Pragmatic and ever the realist, the teenager would surely have dismissed his story as an older man's boastful attempt at seduction. Her companion, Kate learned, was a house guest of the Liddell family and had arrived on a steamer from his native Belgium a day or two before the death of Henry George Liddell, the Earl of Ravensworth.

COACH ROAD RAVENSWORTH GATESHEAD

The Coach Road to Ravensworth Castle, and down which Kate McMullen's "gentleman" lover walked to meet her. This picture was taken in 1905—at the height of the affair.

The second Earl had been a doctor of civil law and a justice of the peace and, like many of the Liddells, a military man. He was colonel and honorary colonel of the Northumberland Hussars Yeomanry. When he succeeded to the barony in 1878 Henry Liddell resigned his twenty-six-year tenure as member of parliament for South Northumberland. Although married twice, Henry Liddell failed to father any sons. In August, 1903, his brother Athol Charles John Liddell became the third Earl of Ravensworth.

Two decades earlier, while the future Earl was touring Europe, he was introduced to the art-loving and rebellious elder son of a Belgian aristocratic family. As a teenager Liddell's new friend constantly sketched and painted the miners and their families and the grubby streets of industrial south-eastern Belgium. But it was his determination to become a professional artist and turn his back on his father's Ardenne mining

Ravensworth Castle, where Catherine was misled into believing her father had worked as a footman.

empire which prompted a bitter family rift. Obviously talented, his pictures never sold well. The subjects were too gritty and honest to sit comfortably with his peers among the Walloon gentry. For years he survived on a secret stipend from his mother.

It was Alex's mother—and her fear for her son's life—who eventually persuaded him to cross the Channel and, indirectly, to change the course of English literature. Following the attempted assassination on King Leopold II the previous November, several minor royals had been killed or injured. For seven months Alex's mother desperately tried to get her strong-willed eldest son to leave Belgium. As a distant cousin of the King, the countess was certain it was only a matter of time before her son would himself become a target of the revolutionaries. He would be safer in England.

Alex never became a regular at the Ravensworth Arms, but planned his visits to coincide with Kate's free time and treated her to outings and excursions. For a few brief hours each month Kate become "a lady". Never dazzled by the dream, she was well aware the distance between them on the strict social ladder of the time was unscalable.

For two years, month by month, Kate allowed herself to be seduced. Her companion's kisses became more urgent. Finally, in the last two weeks of September 1905, Kate surrendered. She was a virgin. The result of this single, sexual encounter, at the age of twenty-one, soon became apparent. By the end of October Kate began to suspect the worst. During November she knew she was pregnant.

She returned to break the news to Rose and John McMullen. Her stepfather erupted in hypocritical indignation and Rose had to protect her daughter from a beating. Kate Fawcett would never see her lover again. Their daughter was born on 20th June, 1906, a balmy Wednesday morning, in the bedroom of 5 Leam Lane, Tyne Dock.

Kate arrived at South Shields Register Office on 13 August with several misgivings. In her step-father's eyes she had already committed the most heinous of offences against her family—she had given birth while unmarried. Kate was about to commit a second crime.

She had left the registration of her daughter to the last minute. A bout of milk fever had delayed her even more. Her only concern now was to bequeath the child at least the makings of respectability. Convinced she would be prosecuted for the late registration—it was already fifty-five days after the child's birth—Kate claimed her daughter had been born a week later on 27 June. To hide the illegitimacy Kate invented a new and respectable persona for herself. She gave her name as Mrs Catherine Davies, living at 5 Leam Lane. Her husband, the child's father, she claimed was Alexander Davies, a commission agent. Kate gave her maiden name as Fawcett which, at least, was true.

For years Catherine Cookson credited her absent father with her interest—her latent talent—for art. But there was much more: Her energy; her ambition; her rebellious, sometimes reckless determination to succeed; her compassion; her "painful sensitivity ... without which what I sensed in others would have remained an indescribable mass of feelings".

Sadly, she would also inherit a disease which would have crippled a less determined person. There is no evidence to suggest Kate's lover showed any of the classic symptoms of haemorrhagic telangiectasia. Neither Kate, nor her sister Mary, made any comment on Alex's appearance. With medical hindsight it is safe to assume he would have been thin and pale, almost anaemic looking. The chances of inheriting telangiectasia from a parent have been rated at fifty per cent. If the son or daughter of a confirmed sufferer is found to be free from the genetic disorder there is no chance of it being passed on to future generations—conclusive proof that Catherine's father must also have inherited the disorder and a fact which brings his behaviour, and the couple's prolonged courtship, into sharper focus.

Alex blamed the long periods between his meeting with Kate, some as long as two months, on his painting expeditions across the North East. It is equally possible that he, like his future daughter, was forced to spend weeks confined to bed recovering from a bleeding attack. His condition, which he shared with other members of Belgium's ruling family, might also explain why, approaching his forties, he was still unmarried. A sensitive and kind man who shunned marriage for fear of passing on such a frightening condition would almost certainly have thought long and hard before embarking on a casual affair.

Confronted by the news of Kate's pregnancy there was no reason for Alex to remain in England. Kate had returned to her family at Leam Lane End. Alex's friend and benefactor, the fourth Earl, was already dead, just seven months after inheriting the Ravensworth title. The Belgian painter was now a tolerated, if not unwelcome, guest at the castle.

The fifth Baron, Arthur Thomas Liddell, died in 1919. His heir, Gerald Wellesley, left Ravensworth to live at Eslington Park, near Alnwick. The following year the contents of the castle were sold off. Among the furniture and bronzes and china were scores of painting. One, a Rembrandt entitled *The Baptism of the Eunich*, sold for £10,000. The cataloguer listed six other pictures: "Oil paintings of Newcastle, Jarrow and South Shields street scenes by un-named Belgian artist."

Perhaps the strongest indication that Catherine was aware of her father's true identity—and did not accept Bella Thompson's compassionate explanation—came in 1950 with the publication of her first novel.

Kate Hannigan has been brought up believing she is the daughter of Tim and Sarah Hannigan. One day her mother admits a brief and disastrous affair with a lodger. The man was short and greying and in his late thirties, a wandering artist who painted the slums and docks and the Tyneside street life. He spoke "differently", just as Kate McMullen's lover had. A few years later Sarah Hannigan learns of the artist's death through a half-page newspaper obituary.

Kate Hannigan is Catherine Cookson's most autobiographical novel. There are no less than sixty-two instances in the novel directly related to Catherine's own life. The majority of the story takes place within the narrow environment of Catherine's own early years, from the fictitious Fifteen Streets at East Jarrow—only yards from the New Buildings—to the luxury of Westoe.

The book opens with Kate Hannigan in labour, about to give birth to a bastard child—Catherine's mother was also called Kate. She is attended by a young physician, Dr Rodney Prince, as was Kate Fawcett by Dr McHaffie; both doctors drove cars. Downstairs, Tim and Sarah Hannigan wait in the kitchen for the baby's delivery, "Tim Hannigan sitting in his chair by the fireside, wearing his look of sullen anger" and Sarah with "her weary face", exactly as John and Rose McMullen must have done. Catherine calls the child Annie, her own middle name. Kate Hannigan's kindly neighbour is called Mullen, instead of McMullen.

In the late 1940s when Catherine was writing *Kate Hannigan* she had no notion of literary fame. The story—the true story of her father—would, like the rest of her early life, be woven into the pages of her fiction.

A Cookson Chronology

1850-1856

John McMullen—Catherine Cookson's step-grandfather—is born in a southern county of Ireland, one of triplets and with thirteen brothers.

1858

Rose Ann McConnell—Catherine Cookson's grandmother—is born in Gateshead.

1878

Rose McConnell marries William Fawcett.

1884

Birth of Kate Fawcett, Catherine Cookson's mother.

1888

William Fawcett dies of tuberculosis, leaving Rose and their five daughters destitute.

1890

4th May: John McMullen marries Rose Fawcett.

December: Jack McMullen—Catherine's step-uncle—is born.

1902

Summer: Kate Fawcett joins her sister Mary as barmaid at the Ravensworth Arms, in the village of Lamesley, south Gateshead.

1903

Winter: Kate begins her two year affair with a "gentleman" customer at the Ravensworth Arms.

Lamesley village, c.1906. A year earlier Kate would have walked the same country lanes with her "gentleman" lover.

The Ravensworth Arms, Lamesley.

Leam Lane End: taken in 1906—the year of Catherine's birth—this picture was taken from the Jarrow Road looking up Simonside Bank. The little girl is standing opposite Number 5 Leam Lane.

1905

The McMullen family move into Number 5 Leam Lane, Tyne Dock. It is their ninth home since their fifteen-year marriage.

November: Kate Fawcett discovers she is pregnant and returns to her family at their new Leam Lane End home.

1906

20th June: Birth of Catherine Cookson at Number 5 Leam Lane, Tyne Dock.

13th August: Kate registers her daughter's birth at South Shields register office. She falsely gives her own name as "Mrs Catherine Davies", whose husband "Alexander" is a commission agent. Kate records her child as "Catherine Ann Davies". She also claims her daughter was born one week later, on 27th June.

1910

2nd September: Catherine attends Simonside Protestant School.

1912

Thomas Henry Cookson is born in Essex, the son of a verger.

June: John, Rose and Jack McMullen and Catherine move to an upstairs house in William Black Street, East Jarrow.

July: The family moves to Number 10 William Black Street.

Summer: Rose suffers from dropsy and her daughter Kate leaves service to run the McMullen household.

1913

Spring: Catherine is moved to The Meases School, East Jarrow.

June: She changes school again, this time to St Bede's Infants School, Monkton Road, Jarrow.

Autumn: Catherine is confronted with her illegitimacy for the first time while playing with friends; Kate admits she is her mother.

1914

Spring: John McMullen receives £100 injury compensation and retires.

Summer: Catherine is sexually assaulted by her mother's boyfriend.

4th August: First World War; within weeks Jack McMullen joins the army and is posted to the Durham Light Infantry.

1915

Summer: Catherine is refused entry to a friend's birthday party, allegedly because of her illegitimacy.

Summer: Catherine writes her first story, *The Wild Irish Girl*.

1916

Spring: Catherine is moved to Saint Peter and Paul's Catholic School, Tyne Dock.

1917

13th December: Rose McMullen dies at Number 10 William Black Street. Her grand-daughter is asleep in the same room.

1918

5th September: Jack McMullen dies from "wounds received in action" while serving in France.

1919

December: Catherine injures her leg in a playground fall; she never returns to school. She will suffer with the damage to her leg for the rest of her life.

1920

Summer: Catherine enters services with the Sowerby family at 27 Simonside Terrace; she also considers training as a nurse.

Autumn: After a thirty-minute art lesson she quits domestic service and starts her own business pen painting cushion covers.

1922

Catherine completes her first long story, *On the Second Floor*. The 16,000 word story is rejected by the *Shields Daily Gazette*.

1923

30th June: Kate marries David McDermott.

1924

June: Catherine suffers from lead poisoning and is forced to give up her pen painting business.

Summer: She finds work as a companion-maid; the work is exhausting; Catherine shows the first signs of her inherited blood disorder.

22nd October: Catherine begins work at Harton Workhouse as a laundry checker.

Catherine's grandmother and step-grandfather, John and Rose McMullen, with their only son, Jack. The picture was taken in the back yard of Number 5 Leam Lane.

1925

Summer: Catherine makes her second attempt to enroll as a nurse; she is shortlisted for training by a Newcastle hospital.

1926

Summer: Catherine submits a play to a national correspondence school; it is returned with the comment: "Strongly advise author not to take up writing as a career."

1927

September: When the workhouse assistant laundress leaves Catherine is promoted to take her place at £3 12s 6d a month (£3.62p). Four months later her application to become the laundress is refused.

The Hastings shop where Catherine rented a first floor bedroom in 1930.

1927

Autumn: Catherine discovers Lord Chesterfield's *Letters to His Son* while reading Elinor Glyn's *The Career of Katherine Bush*.

1929

April: Catherine applies for the post of laundress at Tendring Workhouse, near Clacton; she is appointed at £43 10s [£43.50p] a year. Before she leaves the north she returns to Lamesley to learn more about her "gentleman" father.

29th May: Catherine starts work at Tendring Workhouse.

19th December: She is interviewed for the post of head laundress at Hastings Poor Law Institution, formerly the town's workhouse.

1930

1st February: Catherine leaves the Tendring Workhouse after "eight lonely months"; she reports for duty at Hastings two days later at a salary of £156 a year. Her first lodgings are above C.E. Morris' grocer shop in Clifton Road.

18th April: John McMullen dies at Number 10 William Black Street. Catherine decides not to attend her step-grandfather's funeral.

1931

December: Catherine moves to a flat in West Hill House, Hastings.

1932

Spring: Kate visits her daughter in Hastings; she persuades Catherine to let her move south permanently.

September: Tom Cookson is awarded a scholarship to St Catherine's College, Oxford.

1933

Catherine buys The Hurst, a run-down "gentlemen's residence" in Hoads Wood Road, Hastings.

1935

July: Tom Cookson graduates from St Catherine's College, Oxford with a second-class honours degree in mathematics.

1936

September: Tom Cookson joins the staff of Hastings Grammar School; Catherine and Tom meet for the first time.

1937

Summer: Kate returns to Tyneside; Tom Cookson joins the other lodgers at The Hurst.

Summer: After the disapproval of a Hurst guest Catherine destroys all her notes, short stories and manuscripts.

1938

5th September: David McDermott dies after falling into the River Tyne.

1939

August: Catherine resigns job as head laundress at Hastings Poor Law Institution, to concentrate on running The Hurst.

3rd September: Outbreak of the Second World War; The Hurst is requisitioned by London County Council for blind refugees.

1940

1st June: "Catherine Ann Davies" marries Thomas Henry Cookson, at Hastings.

Summer: Hastings Grammar School evacuated to Hertfordshire; Tom and Catherine take a flat in Victoria Street, St Albans.

7th December: Catherine's first child, a boy, is born dead after nine days of premature labour.

1941

August: Tom enlists in the Royal Air Force.

Autumn: The couple move to Sleaford, Lincolnshire where Catherine suffers a miscarriage.

1942

Autumn: Tom is posted as an instructor to RAF Madley, near Hereford; the Cooksons are billeted at 31 Ryelands Street, Hereford.

December: Catherine sells the first of her sketches for £5 to J. Arthur Dixon, an Isle of Wight greetings card publisher.

1943

Catherine suffers a second miscarriage.

The Hurst, Hoads Wood Road, the fifteen-room Hastings mansion the twenty-three year old Catherine bought on a wage of £3 a week.

1944

Spring: Catherine works at the Rotherwas ammunition factory; after five weeks she develops cordite poisoning and leaves.

Autumn: Confined to bed with phlebitis, the guilt of her lost babies and her own illegitimacy trigger the first signs of Catherine's mental breakdown.

1st June 1940, Mr and Mrs Cookson leave the church after their Hastings wedding ceremony. In the doorway is George Silverlock, the workhouse master, who gave Catherine away.

1945

May: Catherine is admitted as a voluntary patient to St Mary's psychiatric hospital at Burghill, near Hereford; she discharges herself after six weeks.

July: Catherine returns alone to Hastings to rebuild The

Hurst. Tom, still in the RAF, visits at weekends.

Autumn: Her fourth pregnancy ends in another miscarriage.

1946

February: Tom Cookson is demobbed from RAF. Catherine struggles to cope with her ever deepening breakdown.

December: Catherine starts work on her first novel, *Kate Hannigan*.

1948

Spring: After the loss of four babies Catherine undergoes an operation on her womb.

Catherine joins Hastings Writers' Circle.

Catherine reads the early drafts of *Kate Hannigan* and the episodes from her future *Mary Ann* stories to meetings of Hastings Writers' Circle.

1949

Summer: A second operation on her womb proves unsuccessful.

Autumn: Catherine Cookson signs with her first literary agent, John Smith at Christy & Moore.

15th August: *Woman's Hour* broadcasts Catherine's talk, *I Learned to Draw at Thirty*.

All fifty short stories Catherine wrote during the year are rejected by magazines and newspapers.

1950

Spring: Catherine undergoes a third operation on her womb.

30th January: *Woman's Hour* broadcasts Catherine's second talk, *Making Dreams Come True*.

June: *Kate Hannigan* is published by Macdonald; she receives £100 advance.

Autumn: Macdonald rejects Catherine's second book, *Annie Hannigan*.

1951

May: *Woman's Hour* broadcasts Catherine's third talk, *Buying Secondhand Furniture*.

1952

March: *The Fifteen Streets* is published.

21st March: *Woman's Hour* broadcasts Catherine's latest talk, *Getting Your Nerves Under Control*.

1953

Colour Blind published.

1953

Summer: Kate—suffering from terminal cancer—moves from Tyneside and into The Hurst.

1954

November: Catherine, Tom and the dying Kate move to a new Hastings home, Loreto.

Catherine at forty-seven, in 1953.

The Fifteen Streets

I was alone and I thought and thought but didn't have an idea in my head.

I'd given up God at that time and I was still fighting my breakdown, but as I sat in the room I suddenly had this feeling that I wanted to talk to something—someone.

I can remember looking up at the ceiling and saying, "Well, if there's anything there, then give me a story." It sounds phoney now, but that's what happened.

Within an hour I had the whole story of The Fifteen Streets, right from the opening to the very last words. Every character, every incident and definitely the background. It was all there. I won't say I couldn't believe it. I just accepted it. I knew here was a complete story and I must get it down straight away.

I went from there into the dining room, where I usually did my writing on the table, and with my frozen fingers I wrote the title, "The Fifteen Streets". From that moment until months later when I finished that story, I can say with truth I never altered a character, an incident, or anything else in the whole plan. I worked on it practically night and day.

I worked on it through bleedings and flu and desperate tiredness, but I got everything down as it had been given to me, when I asked for it on that particular morning.

I never had to alter a word of it and I still think it's a good story. It's never happened to me again, but I took it as a sign that I was meant to go on writing.

❧ *Catherine Cookson*

Loreto, St Helen's Park Road: Catherine and Tom, and their dog Simon in the garden of the Hastings house in which Kate died in September 1956.

Maggie Rowan and *A Grand Man* published.

May: Film rights to *A Grand Man* are sold to J. Arthur Rank for £750.

1956

23rd September: Kate McDermott dies at Loreto as Catherine holds her mother's hand.

The Lord and Mary Ann published.

Spring: The film rights to *Rooney* are sold to J. Arthur Rank.

Summer: *Jacqueline*—retitled from *A Grand Man*—gets its first showing in British cinemas; Queen Elizabeth, the Queen Mother, orders a special screening at Buckingham Palace.

September: Catherine begins work on her autobiography, *Our Kate*.

1957

Rooney published.

1958

The Menagerie and *The Devil and Mary Ann* published.

Spring: *Rooney*—filmed from the book of the same name—is released; Corgi issue the novel as a paperback.

Autumn: Catherine completes a short novel—*The Bonny Dawn*—which remains unpublished for thirty-eight years.

October: *Woman's Hour* begins a serialisation of *The Adventures of Mary Ann Shaughnessy*.

1959

Fanny McBride and *Slinky Jane* published.

Summer: *The Lady on My Left* is completed but not published until the late 1990s.

1960

March: Ill health forces Catherine to withdraw from delivering a South Shields Lecture & Literary Society speech entitled: *From Paupers to Pinewood*.

11th November: Recovering from pneumonia Catherine returns to Tyneside after being elected president of the South Shields Lecture & Literary Society; her acceptance speech is called *Child of the Time*.

Fenwick Houses published.

Spring: Several film companies reject *The Fifteen Streets*; it is twenty-nine years before the novel is adapted for television.

1961

May: After writing her first sixteen books in longhand, writer's cramp forces Catherine to dictate her stories on to a tape recorder; she never "writes" again.

Love and Mary Ann published.

Spring: *Woman's Hour* serialises *Fanny McBride*.

Spring: The first Catherine Marchant story—*The Fen Tiger*—is serialised in *Woman's Own*.

Summer: *Woman's Own* publishes two more Catherine Marchant stories, *Heritage of Folly* and *House of Men*.

Autumn: *Woman's Hour* serialises *Love and Mary Ann*.

1962

March: Catherine Cookson is interviewed live as *Woman's Hour* guest of the week.

Life and Mary Ann and *The Garment* published.

June: Catherine reads an extract—*The Day of the Party*—from her still unpublished autobiography for *Woman's Hour*.

December: *Woman's Hour* begins an eight part reading from *Life and Mary Ann*.

1963

The Blind Miller published.

The Fen Tiger and *Heritage of Folly* published as Catherine Marchant novels.

Heritage of Folly published in the United States under the pen name Katie McMullen.

Spring: *Woman's Hour* broadcasts a second extract from the *Our Kate* manuscript entitled *The Train to South Shields*. It is rebroadcast on *Home for the Day*.

September: *Woman's Hour* broadcasts *Me Granda* another *Our Kate* extract.

1964

Hannah Massey and *Marriage and Mary Ann* published.

House of Men published as a Catherine Marchant novel.

House of Men published in the United States under the pen name Katie McMullen.

March: *Woman's Hour* broadcasts *Up the Creek*, another *Our Kate* extract.

1965

Catherine publishes her first children's book, *Matty Doolin*.

Mary Ann's Angels and *The Long Corridor* published.

Evil at Roger's Cross published in the United States as a Katie McMullen novel.

Spring: After fifteen years of live broadcasts Catherine makes her first recorded contribution for *Woman's Hour*, *Thursday's Child Has Far to Go*.

Autumn: *Woman's Hour* broadcasts *Playgrounds*; repeated on a morning edition of *Home for the Day*.

1966

The Unbaited Trap published.

1967

May: An attack of phlebitis forces Catherine to cancel a Harrogate literary lunch and a North-East promotion tour.

Mary Ann and Bill published.

25th May: *Katie Mulholland* is published. At 275,000 words, it is Catherine's longest book so far. Corgi, the US-based paperback publisher agrees to issue an American edition—but only if she cuts 50,000 words.

1968

Joe and the Gladiator published for children.

Spring: *The Round Tower*—her thirty-sixth book—is named the year's Best Regional Novel and its author is awarded The Winifred Holtby Prize by the Royal Society of Literature.

1969

The Nice Bloke published.

April: *Our Kate* is finally published after thirteen years and numerous rewrites.

Catherine at sixty, in 1966

July: Tom Cookson retires from teaching.

Summer: Catherine rejects a move to Jersey for tax reasons.

1970

February: An emergency operation saves Catherine's life after a prolonged haemorrhage.

The Glass Virgin and *The Invitation* published. *The Nipper* published for children.

1971

The Dwelling Place and *Feathers in the Fire* published.

March: *Joe and the Gladiator* screened as a three-part BBC serial; it is the first Cookson story to appear on television.

Summer: Catherine agrees to donate most of her early manuscripts to the Boston University library—the parcel weighs 220lbs.

1972

Pure as a Lily published. *Blue Baccy* published for children.

March: Catherine returns to the North East for a book signing tour; one South Shields store sells one thousand Cookson paperbacks in less than an hour.

Winter: Catherine's agent, John Smith, retires and sells his client list to Anthony Sheil; her new agent immediately signs a new publishing deal with Heinemann.

1973

21st January: Tyne Tees Television asks Catherine to make a last minute guest appearance on its *Challenge* programme after the actress Moira Shearer is injured in a car accident.

The Mallen Streak published.

February: *The Mallen Streak* is voted *Daily Express* Book of the Month; in less than a year the novel sells 1,027,000 copies.

1974

March: South Shields grants Catherine the Freedom of the Borough.

The Mallen Girl and *The Mallen Litter* published. *Our John Willie* published for children.

1975

The Invisible Cord and *The Gambling Man* published.

Miss Martha Mary Crawford published as a Catherine Marchant novel.

Our Kate is dramatised and filmed by students from Harlow College of Technology and Art. Catherine helps pay for the £900 project.

October: The Cooksons purchase 39 Eslington Terrace, Jesmond; they commute between Hastings and Newcastle.

October: Catherine interviewed on Tyne Tees Television and describes herself as "the best-paid bastard in the business".

1976

April: Cookson fans outnumber students twenty-to-one during a Durham City Technical College lecture entitled *Old John McMullen versus Lord Chesterfield*.

May: Loreto is sold; Catherine returns permanently to the north and a converted church near Morpeth, Northumberland.

Autumn: The Cooksons purchase High Barns in Corbridge, Northumberland; they also buy adjacent Trinity Barns.

The Tide of Life—initially published as a Catherine Marchant story—is reissued as a Cookson novel. *Mrs Flannagan's Trumpet* published for children.

The Iron Facade published as a Catherine Marchant novel. It is followed by *The Slow Awakening*—the last Catherine Marchant story.

1977

Summer: Catherine agrees to return to the scene of her birth to demolish William Black Street for a television *Lifestyle* documentary.

The Girl published.

1978

The Cinder Path published. *Go Tell it to Mrs Golightly* published for children.

1979

Spring: Hastings Writers' Group announces the annual Catherine Cookson Short Story Competition.

Spring: Catherine's sketches, pastel works and oil seascapes are included in a five-week Women Artists of the North-East exhibition at the Metal Art Precinct, South Shields.

The Man Who Cried published.

June: Granada Television screens a three-part adaptation of the *Mallen* trilogy.

1980

February: The Cooksons donate £27,500 to Newcastle Haemophilia Research Centre, part of the Department of Medicine at Newcastle University.

Autumn: Catherine is admitted to hospital after a severe bleeding attack; her treatment forces her to withdraw as a *This Is Your Life* guest for football manager Laurie McMeneny.

Tilly Trotter published.

January: The BBC screens a five-part serial of *Our John Willie*.

1981

12th January: Burglary at Trinity Barns; the property is sold and the Cooksons buy Bristol Lodge at Langley, ten miles from Hexham, Northumberland, as a retreat.

January: A £12,800 gift from the Cooksons buys life-saving baby care equipment for Newcastle General Hospital.

Summer: Former agent John Smith abandons a biography of Catherine Cookson after pressure from the author.

22nd September: Catherine is booked to open a £500,000 housing project for the elderly at Simonside, within sight of her Leam Lane birthplace; she is forced to pull out because of ill health.

Tilly Trotter Wed published. *Lanky Jones* published for children.

Summer: Corgi presents its best-selling author with a trophy after her paperback sales reach 27,500,000.

Catherine Cookson at seventy-seven, 1983.

This is Your Life. Just before Christmas 1982 Catherine arrived at Tyne Tees Newcastle studios expecting to take part in a live two-minute interview—instead she was confronted by Eamonn Andrews.

1982

October: The Variety Club elects Catherine Cookson Woman of the Year.

October: Readers of *Woman's Own* vote Catherine their favourite creative writer in the magazine's Women of Achievement Awards.

22nd December: Catherine arrives at the Newcastle studios of Tyne Tees Television expecting to take part in a two-minute interview. Instead she is greeted with the words: "Catherine Cookson ... This Is Your Life."

Tilly Trotter Widowed published. *Nancy Nuttal and the Mongrel* published for children.

1983

The Whip and *Hamilton* published.

January: Asked to pay for more baby care equipment for

Newcastle General Hospital, Catherine agrees to pay for the building of a £40,000 ward.

February: When an appeal to buy a £60,000 Cavitron ultra-sonic scalpel falters, the Cooksons step in with a £20,000 donation.

February: Catherine is rushed to hospital from her Corbridge home after suffering a violent bleeding attack.

Spring: Visits to "Catherine Cookson's Corbridge" appear in several North American holiday brochures. In despair the Cooksons sell High Barns and move permanently to Bristol Lodge. Catherine also blames the move on a hate campaign by other Corbridge residents.

13th May: Catherine is awarded an honorary Master of Arts degree by Newcastle University.

29th September: Stage adaptation of *Katie Mulholland* opens at Newcastle's Playhouse Theatre; two days before the first night only 400 of the 12,572 seats are unsold.

11th November: The Variety Club of Great Britain vote Catherine Cookson its North-East Female Personality of the Year.

20th November: Catherine Cookson is the subject of a fifty-four minute *South Bank Show*.

December: Catherine Cookson House, a block of retirement flats at Westoe Village, South Shields, is named by the Guardian Housing Association.

1984

The Black Velvet Gown and *Goodbye Hamilton* published.

January: When the first return from the Public Lending Right is published Catherine Cookson is named as Britain's most borrowed author; thirty-three of the top 100 books are Cookson novels. Catherine donates her £5,000 payment to the Royal Literary Fund.

Northern Echo

Master of Arts: Only weeks before her seventy-seventh birthday, Newcastle University awards Catherine an honorary degree.

Spring: When an American magazine nominates Catherine Cookson for its annual romantic writer award Catherine demands to be taken off the the shortlist—"you can't get romantic about a pit lad earning 3s 6d a shift", she says.

24th June: Catherine lays the foundation stone for a sports

centre for the disabled at Hexham General Hospital; she launched the appeal with a £2,500 donation.

September: Catherine agrees to allow a new hybrid tea rose to be named after her—only if a proportion of the profits are donated to charity.

10th October: The Cooksons give £5,500 for baby monitoring equipment to South Shields General Hospital.

November: The Variety Club of Great Britain votes Catherine Cookson its Regional Female Personality of the Year for the second year running.

1985

A Dinner of Herbs and *Harold* published.

January: Catherine Cookson retains her place at the top of the library list; thirty of the 100 most borrowed books are Cookson novels.

April: Limited Corgi edition of *The Black Velvet Gown* issued to mark the publication of the fiftieth Cookson paperback.

15th June: Catherine Cookson awarded an OBE in the Queen's Birthday Honours List.

August: South Tyneside Council receives "official" approval to launch Catherine Cookson Country; within a year thousands of fans are walking the Cookson Trail.

Summer: Catherine refuses to allow the name of The Allison Arms—the only public house left in East Jarrow—to be renamed the Catherine Cookson.

September: A Cookson cheque for £32,000 creates four new jobs at Newcastle University library.

5th September: *The Gambling Man* opens at Newcastle Playhouse; the sell-out adaptation was Catherine's own choice.

2nd December: Catherine is admitted to Newcastle's Royal Victoria Infirmary with intestinal bleeding.

4th December: From her hospital bed she signs three cheques: The first, for £250,000, will be used to launch the Catherine Cookson Foundation; a £40,000 cheque will be used to buy surgical laser equipment, and £50,000 will help treat deaf children.

December: *The Times* claims Catherine Cookson is now Britain's fourteenth richest woman with a personal fortune of at least £20m; Catherine dismisses the statement as "ludicrous".

1986

Catherine Cookson Country, her *Pictorial Memoir*, and *The Moth* and *Bill Bailey* published.

January: Twenty-five of the 100 most borrowed library books are Cookson novels.

6th February: Prince Charles presents Catherine's OBE during a Tyneside visit.

25th May: Cliff Michelmore talks to Catherine in the Galilee Chapel of Durham Cathedral; she chooses some of her favourite music for the BBC television interview.

20th June: Catherine Cookson's eightieth birthday. Three publishers honour her with a celebration lunch and the author marks the occasion by giving away £160,000. The money will be added to the Catherine Cookson Foundation and used to establish the Catherine Cookson Lectureship in Molecular Haematology.

25th June: The Catherine Cookson display opens at South Shields Museum; it includes a reproduction of the kitchen at No 10 William Black Street.

October: Bantam Press, an imprint of Transworld, outbids Heinemann for the next ten Catherine Cookson novels in a £4m deal.

Our Kate. In 1986 Catherine stepped back in time to open a £50,000 Cookson exhibition at South Shields' Ocean Road Museum. The display included a full-scale replica of the William Black Street kitchen.

Northern Echo

1987

The Parson's Daughter and *Bill Bailey's Lot* published.

January: Twenty-nine of the 100 most borrowed library books are Cookson novels.

Spring: A stage adaptation of *The Fifteen Streets* opens at the Belgrade Theatre, Coventry, and is followed by two national tours.

23rd April: The Variety Club of Great Britain names Catherine Cookson its Female Personality of the Year for the third time in four years.

May: Royal Doulton issues the first in a series of Cookson character figures; the first is Kate Hannigan.

15th December: Newcastle University renames a seven-storey campus block The Catherine Cookson Building.

18th December: A Cookson donation of £100,000 allows work on conserving rare books at Newcastle University Library to continue and throws a lifeline to the university's Hatton Gallery.

1988

The Cultured Handmaiden and *Bill Bailey's Daughter* published.

January: Twenty-eight of the 100 most borrowed library books are Cookson novels.

2nd January: Catherine suffers a series of bleeding attacks; they continue almost daily until the end of February.

February: Catherine voted Writer of the Year in the Woman of Achievement awards.

19th February: Catherine Cookson is the celebrity guest on the first *Woman's Hour* broadcast from the BBC's Newcastle studios.

20th May: *The Fifteen Streets* opens at The Playhouse, London; it runs for five-and-a-half months.

Summer: Catherine donates £50,000 to the Royal Victoria Infirmary's department of dermatology—provided it is used directly for the treatment of patients.

Summer: The Cooksons take their first holiday in twenty years; they spend five days in the Lake District.

September: Tom Cookson collapses; doctors discover heart and circulatory problems and suggest he "retires".

December: Catherine begins a series of Saturday night Tyne Tees epilogues. The demand for copies of the scripts and poems is so overwhelming her publisher agrees to issue the collection as *Let Me Make Myself Plain*.

Christmas: Tyne Tees Television screens a thirty-minute documentary on Catherine Cookson. Its title is *Let Me Make Myself Plain*.

1989

The Harrogate Secret and *The Black Candle* published.

January: Thirty-five of the 100 most borrowed library books are Cookson novels.

25th February: The Cooksons donate £40,000 to the North East Council on Addictions.

March: A £150,000 appeal to upgrade South Shields General Hospital postgraduate medical centre is topped up with a £25,000 Cookson cheque.

June: Catherine and Tom agree to be godparents of Elisabette Karina de Roumanie Medforth-Mills, daughter of Princess Helen of Romania.

July: A yellow and pink Catherine Cookson carnation is registered with the Royal Horticultural Society.

Summer: Catherine refuses to sanction an official Catherine Cookson Fan Club.

20th August: An ITV adaptation of *The Fifteen Streets* attracts ten million viewers. It is named Best Network Programme by the Royal Television Society and is short listed for an Emmy award.

1990

The Wingless Bird and *The Gillyvors* published.

January: Thirty-two of the 100 most borrowed library books are Cookson novels.

Spring: A joint Northern Blood Transfusion Centre and British Bone Marrow Donor Appeal receives a £25,000 Cookson cheque.

5th May: Catherine suffers a heart attack while working at Bristol Lodge; she is treated at Hexham General Hospital.

1st June: Catherine and Tom celebrate their golden wedding anniversary with a private party at Bristol Lodge.

9th August: Despite medical advice Catherine keeps to her daily writing schedule and suffers a second heart attack.

1991

My Beloved Son and *The Rag Nymph* published.

January: Twenty-two of the 100 most borrowed library books are Cookson novels.

10th February: Catherine receives emergency hospital treatment after a haemorrhage; she has been "very poorly" for almost two months.

4th March: The Cooksons sell Bristol Lodge and move to White Lodge, a bungalow in Glastonbury Grove, Jesmond, Newcastle. Catherine dubs their new home "the box".

Spring: Sunderland Polytechnic award Catherine an honorary doctorate.

26th May: A television adaptation of *The Black Candle* is screened as part of a Cookson mini-series and attracts 10.8 million viewers.

2nd June: *The Black Velvet Gown* is watched by 12.8 million viewers—sixty-one per cent of the national audience—and shares the number one spot with *Coronation Street*. It is awarded an Emmy.

9th June: *The Fifteen Streets* concludes the three-film Cookson run.

Summer: Four South Shields catering students name their entries in a national Taste of Britain competition after the writer's characters—Mulholland Mussels, Fanny McBride's Braised Lamb and Calfclose Mousse.

Summer: Tom destroys seventeen years of his wife's personal diaries to forestall any biography; only medical notes remain.

August: The Cooksons buy a £65,000 laser for Newcastle's Freeman Hospital; it is the only one of its kind in Britain.

October: Catherine is admitted to the Freeman Hospital, Newcastle, with a "heartbeat irregularity".

1992

The House of Women and *The Maltese Angel* published.

January: Twenty-four of the 100 most borrowed library books are Cookson novels.

February: The annual £10,000 Catherine Cookson Fiction Prize is announced.

March: Sunderland Polytechnic's Tropical Disease Research Unit receives a £100,000 Cookson cheque to investigate traditional Indian remedies for arthritis.

Summer: *The Black Velvet Gown*—screened a year earlier—wins a first prize at the Umbria Fiction TV Festival.

July: Tom collapses with fatigue and is treated in hospital; the Cooksons announce they will no longer consider private "begging letters".

Autumn: The Cooksons donate £120,000 to a Freeman Hospital campaign to build a liver transplant centre.

1993

The Year of the Virgins and *The Golden Straw* published.

January: Sixteen of the 100 most borrowed library books are Cookson novels.

January: Television screening of *The Man Who Cried*.

1st January: Catherine Cookson is made a Dame of the British Empire in the New Year's Honours List.

1994

Justice is a Woman and *The Tinker's Girl* published.

January: Seventeen of the 100 most borrowed library books are Cookson novels.

February: Catherine Cookson is awarded a Lifetime Achievement Award in recognition for her worldwide multi-million sales at the annual British Book Awards

April/May: ITV adaptation of *The Cinder Path*.

May: ITV screening of *The Dwelling Place*.

1995

A Ruthless Need, *The Obsession* and *Plainer Still* published.

Final curtain: Rob Bettinson's adaptation of the Fifteen Streets returned to South Shields in 1996 after a London season and two tours.

January: Sixteen of the 100 most borrowed library books are Cookson novels.

January: Television adaptation of *The Glass Virgin*.

February/March: ITV screening of *The Gambling Man*.

1996

The Branded Man, *The Bonny Dawn* and *The Upstart* published.

January: Sixteen of the 100 most borrowed library books are Cookson novels.

January: Television adaptation of *The Tide of Life*.

February/March: ITV screening of *The Girl*.

20th June: *The Fifteen Streets* opens for a three week run at The Customs House, South Shields.

November: Catherine issues *Her Way*, a sixty-seven minute cassette of songs and reminiscences.

1997

The Bondage of Love, *The Desert Crop* and *The Lady on My Left* published.

January: Sixteen of the 100 most borrowed library books are Cookson novels.

January: Television adaptation of *The Wingless Bird*.

February/March: ITV screening of *The Moth*.

October: *The Rag Nymph* becomes the third Cookson adaptation screened during 1997.

1998

The Solace of Sin and *Riley* published.

January: Twelve of the 100 most borrowed library books are Cookson novels.

January: Television adaptation of *The Round Tower*—thirty years after it was named Best Regional Novel.

11th June: Dame Catherine Cookson dies at her Jesmond, Newcastle, home with her husband holding her hand. She is ninety-one years old.

16th June: A close circle of family and friends attend Catherine Cookson's funeral at Newcastle's West Road Crematorium.

23rd June: Tom Cookson is admitted to the Royal Victoria Infirmary hospital, Newcastle.

28th June: Tom dies in hospital from heart failure seventeen days after Catherine's death.

24th November: More than six hundred relatives, friends and fans attend a memorial service at St Mary's Cathedral in Newcastle to Catherine and Tom Cookson.

16th, 22nd and 23rd December: *Colour Blind* is screened as three one-hour television episodes.

1999

January: Television adaptation of *Tilly Trotter*.

The Books

Kate Hannigan
The Fifteen Streets
Colour Blind
Maggie Rowan
Rooney
The Menagerie
Fanny McBride
Fenwick Houses
The Blind Miller
The Long Corridor
The Unbaited Trap
Katie Mulholland
The Round Tower
The Nice Bloke
The Glass Virgin
The Invitation
The Dwelling Place
Feathers in the Fire
Pure as the Lily
The Garment
Slinky Jane
Hannah Massey
The Invisible Cord
The Gambling Man
The Girl
The Man Who Cried
The Cinder Path
The Whip
The Black Velvet Gown
A Dinner of Herbs
The Moth
The Parson's Daughter
The Cultured Handmaiden
The Harrogate Secret
The Black Candle

The Wingless Bird
The House of Women
The Gillyvors
My Beloved Son
The Rag Nymph
The Maltese Angel
The Year of the Virgins
The Golden Straw
Justice is a Woman
The Tinker's Girl
A Ruthless Need
The Obsession
The Upstart
The Branded Man
The Bonny Dawn
The Desert Crop
The Lady on My Left
The Solace of Sin
Riley
The Blind Years

Tilly Trotter Trilogy
Tilly Trotter
Tilly Trotter Wed
Tilly Trotter Widowed

The Bill Bailey Series
Bill Bailey
Bill Bailey's Lot
Bill Bailey's Daughter
The Bondage of Love

The Mallen Trilogy
The Mallen Streak
The Mallen Girl
The Mallen Litter

The Hamilton Trilogy
Hamilton

Goodbye Hamilton
Harold

Autobiography
Our Kate
Catherine Cookson Country
Let Me Make Myself Plain
Plainer Still

For Children
Lanky Jones
Our John Willie
Mrs Flannagan's Trumpet
Matty Doolin
Go Tell It To Mrs Golightly
Joe and the Gladiator
The Nipper
Rory's Fortune
Nancy Nuttal and the Mongrel
Bill and the Mary Ann Shaughnessy

The Mary Ann Novels
A Grand Man
The Lord and Mary Ann
The Devil and Mary Ann
Love and Mary Ann
Life and Mary Ann
Marriage and Mary Ann
Mary Ann's Angels
Mary Ann and Bill

Writing as Catherine Marchant
House of Men
The Fen Tiger
Heritage of Folly
Miss Martha Mary Crawford
The Slow Awakening
The Iron Facade

Catherine Cookson
alias *Catherine Marchant* alias *Katie McMullen*

EARLY IN 1984 Catherine heard an American magazine had nominated her as a candidate for its annual romantic writer award. She hastily wrote back, refusing even to be considered. She was not, the editor was curtly informed, a "romantic" writer—"I'm a story-teller, a novelist ... you can't get romantic about a pit lad or dock worker earning 3s 6d a shift."

As Cookson paperbacks began to sell in their millions American and Australian critics—eager to perpetuate the myth of swashbuckling English lords and innocent beauties—quickly dubbed her novels "bodice rippers". Catherine always defended them as unromantic, unsentimental social histories of the north. "It's a prejudice. I've written as Catherine Marchant for a woman's magazine because they wanted lighter stories. They could be called romantic," she explained. "But I wouldn't write them under the name Catherine Cookson. Catherine Cookson is not a romantic writer."

The first self-styled Cookson "romance" appeared in 1961. John Smith, her agent, had been asked if his client would consider writing a romantic novel. The advance on offer was £150 and the story would be serialised before publication as a book. "I couldn't think of a name so John said he would find me one," explained Catherine. "In the end he came up with Marchant. I thought it was terrible. I hated it."

Attempts to drain the trackless fens of eastern England several centuries earlier had been harassed by independent and solitary men who inhabited the windswept wastelands. They employed cunning and craftiness to halt the excavation of their domain and frequently resorted to murder. These early environmental guerrillas had earned the name "Fen Tigers".

The legend fascinated Catherine as she and Tom cruised the Fenland waterways on their summer holidays. Transposing the character of these rough, crude individuals to the present day, she created Michael Bradshaw, the "Fen Tiger" of the title.

The story appeared in 1961 as a *Woman's Own* serial. It was published in Britain two years later as her first Catherine Marchant novel, followed the same year by *Heritage of Folly*, another story written for the magazine's weekly readership.

Another *Women's Own* story—*House of Men*—originally written and published in 1961 appeared as a Catherine Marchant book in 1964.

When her agent persuaded a US publisher to try some of his client's books on the American market

Catherine demanded they abandon the irritating Marchant pseudonym. Instead she delved into her childhood for a new—and "more honest"—pen name.

Fifty years earlier the eight year old Katie McMullen had stood bare foot on the kitchen clippy mat at Number 10 William Black Street toasting her back with the warmth of the range.

"Granda," she said catching John McMullen's attention. "You know that little man you tell me about, the one that sits on the wall in Ireland, no bigger than your hand. You know, him with the green jacket and the red trousers and the buckles on his shoes, and the high hat and the shillelagh as big as himself; you remember Granda?"

"Aye, what about him?"

"Well, I've seen him Granda."

"You have, have you?"

"Aye Granda. He was round the top corner."

"He was, was he? And I suppose he spoke to you?"

"Aye Granda, he did."

"And what did he say?"

"Well, he said: 'Hello Kate'"

"And what did you say to him?"

"I said: 'Hello mister, my Granda knows you.'"

John McMullen wiped his moustache with the back of his hand and raised his white eyebrows. "You know what you are Katie McMullen, don't you, you know what you are? You're a stinking liar. Go on, go on. Either into the clink or into the money."

Her American books, Catherine decided, should be issued under her childhood name of Katie McMullen.

The first two, *Heritage of Folly* and *House of Men*, were simply reissues of her British Marchant stories. Her third would not be available for Catherine's British readers for another twelve years. Published in American as *Evil at Roger's Cross* the story was finally released in the mid-1970s as *The Iron Facade*— Catherine Marchant's last novel.

By the time she left Loreto, her second Hasting's home, and returned north in 1976, Catherine had published forty-one Cookson novels, five as Catherine Marchant and three in the United States as Katie McMullen.

Working Titles

I N A ROOM on the first floor of her Hastings home Catherine Cookson had collected the typescripts of thirty of her books.

Stacked in neat piles across the green baize of the full-sized billiard table was the original working copy of *Kate Hannigan*, next to it the thicker manuscript of *Katie Mulholland*. The most recent was *The Glass Virgin*, published the previous year in 1970.

After weeks of sorting the thousands of sheets into order, they were finally ready to ship. Some were neatly bound, others tied into loose-leaf bundles. All thirty—weighing 220lbs—were destined for the austere library of Boston University.

"They just sent and asked if they could have them. Out of the blue," Catherine explained. "I had dumped them in the attic and often wondered what on earth I was going to do with them all. I thought maybe I should make a bonfire of them now or let someone else do the job when I was dead."

Unknown to their author the manuscripts and working notes to some of the world's most popular fiction remained unopened and unread for almost thirty years. The parcel from Sussex had been signed for and paid for and dumped in a basement corner of the Massachusetts library. Additional manuscripts, sent as part of the on-going agreement, were abandoned nearby.

Examining the typescripts—and their scribbled corrections—highlights the considerable gap between the completion of a story and its publication. *The Lady on My Left* was written in the late 1950s, yet never issued until 1997. It took six years for *The Moth* to appear and eight years for *The Gillyvors*.

As Catherine's health and energy diminished she came to rely more and more on the store of the books—the "books in the bank"—she had created years before. At least half the Cookson novels published in the last decade of her life had been written in the 1970s and 80s.

The library collection also reveals a secret rarely shared between a writer and his or her readers, some of the working titles she adopted for her stories—and fought against changing.

From the conception, and throughout the six months of work on one of her novels, Catherine had adopted the title *Freddie Musgrave*. After the story had been completed, but while the manuscript was under revision, its name was changed to *The Runner*. The book finally appeared in 1989 as *The Harrogate Secret*.

The working title of another book smouldered into a last minute stand-off between Catherine and her publisher.

One of her late 1960s stories tells of the comic rise through the social order of a Fellburn family. The novel opens with an invitation from the Duke of Moorshire. For some unexplained reason Catherine set her mind on calling the book, *Bugger the Duke*.

Both her agent and publisher repeatedly failed to get Catherine to change her mind. With publication only weeks away—and with the possibility of Transworld refusing to publish the book—she finally relented and allowed it to appear as *The Invitation*.

Published Title	Year	Working Title
Fanny McBride	1959	The Ladies
Fenwick Houses	1960	Christine
The Garment	1962	Deeds of Mercy
Katie Mulholland	1967	The Steel Heart
The Invitation	1970	Bugger the Duke
The Black Velvet Gown	1984	The Black Velvet Dress
Harold	1985	Hello Harold
The Moth	1986	Thorman's Moth
The Parson's Daughter	1987	The Parson's Prig
The Harrogate Secret	1989	Freddie Musgrave *then* The Runner
The Gillyvors	1990	The Dagshaw Gillyvors

Collectable Cookson

I N 1912—six years after Catherine Cookson was born—Royal Doulton designed and sold its first collection of figures.

For seventy-five years the Stoke-on-Trent pottery added to its catalogue of classic literary characters, politicians and royalty. But in 1987 the company broke with tradition and decided for the first time to design a character taken from the works of a living author.

The character Royal Doulton chose was Kate Hannigan, the heroine of Catherine's first published novel: " ... and none of them stood like Kate did, or walked like her, she stood very straight and, when she walked, her skirts danced".

The man given the task of interpreting and fashioning Catherine's words into a nine-inch figurine was Eric Griffiths, Royal Doulton's art director of ceramic sculpture.

Despite numerous book jackets and illustrations since Kate Hannigan made her first appearance in 1950, only Catherine could focus the largely autobiographical character in her mind's eye.

Miniature classic: Catherine discusses the design of the Kate Hannigan figure with Royal Doulton's art director Eric Griffiths.

Even before making his initial sketches Griffiths travelled to the Cookson's isolated home on the Northumberland fells to hear the writer describe her creation in her own words. Repeat visits to Bristol Lodge followed each production stage of the statuette, from clay prototype to the finished bone china figure.

"The likeness to my own imagination is amazing," said Catherine.

Issued just days before her eighty-first birthday, the figure—which had been commissioned by Lawleys-by-Post—went on sale for £79.95.

*Royal Doulton model number: HN 3088.

Cookson on Loan

I N 1983 Catherine Cookson added a new record to her list of ever increasing literary achievements—and kept it for the next fifteen years.

For the first time in Britain writers were being paid every time one of their books was borrowed from a public library. When the Public Lending Right scheme began in the early 1980s only 6,113 authors had registered. The maximum annual payment any author could receive was £5,000. Catherine agreed to donate her cheque to the Royal Literary Fund to help struggling writers and poets.

The long fought for scheme also provided an instant league table of the country's most widely read authors. Of the 100 most borrowed books between January and June—future surveys would cover a full twelve months—the Register of Public Lending Right showed no less than thirty-three were Cookson novels. Second, with just nine books, was the historical novelist Victoria Holt.

Characteristically she shrugged off the official compliment: "I don't think about numbers," Catherine said, "I just carry on writing."

She has remained at the top of Britain's most borrowed books chart ever since. In one year during the 1980s libraries nationwide notched up more than five million Cookson loans—three million more than her nearest rival.

"Catherine Cookson is now part of PLR and library history," says the scheme's registrar, Dr James Parker. "In many ways she has become an institution."

Sixteen others countries now operate funds to reimburse writers for allowing public access to their books. Canadian authors are paid every time a library purchases a copy of a registered book. In Britain, annual PLR cheques are calculated on the number of times individual titles are borrowed from an ever-changing sample of libraries.

It is a unique survey which places Catherine Cookson—long established as an international best-selling novelist—in a unique position as possibly the world's best read writer.

Since 1990 the PLR figures have recorded a steady decline in the number of books borrowed from public libraries. Although always holding the number one slot, Catherine's 1983 high of thirty-three books has now fallen to twelve. One reason for the reduction, suggests Dr Parker, is her own continued popularity.

"When the Cookson stories were first issued as paperbacks and her fame began to take off she was very much on her own as a story teller," he explains. "She created a genre and a style which captured the public's imagination.

"At first, it was natural she would be copied as other writers and publishers decided to cash in on the her brand of gritty nostalgia. Now they are less reserved about it and are openly using her name." With more and more novels "in true Cookson style" or boasting "a story Catherine Cookson would be proud of", he feels it was inevitable her readers should be tempted by other writers.

From July, 1996, the Public Lending Right analysed library loans on a regional basis. Not surprisingly Catherine Cookson's novels featured heavily in all four test regions.

One unexpected result was that people in the rural counties of Cornwall and Devon borrowed more Cookson books than readers in her native North-East.

Not unexpectedly the London area recorded the lowest Cookson readership with just six of the capital's most borrowed fiction titles—but with two stories still making the top ten.

Cookson Bestsellers

B ETWEEN JUNE, 1950, and 1997 an estimated ninety-five million copies of Catherine Cookson's novels, children's stories and personal recollections had been sold worldwide. An average of 5,538 books every day—231 copies every single hour.

Literary records were nothing new for Britain's best-loved and best-read writer.

In the twenty-one years between 1974 and 1995 no less than four of her novels went straight to number one in the hardback fiction charts. For almost two decades a Cookson title remained a permanent fixture of the *Sunday Times* bestseller list.

By the mid-1990s Catherine Cookson's top ten UK bestsellers were:

Estimated sales

The Mallen Streak	1,027,000	The Mallen Litter	912,000
The Black Velvet Gown	962,000	The Fifteen Streets	910,000
The Mallen Girl	937,000	A Dinner of Herbs	909,000
Katie Mulholland	929,000	The Moth	874,000
The Girl	914,000	The Dwelling Place	858,000

Cookson on Screen and Stage

CATHERINE COOKSON was finding it more and more painful to work. Her fifteenth novel—*Life and Mary Ann*—had just been published and for the first time she began to wonder if her writing career might be over. In the early days she would cover sheets of paper with almost illegible scribble, writing so frantically and pressing so hard that her middle finger became bent and deformed. An attempt at typing ended within a few days when the slowness of the process proved more frustrating than productive. Now, writer's cramp and a progressively worsening bout of frozen shoulder were making using a pen and paper a painful practice.

The answer, Tom suggested, was a tape recorder. Within days a bulky, reel-to-reel tape recorder had been set up in Catherine's study. On her best day she produced almost 15,000 words—"I didn't know then what a new world was opening up for me, "because while talking my northern characters down I could see them acting."

The circle was complete. Catherine had returned to her Irish-Tyneside roots of kitchen story telling and unwritten family legends passed from parent to child. But the characters and incidents she created—"I talk every piece of dialogue. I make love. I fight. I laugh and cry with them"—demanded a wider audience than her books.

Her first encounters with the film industry were not happy. In May, 1954, her agent had sent a proof copy of *A Grand Man* to Group Film Productions, a J. Arthur Rank company based at Pinewood Studios in the Buckinghamshire countryside west of London. Rank immediately signed an option on Catherine's fifth book and announced filming would begin early the next year.

The part of Mary Ann Shaughnessy would go to twelve year old Jacqueline Ryan, a Dublin convent schoolgirl and daughter of former actress Phyllis Ryan. Her alcoholic father would be played by John Gregson. And Father Owen, the parish priest, would be played by Noel Purcell, an Irish character actor. Although Catherine had no quarrel with the cast, she was unhappy about two of Rank's other decisions. It was rumoured that pressure from the child star's agent and famous mother was behind a decision to call the film *Jacqueline* instead of *A Grand Man*. Rank also announced it would be setting the film in Belfast instead of Tyneside. Roy Baker, the film's director, explained that with so many Irish actors and actresses among the cast it would have been "confusing" to stay with the original location.

Catherine worked hard to distil the book into a film script. She also flew to Belfast with production staff

It's a happy family that has such a wonderful father, thinks young Jacqueline Ryan as she whispers something to John Gregson while Kathleen Ryan watches in amusement in this scene from the Pinewood production "Jacqueline"

JAC-2 ... 7/3d

John Gregson stars as the good-natured but hard-drinking Irishman in Pinewood Studios' tender story. "Jacqueline," a heart-warming tale of an Irish family in Belfast

The Irish smile and sparkling eyes belong to lovely Kathleen Ryan, starring with John Gregson in "Jacqueline"

JAC-4 ... 6/3d

SPECIAL PRESS SERVICES

Below are listed the district associations of some of the people who made "Jacqueline." If any of these are of special interest to your area we will be pleased to supply additional material at your request.

Full background stories and biographies can also be supplied to papers. Just state subject and deadline, together with any particular angle you would like the story to follow.

Please address your requests to the Press Officer, J. Arthur Rank Film Distributors Ltd., 127-133 Wardour Street, London, W.1.

BELFAST :
Scenes from film that have, at dockyards.
Rita Begley (Sarah Flannagan) lives here.
CHISWICK, LONDON :
Richard O'Sullivan (Michael McNeil) lives here.
DUBLIN :
Kathleen Ryan (Elizabeth McNeil) born here, and attended University College and the Abbey School of Acting.
Myrie Kean (Mrs. Flannagan) educated at Loretto College, Dublin.
Noel Purcell (Mr. Owen) born here.
Jacqueline Ryan (Jacqueline McNeil) born here.
Cyril Cusack (Mr. Flannagan) attended University College here.
Barry Keegan (Bob Quinton) born here.
DUNDALK, COUNTY LOUTH :
Rita Begley (Sarah Flannagan) born here.
GLASGOW :
Maureen Swanson (Maggie Flannagan) born here.
HASTINGS :
Catherine Cookson, author of novel "A Grand Man" from which film is adapted, lives here.
KILKENNY, IRELAND :
Maureen Delaney (Mrs. McBride) born here.
LIMERICK :
Kathleen Ryan (Elizabeth McNeil) lives here.
LITTLE MARLOW, BUCKS :
George Brown (producer) lives here.
LIVERPOOL :
John Gregson (Mike McNeil) born here.
RUSH, COUNTY DUBLIN :
Myrie Kean (Mrs. Flannagan) born here.
WINDSOR :
Tony Wright (Jack McBride) in repertory here.

Elfin-like Jacqueline Ryan plays the title role in the Pinewood comedy-drama, "Jacqueline," which stars John Gregson and Kathleen Ryan in the heart-warming story of a little girl and her great devotion to her hard-drinking father

JAC-5 ... 6/3d

Maureen Swanson and Tony Wright are the young lovers in "Jacqueline," a warm family comedy set near the dockyards of Belfast. John Gregson and Kathleen Ryan star in this Pinewood production

JAC-6 ... 6/3d

It's a good piece of advice coming from Noel Purcell and winsome Jacqueline Ryan takes it to heart in this scene from "Jacqueline," a family story set in the dock area of Belfast, starring John Gregson and Kathleen Ryan

JAC-7 ... 6/3d

to "get the feel of the place" and made a series of visits to Pinewood where, by March 1955, the last scenes of the film were shot before editing.

News of the film contract also put Catherine in the firing line as far as newspapers were concerned. Ironically her first mauling at the hands of the press came from the Newcastle-based *Journal*. Her agent, John Smith, telephoned to warn her that a reporter from *The Journal* had attempted to pressure him into giving away how much Catherine had received from Rank for *A Grand Man*. Smith had refused, only to be told the journalist would ask Catherine direct.

"A few minutes later the telephone rang again," recalled Catherine. "I took John's advice and refused to tell him the amount. Anyway the *Journal* carries a story claiming I had received £5,000, which was a ridiculous figure. You could retire on £5,000 in those days."

The cheque from J. Arthur Rank had actually been for £750, of which her publisher Macdonald was entitled to twenty-five per cent and her agent ten per cent of the remainder. For little over £500 Catherine produced the first draft of the script, which consisted largely of dialogue lines, a second revised version, and travelled to Belfast to help with selection of locations.

Although she kept her concerns private, Catherine was also unhappy about the choice of Jacqueline Ryan to play the title role. She still saw life through Mary Ann Shaughnessy's eyes as very much her own. "That girl was all wrong," Catherine admitted years later. "She was a pudding and I was thin, very thin. She had a mop of hair and I had ringlets."

Rank had also decided change the family's name from Shaugnessy to McNeil. The film's campaign book—issued to all cinema managers—remained enthusiastic about the story and cast:

> In one of the outstanding performances of his career, John Gregson brings penetrating pathos and a touch of whimsy to *Jacqueline*, a harsh, yet at times, tender drama of a man-of-the-soil, wasting away in a big city.

Jacqueline: A page from the film's publicity book. Adapted from Catherine Cookson's A Grand Man—and shot in Belfast not Tyneside—it starred John Gregson and Kathleen Ryan.

Gregson plays Mike McNeil, a good-natured Irish farmer who is forced to work in the shipyards at Belfast in order to support his wife and children. A man used to having his two feet planted firmly on the ground, he finds the dizzy heights at which he must work, too much for him.

Jacqueline is a stirring film of family problems. It is a story of a young daughter who is determined that her father will become in reality what he is in her dreams—and nothing will stop her from making this so. It is also the story of a patient wife, standing by a husband whom the neighbours condemn as a drunkard and a wastrel.

Audiences will feel a part of the McNeil family; will rejoice in their good fortunes, shed tears in their troubled times. They will be caught up in the merry Coronation celebration in the drab little street the family calls home, and will participate on a gay night out at the fair.

Women will feel keenly the despair of Kathleen Ryan as Mike's wife, when she learns that the head of the family is out of work—will share her anguish when Mike returns home roaring drunk. They will remember this moving performance.

Men will sympathise with Mike and recognise his feeling of futility when he cannot find a job to keep his family in food.

All will love pixie-faced Jacqueline Ryan in the title role, as Mike's devoted daughter. She is nothing short of captivating, whether in her numerous street battles in defence of her father, or singing with a crystal-clear soprano voice in the church choir—a perfect angel with a devilish streak hidden away, ready to burst forth at any provocation.

In the spring of 1956—just months before *Jacqueline*'s release—Rank expressed an interest in a second Cookson story, *Rooney*. George Brown, who had produced *Jacqueline*, claimed in a newspaper interview that he and Catherine were firm friends. It was to prove a prophetic assumption.

"I bought *A Grand Man* because I was captivated by its warmth and humanity," said Brown. "Catherine Cookson writes from the heart. She is one of the few people who can write about working people without being patronising. Her characters are real human beings." John Gregson once again agreed to play the lead and filming began in the late summer of 1957.

The book was inspired by the scavengers whose longhandled shovels had unseated anyone making use of the backyard toilets at East Jarrow and later the dustmen who emptied the bins at Catherine's Hastings home. "I thought to myself surely they are entitled to one day of love, one day of happiness. Every working man is entitled to that."

During filming at Pinewood Studios Barry Fitzgerald—an Irish-American actor visiting Britain—persuaded the producer and director that he should step into the role of "the father". It had already been cast with another actor. Catherine was asked to rewrite the script. Despite being ill at the time and committed to other work she agreed. "It was a hard slog," she said. "I worked at it non-stop for three or four days, with Tom feeding me endless cups of coffee."

Several weeks later John Smith telephoned to ask Catherine if she had received a cheque from the film company. Traditionally all payments were made through her agent. When Smith contacted Rank to find out why Catherine had not been paid for the additional work, he was told they had assumed she "would do it for nothing" as part of the original deal. "All I got from them was a bunch of flowers," she added.

THE RANK ORGANISATION PRESENTS

ROONEY

Rank also apparently took Catherine for granted when *Rooney* was released. Despite her long hours working on the script the screenplay credit went to Patrick Kirwan. In all she receives just one acknowledgement—"from the novel by Catherine Cookson". Instead of the VIP treatment offered to the Cooksons for the premiere of *Jacqueline*, the couple found themselves sitting with the critics at the second film's London premiere. In Ireland all mention of Catherine and the original book was dropped from the publicity material.

Rooney's mainland publicity brochure attempted to make the connection just as difficult:

> *Rooney*'s the name—and did ever a bachelor have such troubles? He's as fine a figure of a man as ever walked down O'Connell Street, Dublin.
>
> He has a good steady job with the City Corporation. He's a champion at the sport of Hurley. But his trouble is with the ladies—and the landladies most of all. They start by renting him a room, and finish by wanting to share his life.
>
> Five times in eleven months he has moved to new lodgings. His removal van is a dustcart: for James Ignatius Rooney is a dustman, and proud of it.

At the time Catherine diplomatically said she had "enjoyed" the film. Years later she admitted, "*Rooney* was very disappointing. It was not my story." Artistically *Rooney* was a flop. For Rank it became a financial disaster. The experience left Catherine bitter. "The way they treated me was scandalous," she said. "I vowed then that I would never deal with J. Arthur Rank again and I never have. I would not let them film one of my books even if I was starving."

Her treatment by J. Arthur Rank had left her embittered, but it also left her with a taste for screenwriting. More than ten years after she had turned her back on the stilted characters of her stage plays, Catherine began exploring a new way of bringing her stories to the screen.

Using the experience she had gained writing the screenplays for *Jacqueline* and *Rooney*, Catherine started work on the first of two plays for television. Both scripts initially found favour. "The producer, who liked them very much, intended to use them," said Catherine. "But with a change of producer they were put 'on one side' and I never afterwards bothered about them."

There was another reason for their ultimate rejection. The public, it was deemed, wanted reality not nostalgia. If they were to be made to feel guilty, they should at least get a thrill from the experience. A young television executive at the time recalls: "They [the scripts] were certainly well written—but there wasn't enough sex in them."

It was another twelve years before the BBC, which for years had adapted Catherine stories for radio, announced it wanted to turn her children's novel *Joe and the Gladiator* into a three part series. The adventures of Joe Darling, who meets a rag-and-bone man, Mr Prodhurst, and his intelligent horse, the Gladiator, were to be filmed on Tyneside. It took two years for the BBC crew to arrive in Newcastle, but only after Catherine had spent hours poring over local maps to pinpoint locations with the story's adaptor, Anna Howe.

Eighteen months later a ten-man BBC crew descended on the village of Westoe where, as a teenager, Catherine had turned her back on the chance of a trip to Italy because of her religion. As part of her consent to the adaptation of her children's story *Joe and the Gladiator*, Catherine had insisted all the exterior sequences of the film should be shot in and around South Shields. It was the first time a Cookson story would be seen by television viewers. Not only were the locations authentic—South Shields beach and terraced houses about to be demolished—but many of the cast were also Geordies. The part of Joe was given to nineteen year old Dennis Lingard from Wallsend, Newcastle. Even the Gladiator was played by Peggy, a thirteen year old mare who, in real life, had just been bought by a retired miner for his part-time rag-and-bone business.

Tyneside was also the backdrop for another Cookson story—this time of Catherine's own childhood. Early in 1975 the writer gave permission for a semi-documentary film based on *Our Kate*. The £900 project was to be produced by a nine-strong student film crew from Harlow College of Technology and Art. Its director and editor, John Cheyne, had decided to focus on Catherine's life between the ages of eight and eleven. Her East Jarrow friends would be played by child actors from Backworth Drama Centre, Newcastle, and the film's commentary would be spoken by Catherine herself.

In the Autumn of 1978 executives from Granada Television approached Anthony Sheil about the possibility of adapting the *Mallen* trilogy. Catherine liked the idea. It was the first time one of her adult novels would be serialised. Although the story is set near Alston in Cumbria, the series was filmed in the beauty spots of Derbyshire, close to Dovedale. Ilam Hall, a National Trust property in the valley of Ilam, was transformed into High Banks Hall. Location filming during the harsh 1978-9 winter caused enormous problems for the crew and a team of carpenters was cut off by snowdrifts in the first week of filming. The cast, including Caroline Blakiston, John Duttine, Ian Saynor and John Hallam, fared little better in the freezing conditions.

ITV had scheduled transmission of the first episode for the prime-time slot of nine o'clock on Sunday, 10 June 1979. Some weeks earlier Granada had sent Catherine videos of the first two episodes. She was impressed, but the sensation of watching the images of her mind take on an existence of their own was an eerie one. "When I write, my characters are alive in my mind. The likenesses between some of my characters and the way they are portrayed in the series is uncanny," Catherine said after watching the episodes: "I was full of anxieties and worries about how they would be translated to the screen, but I needn't have been."

Although Catherine had written *Our John Willy* as a children's book, thousands of adult readers rapidly placed the story firmly among the United States top ten sellers. It was soon to become a favourite with British television audiences. BBC director, Marilyn Fox, spent most of the early weeks of 1979 scouring the North-East looking for a yellow-brick row of Victorian cottages. Also on her shopping list were a workhouse, a drift mine and a little-altered rectory dating back to the middle of the nineteenth century. Filming for the five-part serialisation of *Our John Willie* eventually began in May. Taking the part of the deaf and dumb John Willie was thirteen year old Newcastle schoolboy, David Burke. His brother was played by teenager Anthony Manuel.

When confronted a few years later with a project to turn one of her best-read books into a musical Catherine was sceptical enough people would want to see it. She was proved spectacularly wrong. The musical adaptation of Catherine's 1967 bestseller *Katie Mulholland* was the idea of North-East composer Eric Boswell. He had explained his idea when he went to see Catherine at her Corbridge home a year earlier. She liked Boswell, but thought his scheme "pie in the sky".

Within weeks Boswell telephoned to arrange a second appointment, this time to play through several tunes he had composed for the production. Catherine began to take notice. In March, 1983, the musician presented his idea to Blackmore, head and driving force behind the Tyne Wear Theatre Company in Newcastle. Within eight weeks—the kind of speed Catherine admired—Blackmore and the venue's director of production, Ken Hill, had produced a draft script.

Catherine read the script with growing apprehension. "She hated it," admitted Hill. "And Catherine doesn't need a brandy before telling you want she thinks." The problem was obvious. Hill—who at six foot towered over Catherine—had not even read the original novel. "What you have to remember is that

I wasn't even asked to read Catherine's book," he said in defence. "Eric had already had the idea and approached her. It was only then that I became involved … And then, because we were working under such pressure, I had to show her a draft that normally I would have shown nobody. My first script is a very shorthand, stuck-together thing. I had set some scenes in the bawdy house and she hated that … and she was right. I'd probably have cut them, myself."

The second draft, however, was more to Catherine's liking. "I can't speak for Catherine and say she approved of it," said Hill. "But she passed it—put it that way." He also makes the point that there is a considerable difference between writing novels and writing for the theatre. "Sometimes you might have a kind of sub-text going on which isn't immediately apparent on the page, and reading a script requires a certain amount of experience. It's not the same as reading a novel."

After spending two hundred hours auditioning more than three hundred actresses, Blackmore had settled on Malay-born Prue Clarke to star in the first stage production of a Cookson novel. But time was running out. There was just over six weeks from the day that Hill settled on his leading lady to the first two-and-a-half hour production on 29 September. Rehearsals were hard and energetic, but Catherine and Tom made sure the cast relaxed in style. Actor Alan Hockey remembers Catherine sitting quietly watching the rehearsals. "After, she would invite us to dinner at a restaurant—the entire cast—or back to her home at Corbridge," said Hockey.

Management at the 449-seat theatre had not underestimated the pulling power of Catherine Cookson. Two days before the first night only 400 of the 12,572 tickets available remained unsold. By the end of the twenty-eighth performance every seat had been filled. It was the first sell-out in the company's chequered twelve-year history.

Catherine still had doubts. She and Tom attended the first night with a party of twelve friends. "I just hope people will clap," she said drily.

The audiences, who arrived in bus loads from all over the north of England, did applaud. The critics, both local and national, found the musical too parochial. "The show has little hope of repeating its

The Journal, Newcastle

Katie Mulholland: Malay-born Prue Clark is chosen to take the title role in the 1983 musical adaptation of Catherine's best-selling novel.

popular success outside Tyneside," predicted David Isaacs, arts editor of the Newcastle *Journal*. His colleague on the city's evening newspaper, *The Chronicle* was less forgiving. "Were it not for the name of Cookson emblazoned on poster, programme and leaflet ... the theatre would be sparsely attended each night." And he went on, "Having lured their audiences in the performers hoof and mug their way amiably through a musical which at times falls only a degree or two short of pure farce ... Eric Boswell's music is eminently forgettable, trite and frequently so banal as to make one cringe with embarrassment ... Ken Hill meanwhile has given us a cliché-ridden script."

Worse was to come. Most national newspaper critics also, it has to be admitted attracted by the Cookson name, saw it as a "wafer thin attempt at a home-grown show ... appealing only to northerners besotted with Ms Cookson". Plans to tour the musical were abandoned. Catherine, however, continued to defend the production. "This was a book of 200,000 words, remember. It was a colossal task trying to cram all that into a musical," she said. "Anyway I enjoyed it."

Since the sell-out production of *Katie Mulholland*, management at Tyne Wear Theatre Company had not lost sight of the financial necessity of adapting a second Cookson novel. Early in 1985 the company asked Catherine to suggest a suitable follow up. Her choice was *The Gambling Man*. Ken Hill, the Playhouse's resident director, thought the adaptation—as a play rather than a musical—would be an excellent start for the company's 1985 winter season. Before he could finish the script the play had already broken a British box-office record. Three days before the theatre's front office was due to start selling tickets for the September production the company had already received more than 3,000 reservations. The figure represented a fifth of all the seats available during the run and was the highest recorded in advance of an official opening. The cast had not yet been auditioned.

Hill eventually settled on Brendon Price to play the part of Rory Connor—all Price had to do now was learn to speak Geordie. The Coventry-born actor had exactly a month to turn himself into the brash Jarrow lad whose life was governed by chance. "It was one of the most difficult of all regional accents to get right," he remembers. "I went to see a dialect coach in London and listened to tapes of Geordies talking." He also conducted his own research in several Tyneside pubs.

Another dramatist, Rob Bettinson, couldn't sleep one night. He tossed and turned until his frustration solidified into anger. Reaching across the bed he picked up a book his wife, Shirley, had put aside several hours earlier. "I started reading it thinking it would send me to sleep," commented Bettinson. "I thought it would be a nice Mills and Boon-type thing leading up to a happy ending ... But then half-way through there is this great shock ... I couldn't believe it. I thought, 'She can't do this'."

The book was *The Fifteen Streets* and the dramatist knew he had found the story he was looking for. Within days Bettinson, the son of a Cleveland sheetmetal worker, had contacted Catherine. Since its publication in March, 1952, its readers had always found something magical in *The Fifteen Streets*. The latent energy in the book had kept it in print and among her bestsellers for more than thirty-five years. Even so Catherine had "qualms" about Bettinson's stage production. "I was against him doing it," she admitted. "If I had to be asked which book I wanted to go on the stage, that would have been the last one I would have picked."

With a tentative approval Bettinson set about transferring the story of the battling O'Briens. The daily round of writing was not his only battle. He still had to convince potential backers that the story was more than a simple romance—the same image Catherine had been struggling to shed for almost four decades. "The public perception of Catherine Cookson was such a false one," Bettinson admitted later. "Everyone thought she was like Barbara Cartland, but all her stories are deeply rooted in reality … *The Fifteen Streets* may be a microcosm of the North-East, but Catherine knows people like the back of her hand. The main character is not romantic, he is a six-foot-four docker—a man with all his faults."

Many producers feared her stories were too parochial for a West End theatre. In a perverse way they were right. The enthusiasm needed to visualise the transition from page to stage appeared only to be shared by those born or who had lived in the North-East of England. The latest production of *The Fifteen Streets* was no exception. Its first run—extended by three weeks—took place at the Belgrade Theatre, Coventry, early in 1987. Both the leading actor and actress came from the region. Peter Marshall, who portrayed the imposing father in the O'Brien family, and Margo Stanley, who played his wife, had Tyneside connections—Stanley was born in South Shields, less than four miles from Catherine's birthplace.

Like all previous attempts to adapt a Cookson novel for the stage Bettinson's production was applauded by her fans while suffering at the hands of the critics. One commented, "Unfortunately the designer poverty of the young O'Briens

Keith Pattison

Sellout: Katherine Dow Blyton was Mary Llewellyn and William Leslie played John O'Brien in The Customs House, South Shields, production of The Fifteen Streets in 1996.

owed more to Laura Ashley than Tyneside of 1910. Throughout the summer Bettinson, the play's producer and associate director at the Belgrade, had attempted to capitalise on the critical kudos amassed by the Coventry production. Early in December he announced plans to take the Cookson story to London's West End following a national tour.

Bettinson's promise to make the production the first Cookson story staged in London also proved hard to keep. Negotiations with various theatres proved fruitless. It was not until the end of March, less than six weeks before it was due to open in the capital, that *The Fifteen Streets* was finally booked into MP-turned-writer Jeffrey Archer's newly refurbished Playhouse Theatre near Charing Cross station. It eventually ran for five-and-a-half months, but the producer, Philip Talbot, still had plans for the play. After a month's rehearsals it re-opened at York's Theatre Royal in March, 1989, at the start of a nine-month tour. Early in April *The Fifteen Streets*, with a cast of thirty-two including eleven children, returned to the North-East, this time for a booking at Newcastle's Theatre Royal.

Although Catherine had been too ill to attend a Sunderland performance, she insisted she would not miss it this time. Tom reluctantly agreed to drive her the thirty miles from their Northumberland home to Newcastle. Catherine looked tired. As a precaution—and as a "thank you" gesture—she was accompanied by two of her doctors and their wives. "It has been a great effort to get here," she admitted to a friend, "but it is probably my last chance of seeing it."

Despite fears the poverty and petty squabbles of the nineteenth-century working-class family would prove unpopular with affluent 1980s theatregoers around the country, *The Fifteen Streets* played to packed houses. "The further south it went, the more letters I got," Catherine recalls.

Ray Marshall, an enthusiastic Yorkshireman, had been appointed to lead World Wide International Television Productions' move from corporation film-making into small-screen drama. While waiting for an appointment with London literary agent, Anthony Sheil, Marshall noticed a display of Cookson novels. Anthony Sheil, Catherine's new agent, admitted there were no plans for any future adaptation of her books and agreed to arrange a meeting between Marshall and the eighty-two year old writer.

Marshall combined his trip north to Bristol Lodge on the Northumberland fells beyond Hexham with a meeting at Tyne Tees Television. Geraint Davies, director of programmes at the Newcastle-based company, conceded he would be interested in the possibility of backing a Cookson film. Within weeks Marshall was back with plans to turn *The Fifteen Streets* into a made-for-television, two hour drama.

Marshall admits he could not understand why Catherine's stories had not been adapted and screened more widely. "I must confess I was amazed to discover a writer of Catherine Cookson's calibre, who outsells every major British writer, has been largely ignored by television. Her work is ideally suited to television adaptation." Shooting began in April 1989. Marshall asked Rob Bettinson, who had originally adapted the book for the stage, to write the screenplay. He was equally sure about his choice of actor Owen Teale—who had headed the West End cast—for the roll of docker John O'Brien.

The part of the treacherous Dominic O'Brien went to Sean Bean, who had never heard of Catherine Cookson. "Until I read her book I didn't realise how much powerful drama she packs into her work," he commented later. Other members of the cast were equally accomplished. They included Ian Bannen, Clare Holman, Billie Whitelaw, Frank Windsor and Jane Horrocks. The film was directed by Sunderland-born David Wheatley.

One immediate problem facing Wheatley was finding a Tyneside terraced street, still cobbled, and with a shipyard within sight. An impossible task. In the end his team settled on Richardson Street in the Heaton area of Newcastle. The road was cobbled and working gas lamps were fitted. A huge shipyard backdrop was hung across the end of the street. The transformation was so startling that the residents later petitioned Newcastle City Council to have the area renovated in the "Cookson style".

When *The Fifteen Streets* was screened on 20 August, 1989, it attracted more than 10 million viewers. Not everyone was pleased. Catherine endorsed several viewers' complaints about the inclusion of a four-letter word in the script, claiming such words were never used during the period in which the book was set. The Tyne Tees production won almost instant recognition from the public and professionals alike. Book shops nationwide sold out of the novel within a week. Two months later the film won Best Network Programme title at the Royal Television Society's annual regional awards.

To follow *The Fifteen Streets* Marshall had chosen *The Black Velvet Gown*. The story focuses on the prejudices of the last

The Fifteen Streets: John O'Brien (Owen Teale) and Mary Llewellyn (Clare Holman) Christmas shopping in South Shields.

The Black Velvet Gown: Janet McTeer as miner's widow, Riah, and Bob Peck as Miller, the embittered intellectual recluse.

century, with miner's widow Riah Millican moving into the local manor house as the owner's housekeeper. There she discovers love and the fact that it rarely runs smoothly. "It is a complete contrast to *The Fifteen Streets*," said producer Ray Marshall. "It's strong on character and highly visual."

While his latest project was still in production, Marshall received news that *The Fifteen Streets* was among three films shortlisted from over 250 nominations for an Emmy award. The film had already been sold and screened in twenty-two countries worldwide. Video sales of 50,000 had pushed it to number five in the British video charts.

Three days before her eighty-fifth birthday Catherine received the news that a trilogy of Cookson films had attracted almost thirteen million viewers—and nudged the long-running soap opera *Coronation Street* from its number one slot. The Cookson mini-season had begun on 26 May with a screening of Ray Marshall's £1.3 million adaptation of *The Black Candle*. It was followed a week later by *The Black Velvet Gown* and concluded, on the third Sunday by a second showing of *The Fifteen Streets*. Catherine, recovering from a bout of pneumonia, remained laconic. "It's rather wonderful news, but I don't think about figures," she said. "I simply hope that the readers will enjoy my books."

Executives at Tyne Tees Television were less restrained. The company had topped the national ratings for a network programme for the first time in its existence. Their decision to screen the two new Cookson films on consecutive Sundays, followed by a repeat of *The Fifteen Streets*, paid dividends. *The Black Velvet*

Tyne Tees Television

Gown and *The Black Candle* achieved the highest and the second highest figures recorded on any channel for the previous twelve months.

The Black Candle attracted 10.8 million Sunday evening viewers. The next weekend *The Black Velvet Gown* kept 12.8 million viewers glued to their television sets—sixty-one per cent of the national audience—and shared the number one spot with *Coronation Street*. *The Fifteen Streets*, screened on 9 June, also topped the 10.2 million viewers it had attracted when it was first screened two years before.

Again, not everyone was happy with the visualisation of the Cookson stories. Five viewers complained to the Broadcasting Standards Council about the murder scene in *The Black Candle*, in which a man has his head slammed against a tree and is then stabbed and choked. Although the actual blows were hidden from viewers, the victim's bloodied head was shown. The BSC upheld the complaints, ruling the scene was "too long and graphic."

A year after America's Emmy Award judges had shortlisted Tyne Tee's film of *The Fifteen Streets* they were considering a second Cookson story. This time they were unanimous. *The Black Velvet Gown* carried off a prestigious Emmy.

The film also scored a "perfect ten" in three classes at the annual International Film and Television Festival in New York—the first time in the festival's forty-four year history. The production, which starred Bob Peck and Janet McTeer, was awarded the Gold Award for Entertainment and Norman Stone was

The Black Candle: Bridget Mordaunt (Samantha Bond) talks to blacking factory manager Joe Skinner (James Gaddas).

honoured with a Gold Medal as best director. When Catherine heard the news she burst into tears.

As so often happened during her writing career a woman had had a hand in Catherine's successes. Stone's wife, television personality Sally Magnusson, read *The Black Velvet Gown* while confined to bed through illness. She was so enthusiastic about its possibilities she convinced Stone to consider it.

A year later, in 1992, the Tyne Tees-World Wide film added yet another honour to its list. This time a first prize at Umbria fiction TV festival.

Ray Marshall, whose company had been renamed Festival Films-World Wide to reflect the America awards, had decided on *The Man Who Cried* as his fourth Cookson project. Scheduled for screening in January, 1993. It would be the first Cookson adaptation to include location shots filmed away from Tyneside.

The £1.5 million epic would be the most modern of Marshall's adaptations. Spanning the years between 1932 and 1943, actor Ciaran Hinds played the central character of Abel Mason who leaves his shrewish wife in Hastings to search for work in the North-East, taking his young son with him. His luck changes when he befriends a wealthy garage owner. But Abel is soon involved in romance, deception and bigamy. Other members of the cast included Daniel Massey and Gemma Craven.

In the next five years Marshall produced twelve more Cookson adaptations, each with a budget as frugal as Catherine's own childhood—none cost more than £2m to make.

But, says Marshall, there is another magic ingredient. "There is nowhere like the North-East for location work. These films could not have been made anywhere else but here and kept the same sense of authenticity."

By the autumn of 1998—ten years after *The Fifteen Streets* was screened and just a few months after Catherine's death—Ray Marshall's exclusive contract to adapt and produce Cookson stories expired. It was time, he admitted, for "a pause for breath".

From Page to Stage

1956 *Jacqueline*—adapted as a film and renamed from *A Grand Man*.

1958 *Rooney* filmed from the book of the same name.

1971 *Joe and the Gladiator* adapted by the BBC as a three-part children's serial.

1975 *Our Kate* dramatised and filmed by students from Harlow College of Technology and Art.

1979 *The Mallens* shown as a thirteen episode adaptation over two series by Granada Television.

1980 *Our John Willie* adapted by the BBC as a five-part children's serial.

1983 *Katie Mulholland* adapted as a musical and staged at Newcastle Playhouse. Every show is a sell out.

1985 *The Gambling Man* adapted as a play by Tyne Wear Theatre Company, produced at Newcastle Playhouse.

1987 *The Fifteen Streets* adapted as a play at the Belgrade Theatre, Coventry. It is followed by two national tours.

1988 *Let Me Make Myself Plain* a Tyne Tees Television documentary.

1988 *The Fifteen Streets* opens at The Playhouse, London. It runs for five and a half months.

1988 Catherine begins a series of Saturday night Tyne Tees epilogues. The demand for copies of her scripts and poems is so overwhelming that her publisher agrees to issue the collection as *Let Me Make Myself Plain*.

1989 *The Fifteen Streets* adapted as a film and shown on Independent Television.

1991 *The Black Candle* adapted as a film and shown on Independent Television.

1991 *The Black Velvet Gown* adapted as a film and shown on Independent Television.

1993 *The Man Who Cried* adapted as a film and shown on Independent Television.

1994 *The Cinder Path* adapted as a film and shown on Independent Television.

1994 *The Dwelling Place* adapted as a film and shown on Independent Television.

1995 *The Glass Virgin* adapted as a film and shown on Independent Television.

1995 *The Gambling Man* adapted as a film and shown on Independent Television.

1996 *The Tide of Life* adapted as a film and shown on Independent Television.

1996 *The Fifteen Streets* opens at The Customs House, South Shields. It runs for three weeks.

1996 *The Girl* adapted as a film and shown on Independent Television.

1997 *The Wingless Bird* adapted as a film and shown on Independent Television.

1997 *The Moth* adapted as a film and shown on Independent Television.

1997 *The Rag Nymph* adapted as a film and shown on Independent Television.

1998 *The Round Tower* adapted as a film and shown on Independent Television.

1998 *Colour Blind* adapted as a film and shown on Independent Television.

1999 *Tilly Trotter* adapted as a film and shown on Independent Television.

The ITV Saga

The Fifteen Streets
Screened: August, 1989.
Starring: Clare Holman, Owen Teale, Sean Bean.
Location filming: South Shields and Jarrow.

The Black Candle
Screened: May, 1991.
Starring: Samantha Bond, Nathaniel Parker.
Location filming: Wallsend and Cragside.

The Black Velvet Gown
Screened: June, 1991.
Starring: Janet McTeer, Bob Peck, Geraldine Somerville.
Location filming: Wynyard Hall.

The Man Who Cried
Screened: January, 1993.
Starring: Ciaran Hinds.
Location filming: Jesmond and Newcastle.

The Cinder Path
Screened: April / May, 1994.
Starring: Catherine Zeta Jones, Lloyd Owen.
Location filming: War scenes at Tow Law.

The Dwelling Place
Screened: May, 1994.
Starring: Tracy Whitwell, Ray Stevenson.
Location filming: Duke of Northumberland's Estate.

The Glass Virgin
Screened: January, 1995.
Starring: Emily Mortimer.
Location filming: Newcastle and Beamish Museum.

The Gambling Man
Screened: February / March, 1995.
Starring: Robson Green, Bernard Hill.
Location filming: South Shields.

The Tide of Life
Screened: January, 1996.
Starring: Gillian Kennedy, Ray Stevenson, James Purefoy.
Location filming: South Shields and Beamish Museum.

The Girl
Screened: February / March 1996.
Starring: Siobhan Flynn, Jonathan Cake.
Location filming: Burnhopeside near Lanchester.

The Wingless Bird
Screened: January, 1997.
Starring: Claire Skinner, Edward Atterton, Julian Wadham.
Location filming: Durham and Beamish Museum.

The Moth
Screened: February / March 1997.
Starring: Jack Davenport, Juliet Aubrey, Justine Waddell.
Location filming: Eshott Hall near Morpeth; The Mill Dam, South Shields; Tyne Dock and Preston Hall.

The Rag Nymph
Screened: October, 1997.
Starring: Val McLane, Honeysuckle Weeks, Perdita Weeks.
Location filming: Beaufront Castle.

The Round Tower
Screened: January, 1998.
Starring: Emilia Fox, Ben Miles, Keith Barron, Jan Harvey, Denis Lawson.
Location filming: Leamington and Stocksfield.

Colour Blind
Screened: December, 1998.
Starring: Niamh Cusak, Tony Armatrading, Art Malik.
Location filming: Newcastle.

Tilly Trotter
Screened: January, 1909.
Starring: Simon Shepherd, Carli Norris.
Location filming: Simonburn.

Cookson on Air

EARLY IN 1949 Catherine Cookson was walking near her Hastings home when she overheard a woman boast about the carrying power of her voice. By the time Catherine returned to The Hurst she had decided to show that woman just how far her own voice would carry—all over Britain.

By the end of the week she had written a radio talk on discovering artistic talent late in life. The only skill she had yet to discover was the ability to deliver her script without allowing the fear to surface in her voice.

As ever Catherine tackled the problem head on and in secret. Her husband knew nothing of the script. Each morning, after Tom left for his classroom at Hastings Grammar School, Catherine would sit cross-legged on the floor in front of an electric fire. Using the fire's red thermostat light as an impromptu "on air" signal she would painstakingly read and re-read her talk.

It took three months of clandestine "rehearsals" before Catherine considered she was good enough to overcome her nerves and perform in public.

The script was finally sent to the BBC where it was passed to the producer of *Woman's Hour*, an afternoon programme already attracting more than six million listeners. Catherine was called to London for a voice test and on Monday, 15 August, 1949—ten months before the publication of *Kate Hannigan*—she read her talk, *I Learned to Draw at Thirty*, live from Broadcasting House.

That autumn Catherine wrote a second script. Once again it was accepted by the BBC and on 30 January she was back in the capital explaining the knack of *Making Dreams Come True*.

Thoughts of a third radio talk had to be postponed while she worked on *The Fifteen Streets* and plotted her next book. It wasn't until the beginning of May, 1951, that *Woman's Hour* listeners heard her voice again. This time Catherine had chosen a subject which eventually turned into a passion: *Buying Secondhand Furniture*.

On 21 March the following year she went to London to read a *Woman's Hour* talk entitled *Getting Your Nerves Under Control*. It was her fourth and most successful broadcast. Within days she received dozens of letters from listeners, both men and women, struggling to come to terms with mental breakdowns. Catherine replied to each letter personally.

Throughout the 1950s and 60s her books continued to sell. The BBC, eager to keep up, began a long-running tradition of serialising the latest Cookson.

In 1955, as *Jacqueline* was being edited at Pinewood Studios, her agent persuaded *Woman's Hour* to use a two-week serialisation of *A Grand Man*. A year later millions of listeners were treated to *The Lord and Mary Ann*.

By the start of the sixties Catherine had gained enough confidence, not only to take part in unscripted radio interviews and discussions, but also to make use of extracts from the autobiography she still considered "too bitter".

She made two personal broadcasts during 1962. The first in March as a *Woman's Hour* guest of the week and then, three months later, when she agreed to read *The Day at the Party*, a story that would later be published as part of *Our Kate*.

At the beginning of December, 1962, the programme began an eight-part reading from *Life and Mary Ann*, the eighth Cookson story adapted for *Woman's Hour*. This time the actress chosen to narrate the book was Isla Cameron, a Scots-born adopted Geordie.

Between her novels Catherine was still revising the memoir she had started only days after her mother's death. In September, 1963, she tested more of its material by broadcasting *Me Granda* and *Up the Creek*, the last describing how she narrowly escaped death by falling into Jarrow Slake.

Almost sixteen years to the day of her first BBC talk Catherine made her final *Woman's Hour* broadcast. The year before she had read *Thursday's Child Has Far To Go*. In August, 1966, she described her childhood *Playgrounds* in the back alleys of the New Buildings and East Jarrow. Both were taken almost word for word from *Our Kate*.

The Mary Ann Stories

I wrote The Fifteen Streets and brought more in. I brought the docks in, I brought the mines in and I brought the men out of work and everything I'd been brought up with. Still my breakdown was with me.

I should have been rid of these fears. Everything should be clear, it should be marvellous. It wasn't. I couldn't remember one happy incident that had happened in my life. Nothing. Everything I looked back on was black. There was no humour, there was nothing.

And then I thought well, there was humour. Katie laughed. Katie joked, Katie played. And so I wrote the first of the Mary Ann stories. And I thought "This'll do it."

It didn't.

❧ Catherine Cookson

Cookson on Disc

THEY COULD hear John McMullen as he clattered and roared his way down the back lanes of the New Buildings: "I love a lassie, A bonny, bonny lassie; She's as pure as the lily in the dell."

Once inside the cramped kitchen of Number 10 William Black Street he would pick up an iron poker he called "Dennis" and swing it wildly above his head. As the inhabitants scattered and his young granddaughter watched him through the crack of a half-closed door, the irascible Irishman would once again subside into songs of virtuous women and his innocent homeland. Creeping back into the room the young Kitty McMullen found herself lifted on to her grandfather's knee for her own special song—"He would always sing *Danny Boy* to me when he was 'three sheets to the wind'."

More than eighty-five years later Catherine turned the page on a new chapter of her career, by releasing her first audio cassette. Included on the sixty-seven minute tape—titled *Her Way*—was Catherine's own version of John McMullen's drunken favourite, together with several previously unpublished Cookson poems and reminiscences.

The songs were "recorded" in 1986, not long after her eightieth birthday, on an aging reel-to-reel tape recorder. "I experimented with it and discovered that if I put my heart into it, I could sing quite well," admitted Catherine. "When I was thirteen I was picked to sing a Rosary for the school," she added. "But after several rehearsals I still couldn't reach the high notes and told the teacher that I shouldn't be singing that particular song. She said: 'You're right, Katie, you can't sing.' … Ever since, although I would have liked to, I have resisted the temptation to sing. My voice just wasn't good enough."

Ill-health and pressure of work forced the writer to abandon her do-it-yourself recording sessions. Ten years later, in 1996, the tapes were discovered in the attic of the Cookson's Jesmond home. "Tom played them and we were amazed as this woman began to sing," said Catherine. "I couldn't believe it was really me."

Producer Ray Marshall, the man behind the Cookson television adaptations, was also impressed.

The tapes were first sent to EMI's Abbey Road studios—where the Beatles recorded most of their hits—to allow sound engineers to filter out background noises and improve the quality of Catherine's voice. Musician Colin Towns then composed and recorded a musical backing.

Issued in time for Christmas 1996, *Her Way* got its first national airing on BBC Radio 4's *Today* programme and, later the same day, was tipped as a 100-1 outsider to top the holiday charts.

Awards

1968 *The Round Tower*—her thirty-sixth book—is named the year's Best Regional Novel and its author is awarded The Winifred Holtby Prize by the Royal Society of Literature.

1973 *The Mallen Streak* is voted *Daily Express* Book of the Month; in less than a year the novel sells an estimated 1,027,000 copies.

1974 South Shields grants Catherine the Freedom of the Borough.

1981 Corgi presents its best-selling author. with a trophy after her paperback sales reach 27,500,000.

1982 The Variety Club elect Catherine Woman of the Year.

1982 Readers of *Woman's Own* vote Catherine their favourite creative writer in the magazine's Women of Achievement Awards.

1983 Catherine is awarded an honorary Master of Arts degree by Newcastle University.

1983 The Variety Club of Great Britain vote Catherine Cookson the North-East female Personality of the Year.

1984 The Variety Club of Great Britain votes Catherine Cookson its regional female Personality of the Year for the second year running.

1985 Catherine awarded an OBE in the Queen's Birthday Honours List.

1987 The Variety Club of Great Britain names Catherine Cookson its female Personality of the Year for the third time in four years.

1988 Catherine voted Writer of the Year in the Woman of Achievement awards.

1991 Sunderland Polytechnic award Catherine a honorary doctorate.

1991 *The Black Velvet Gown* is watched by 12.8 million viewers —61per cent of the national audience—and shares the number one spot with *Coronation Street* screened as part of the Cookson television mini-series. It is awarded an Emmy.

1992 *The Black Velvet Gown*—screened a year earlier—wins a first prize at the Fiction TV Festival.

1993 Catherine is made a Dame of the British Empire in the New Year's Honours List.

1994 Catherine is awarded a Lifetime Achievement Award at the fifth annual British Book Awards—the literary world's Oscars

1997 Catherine Cookson appointed an Honorary Fellow of St Hilda's College, Oxford.

The Cookson Trail

CATHERINE COOKSON fiercely guarded her good name and reputation. Not only did she vehemently refused to allow a public house to be named after her she even opposed the formation of an unofficial fan club. The latest scheme to bear her name, this time from a local authority, sounded just as dubious.

South Tyneside Council, formed from the amalgamated boroughs which had shared administration south of the River Tyne, announced plans to celebrate its most famous daughter—by inviting visitors to tour Catherine Cookson Country.

With industry in decline and mid-1980s unemployment on the increase the council hoped its £50,000 campaign would attract thousands of Cookson fans into the area. Maps and guidebooks would direct tourists around the borough, while plaques would mark the important sites of Catherine's early years.

"At first Mrs Cookson was afraid the idea might be construed as an ego trip on her part," explained Peter Gillanders, South Tyneside's publicity officer and the man who devised the trail.

"She was wary and it was only because we convinced her of the potential for bringing new jobs and money into the area that she finally agreed to back it. People assumed there was something in it for her, but she got absolutely nothing."

Initially just four plaques were erected: On the site of Catherine Cookson's birthplace; where the New Buildings once stood; at her church and school, and outside the former South Shields workhouse. It was enough. By the next summer more than 100,000 people had followed the Cookson trail on foot or by coach. Within three years the figure had doubled, swelled by fans from around the world. In American and Canadian holiday brochures a visit to Cookson Country was an obligatory part of any British tour.

The start of the trail—each year almost a quarter of a million fans visit Catherine Cookson Country.

Cliff Goodwin

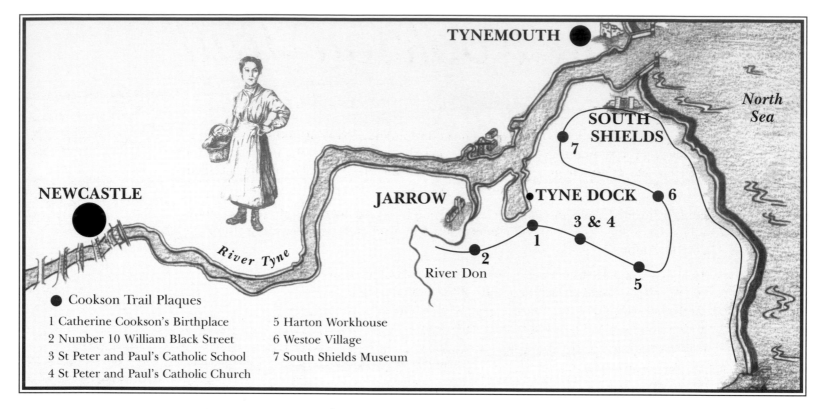

NORTH SEA

TYNEMOUTH

SOUTH SHIELDS
7

NEWCASTLE

JARROW

TYNE DOCK
3 & 4
1
6

River Tyne

River Don
2
5

● Cookson Trail Plaques

1 Catherine Cookson's Birthplace
2 Number 10 William Black Street
3 St Peter and Paul's Catholic School
4 St Peter and Paul's Catholic Church

5 Harton Workhouse
6 Westoe Village
7 South Shields Museum

Cookson Trail Plaques

1 Catherine Cookson's birthplace: At the turn of the century Leam Lane End was a tight-knit community of terraced houses, cottages, front-room shops, a blacksmiths and gas works. It was here, at No 5 Leam Lane, on a warm yet blustery Wednesday morning in June, 1906, that Kate Fawcett gave birth to her illegitimate daughter.

The house was in the middle of a curved terrace on the right-hand side of Leam Lane where it opened out to join the Jarrow Road. The junction was known locally as Leam Lane End. From the front-room window you could look across the street to where another row of houses disappeared around the opposite corner. Looking left, to where Leam Lane started its steep climb up Simonside Bank, there was a second, shorter terrace built six or seven feet above the level of the road and protected by a brick wall. Between the two, leaning against the gable end of the second row, was a blacksmith's shop with a tall, narrow chimney and surrounded by a rough wooden fence.

Northern Echo

Number 5 Leam Lane was a ground-floor house. The three-roomed property above, No 4, was occupied by a family called Angus. George Angus worked as a boiler-maker. The two houses were the only up-and-down homes in the terrace.

Behind the row of houses, built almost into the railway embankment, was a gas works with a single gasometer. It was reached by a track which opened on to Leam Lane next to Lawson's shop. The smell of coal gas crept into every corner of every room. On washdays the women would take metal pails to the gaswork furnace to have them filled with hot cinders to start the wash-house boilers.

In the early 1980s the cluster of buildings known for more than a one hundred and fifty years as Leam Lane End were swept away to be replaced by a petrol station.

2 Number 10 William Black Street: In 1912 Catherine joined her grand-parent's other possessions on the back of a flat horse-drawn cart to be transported the half-mile from her birthplace in Leam Lane to William Black Street.

After a temporary stay at a house further up the street the family finally moved in to Number 10 William Black Street.

The estate was known locally as the New Buildings ... Charles Gidney, the owner of the St Bede Chemical Works, had conceived a plan to build clean modern homes for his employees. He chose a site half-way along Jarrow Road, which connected Tyne Dock with his factory at East Jarrow. Surrounded by open fields, his men and their families would benefit from living away from the overcrowded and fetid streets of Tyne Dock and Jarrow. They would also be less than half a mile away from their place of work.

Left: Leam Lane End, the two men have just passed by Number 5 Leam Lane, Catherine's birthplace.

Right: Trail blazer: by the mid-1980s Leam Lane End had been replaced by a service station—and become the first stop on South Tyneside Council's Cookson Trail.

Gidney's original plan—soon abandoned—had been for fifteen streets to be constructed on the eight acre site south of the main South Shields to Jarrow road and opposite the timber ponds of Jarrow Slake. Only four rows of houses were ever completed:

> Three of the streets on the site ran north to south. On the far left was Lancaster Street. Unlike the other homes the three houses in Lancaster Street had no back lane. Land between them and the front doors of Phillipson Street—intended for more houses—had been left vacant. The back yards of the nine houses in Phillipson Street, one to each household, were separated from the houses in William Black Street by a narrow cobbled lane.

> Reflecting the working-class hierarchy of the time, each street included a larger house for a minor works' official. Number 2 William Black Street, with its gable end facing the enclosed rear of the Larkins' house in Simonside Terrace, was a self-contained seven-roomed house. The remaining houses in William Black Street were separated into upstairs and downstairs homes. The upper homes had four rooms while those who lived beneath were forced to live in three. Both shared a single back yard.

Nothing remains of Catherine Cookson's ground-floor childhood and teenage home. The site is now the Bede Industrial Estate.

3   St Peter and Paul's Catholic School: One day in the summer of 1916 ten year old Kitty McMullen was told she was changing schools. She would be leaving St Bede's Infants School in Monkton Road, Jarrow, and transferring to St Peter and Paul's Catholic School in Belle Vue Crescent beside Tyne Dock railway station.

> The school had opened in the same year as Catherine's birth. The grounds included the presbytery, where Father Bradley lived. He was a long-nosed, righteous man whose toneless voice only added to Catherine's sense of doom. The parish priest had been joined in 1914 by the kinder and quieter Father O'Keefe.

> Of the six hours' teaching each day at St Peter and Paul's a full third would be devoted to religion. The pupils' spiritual and educations welfare was guided by the headmistress, Miss Caulfield, one of three sisters teaching at the school. She was a teacher who appears to have relied on acid sarcasm and her cane to deal with most minor misdemeanours.

> To counter Miss Caulfield's inflexible regime Catherine resorted to bribery. Passing Leam Lane End on her way to school, she would stop at Anne Dixon's house in Leam Lane to buy a pennyworth of flowers from the garden. She would invariably stay too long. When Catherine arrived at school she would present the elder Miss Caulfield with the bouquet, only to be caned for her late arrival.

In 1966 a fire swept through St Peter and Paul's School. It left the building so badly damaged it had to be demolished.

4 St Peter and Paul's Catholic Church: Catherine Cookson continued to hold the rigidity of the Catholic faith and its unbending priests at least partly responsible for her ten year breakdown.

From the age of ten she was mesmerised as much by the faith as she was by the fear of its earthly representatives. Adjacent to her senior school—and still largely unchanged today—St Peter and Paul's Church was the domain of Father Bradley, a man with the unnerving look of someone who could examine your very soul. His assistant was Father O'Keefe and Father Bradley's uncompromising devotion conflicted as much with the younger Father O'Keefe's kindness and generosity as the good and evil they both preached.

It was a powerful message which Catherine used as effectively as any symbolised by the other real-life characters who people her books. In *Kate Hannigan* and *The Fifteen Streets* Father O'Malley and Father

St Peter and Paul's Church and the adjoining Presbytery from which Father Bradley dominated the fearful parishioners.

Bailey cast light and shade—fear and hope—across their parish, just as Father Bradley and Father O'Keefe forced the young Catherine to face the nightmare of a black and white world.

Each Sunday she attended eleven o'clock Mass at St Peter and Paul's Church beside her former school.

She would not walk down Boldon Lane on her way home without kneeling before the alter at St Peter and Paul's to beg Our Lady to keep Kate sober and out of debt. On her way back to the workhouse after an evening or day at William Black Street she would stop and give thanks in the unlit church.

5 Harton Workhouse: The workhouse—and the horror it engendered—loomed over the McMullen household like a cold, grey monolith. Less than a decade before Catherine's birth her out-of-work grandfather had smashed rocks in the workhouse quarry for a shilling a day. John McMullen's abiding fear was that he would die a workhouse pauper. For his teenage grand-daughter the workhouse would offer an escape; first from the claustrophobia of Number 10 William Black Street and, six years later, from the oppressive poverty of the North-East.

Catherine had been recommended for a job in the Harton Workhouse laundry by Father Bradley, the

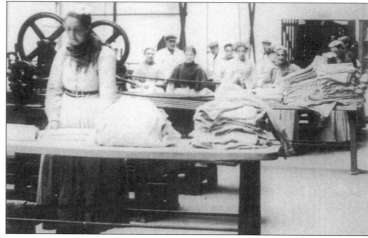
Cliff Goodwin

The main building of Harton Workhouse. It was here the nervous eighteen year old Catherine McMullen was interviewed for her job as laundry checker.

Right: In the Harton Workhouse Laundry.

pious priest at St Peter and Paul's Church. Her arrival was recorded in the House Committee minutes as: "Commenced: 22 October, 1924—Miss K. McMullen [sic]; laundry checker."

She would spend most of her day in a glass-screened corner of the laundry, through which both the dirty and clean linen would pass. Sorting the soiled and foul smelling sheets was left to two illiterate inmate helpers. Catherine would use her childish handwriting to make entries in the ledger.

For this she would have her own room, four meals a day, and earn little over £2 a month. When she retired, after forty years, she would be entitled to a pension of 6s [30 pence] a week.

From her cubicle she could study the rest of the laundry. Only the officers wore black dresses with white aprons, caps and cuffs. They were helped by half a dozen paid hands, also distinguished by their white aprons. The menial tasks were carried out by the inmates, who wore smocks and mop caps.

The equipment was crude but effective. Ironing was done on large benches, down the middle of which ran pipes to feed the wooden-handled steam irons. The two steel-bed presses were driven by exposed leather belts connected to a noisy drive shaft above the bare beams. Crumpled clean linen was dumped on the floor or tables. When it had been pressed it was returned to the main hospital and male and female mental blocks in heavy, square wicker baskets.

Many of the original workhouse buildings, including the laundry, have been demolished. The site is now occupied by South Shields General Hospital.

6

Westoe village: Only days before her eighteenth birthday Catherine arrived at Westoe village convinced her luck had at last changed. She desperately needed a job and signed on at South Shields' employment office. In exchange for her shilling registration fee the dour-faced clerk handed her the name and address of a woman seeking a child's companion.

A mile from the centre of South Shields the tree-lined village street, with its white wooden railings and quiet respectability, looked as though it has somehow survived the first twenty years of the 20th century in sleepy isolation.

Behind the rows of elm trees stood solid, expensive houses, country homes built for town families. These were different to the big houses Catherine had seen on the horse-drawn brake trips to Shotley Bridge or Rowlands Gill in Derwent Valley. The mistresses of these houses would never allow their husbands' work to contaminate their homes.

Westoe village at the turn of the century. Offered work as companion to a Westoe family, Catherine declined the post when she realised she would not be allowed to attend Sunday Mass.

Catherine found the house she had been looking for and introduced herself to the wife of the owner. The woman approved of the shy but proud teenager standing before her. The family, which included a four year old child, was about to embark on a summer tour of Italy. The woman needed a companion for her son, "someone still young enough not to have forgotten how to play, but old enough to have sense".

Suddenly the woman asked her future employee if she was of any particular faith. Catherine readily admitted she was Catholic. And yes, she did attend Mass. The woman, apparently stunned by Catherine's devotion in the face of a remarkable chance to travel, attempted to explain that any childminding duties would include Sundays and High Days. Catherine, however, heard nothing but Father Bradley's admonitions. Miss Mass, the priest was warning her, and you go to hell.

Exactly sixty years later, in 1984, Catherine's "return" to Westoe Village was a little more auspicious. The writer agreed to allow the Guardian Housing Association to name a block of twenty-two Westoe retirement flats after her. The complex is called Catherine Cookson House.

Reconstructions of Cissie Affleck's shop and Number 10 William Black Street, East Jarrow, in South Shields Museum.

7 South Shields Museum: Less than two weeks after launching the Cookson Trail in 1985 South Tyneside Borough Council announced it was also considering opening a Catherine Cookson Museum, possibly in the historic Old Town Hall in the centre of South Shields Market Place, and in the shadow of which the poor but honest Kitty McMullen had returned a pound note to a fellow shopper.

The exhibition—eventually housed in South Shields' Ocean Road Museum—includes a full-size bricks-and-mortar street facade and a reproduction of Cissie Affleck's shop, the name Catherine gave to Jessie Eckford's Phillipson Street shop in *Our Kate*.

The exhibit's centrepiece is an exact replica of the William Black Street kitchen where Kate Fawcett's daughter heard and told and wrote her first stories. "Everything that happened in that kitchen, everything I thought, everything that I have written since, seems to have been bred in that kitchen," admitted the novelist.

At the back of the house was the kitchen warmed by the constant activity, yet never free from the dust and soot given out by the open range. The name of its maker—Grieve & Gillespie, Jarrow on Tyne—was embossed across the top. Each side of the black-leaded range with its heavy oven door was an alcove. In the left-hand space—beside an old chest of drawers—stood an outsize gas cooker Kate had acquired from a hotel; it was never connected to the supply. To the right of the range, tall wooden doors enclosed a cupboard. Beneath the opposite wall, and pressed behind a large leather-topped table, was a six-foot saddle or settee. And spread on the floor between the table and the range lay the family's clippy mat, twisted and sewn from oddments of brightly coloured material.

Catherine helped with the design and layout of the kitchen and agreed to scrutinise items like linoleum and light fittings and door handles to make sure they were as close to the original as possible.

* All extracts taken from *To Be A Lady: The Story of Catherine Cookson* [Century].

The Cookson Legacy

THRIFT AND financial foresight were as much a part of Catherine Cookson's make up as her relentless ambition and artistic talent. From her mid-twenties—and while still living in the North-East—every transaction, both large and small, was noted and tallied in a pocket cash book. If an item, no matter how vital, could not be paid for with cash it was overlooked or disregarded.

Only in the 1950s, when she was an established writer and with one of her stories already sold to a film company, did Catherine reluctantly consent to buying a new washing machine on hire purchase. Throughout the first two decades of her career as a novelist Catherine kept an equal rein on her time. She rarely took an active part in supporting charities because that would take her away from her writing. And if she stopped writing she stopped earning.

By the early 1970, and with the paperbacks of her novels already selling by the millions, Catherine and Tom Cookson found they had the money, but rarely the time. Never a lover of Sundays—"I always work hard on Sundays. It stops me thinking about what day it is"—Catherine broke her rigid work routine to consider hundreds of requests for financial help.

After lunch the couple would sift through the week's letters and decided which appeals should be replied with a cheque. Catherine read every letter. "Some stories would break your heart," she said, "but I had to keep my reason."

In 1976 Catherine ended her forty-six year exile in the south of England and returned to her native Tyneside. Her productivity as a writer never faltered. Nor did her capacity as a patron of worthy causes.

By 1984 the Cooksons had given away at least £250,000 of their own money. The letters and appeals were now arriving by the sackful. To process more formal requests from schools and churches and to ease the poverty within the community, the couple established and launched the Catherine Cookson Charitable Trust. Within twelve months the trust had posted cheques to 120 charities.

The following year the writer donated a another £250,000, this time to launch the Catherine Cookson Foundation. With additional donations,

Catherine Cookson outside the Newcastle University Medical School named after her.

Northern Echo

and the creative use of tax schemes, it meant Newcastle University would eventually receive almost £900,000.

Speculation over Catherine's wealth had rumbled on since she was quizzed by a journalist in the mid-1950s demanding to know how much she had relieved for the film rights to *A Grand Man*. More than thirty years later one unconfirmed report credited her with a personal fortune exceeding £20-million. Another gave her the unlikely title of being the fourteenth wealthiest woman in Britain.

"The only thing I want from money is to die in comfort," commented Catherine. "That I'm looking forward to and I'm really going to get my money's worth."

Ever practical, Tom added: "Since we have no children it would go to charity in the end. It may as well go now."

Late in 1997, and with her health ever worsening, Catherine at last decided she should formalise the donations she and Tom had individually vetted and approved. Catherine signed her final will on 14th October. She had already decided on the mechanics of distributing the vast personal profits from her writing.

Cheque mate: Catherine hands over cheques for £8000,000 to (left to right) Professor Laurence Martin, Dr Chris Record and Dr Hugo Marshall. The money would finance medical research at Newcastle University.

It was always assumed Catherine would die before her husband. For various tax reasons—and to ultimately benefit charities and not the Exchequer—more than £11m was "given" to Tom during the 1980s and 90s. When his wife died this personal fortune was topped-up by the bulk of Catherine's remaining £8,476,174 estate.

Her biggest single bequest was a £250,000 donation to Newcastle University's Medical School. Among the gifts to her personal friends, publishing associates and several of her doctors Catherine left £10,000 to the Harry Edwards Spiritual Healing Sanctuary Trust in Surrey and £5,000 to Sister Catherine Marie living in California. Years of advice from her bank manager was also repaid with a cash gift.

When Tom Cookson died just days after his wife, managers at Newcastle's Medical School found themselves with a second £250,000 donation. The remainder of Tom's £20,222,381 estate went automatically to the Catherine Cookson Trust, which now found itself with millions to donate in the weeks and months after the couple's death.

"It is not exactly difficult to give the money away," explained Catherine's accountant and now trustee William McBrien, "it's deciding where to give it and what to do with it that counts."

Cookson in Character

Compiling the Character List

IT WAS necessary to employ certain rules and criteria in compiling the list of major Cookson characters. The basic qualification for a character to be included in the following A to Z was that he or she must be a 'speaking character'.

No attempt was made to record characters included as part of the general text or mentioned in passing by another character. To simplify and clarify each entry it was decided to include only personal details, relationships to other speaking characters, and brief details of geographic locations. All characters mentioned within a definition—such as children or parents—have an entry of their own.

Because most of Catherine Cookson's novels range over a considerable period in time it was decided that including a character's age would only lead to confusion.

Where a character's name changes during the development of a story, that character has been listed under the name for which he or she is mentioned for the greater part of the book. Should a character marry—such as Louise Barrington in *Riley* or Maria Millican in *The Black Velvet Gown*—then her married name becomes the prime entry.

No attempt was made to include details of plots or storylines, but some entries contain extra points of interest concerning Catherine's relationship with a particular character.

Agnes
    Cook at No 17 Blake Terrace, London, the home of Martha Culmills. *The Branded Man*

Agnes Mary, Sister
    Nun and teacher at the Convent of the Holy Child of Bethlehem, St Leonard's on Sea. *The Devil and Mary Ann*

Aimsford, Mr
    Neighbour of Joseph Dodd and his grand-daughter Bella Dodd. *Go Tell It To Mrs Golightly*

Aiton, Bob
    Area manager for Braithwaite's Grocers in Jarrow. *Fanny McBride*

Allison, Annette
    Daughter of James and Janet Allison and girlfriend of Donald Coulson. *The Year of the Virgins*

Allison, James
    Husband of Janet Allison and father of Annette Allison; friend of Daniel and Winifred Coulson. *The Year of the Virgins*

Allison, Janet
    Wife of James Allison and mother of Annette Allison; friend of Winifred Coulson. *The Year of the Virgins*

Alvarez, Carlos
    Spanish-born music "professor" and husband of Liza Alvarez; lover of Marie Anne Lawson. *The Branded Man*

Alvarez, Liza
    Wife of Carlos Alvarez, a "professor" of music. *The Branded Man*

Ambers, Lady Mary
Eccentric cousin of Lady Sarah Menton. *Justice is a Woman*

Ancliff, Clare
Divorced wife of Peter Jones and mother of David Jones. *Lanky Jones*

Ancliff, George
Husband of Clare Anscliff. *Lanky Jones*

Anderson, PC
Fellburn police officer. *Bill Bailey's Lot*

Andrews, Mrs
Mother of Celia Armstrong, Battenbun's post-mistress and shop keeper. *Slinky Jane*

Annie
Housemaid employed by Janet Fairbrother at No 19 Sweetbanks Gardens, Fellburn. *The Upstart*

Armitage, Francis
Solicitor and executor to John Cornwallis. *Rory's Fortune*

Armstrong
First footman employed by Harry Bensham at High Banks Hall. *The Mallen Girl* & *The Mallen Litter*

Armstrong, Celia
Battenbun's postmistress and proprietor of the village stores. *Slinky Jane*

Armstrong, Dr John
Half-cousin and neighbour of Matilda. *The Man Who Cried*

Armstrong, Fanny
Daughter of Frank Armstrong. *The Mallen Streak*

Armstrong, Father
Fellburn priest; runs the Children of Mary's Youth Club every Thursday evening. *The Invitation*

Armstrong, Frank
Father of Fanny Armstrong and pit owning associate of Thomas Mallen. *The Mallen Streak*

Armstrong, John George
Friend of Rory Connor and fellow rent collector Septimus Kean. *The Gambling Man*

Armstrong, Peter
Miner in charge of the Galloway pit ponies. *The Nipper*

Armstrong, Samuel
Middle-aged father of Robert Robson; lives at Dean Cottages, Hexham. Manager employed by Martha Mary Crawford to run the family's Hexham bookshop. *Miss Martha Mary Crawford*

Arnison, Dr
In the late 19th century the residents of the Cumbrian farms and cottages around Allendale relied for medical treatment on a Dr Arnison. The physician's library had included a book on Allendale and Whitefield written by George Dickinson Jnr and published locally in 1884. Dr Arnison's grand-daughter passed the book on to the writer, whom she had got to know during one of the Cookson's many holidays in the area.

Catherine decided to set her latest story—which eventually appeared in 1977 as The Girl—in the fictitious Pennine foothill village of Elmholm—where the residents are treated by Dr Arnison.

Arnold, Bill
Builder and odd-job man in Rothcorn, Northumberland. *House of Men*

Arthur
Car dealer and one-time lover of Leoline Carter. *Slinky Jane*

Arthur
Rustler associate of Billy Combo. *Lanky Jones*

Atkins, Mary
Housekeeper to Nyrene Riley (née Forbes-Mason). *Riley*

Atkins, Mr
Deputy headmaster of Swandale Preparatory School. *Bill Bailey*

Atkins, Mrs
Neighbour of Maisie Rochester; lives in Wellenmore Terrace, Fellburn. *Hamilton*

Atkinson, Nellie
Slightly-built middle-aged cousin of Grace Howlett, manages Bamford & Brummell's drapery shop, off Green Street, South Shields. Lives at No 71 Filbert Terrace. *Rooney*

Aylmer, Paul
Tall, thick set antique dealer; works and lives with his niece Alison Read; their premises and home is at the top of Tally's Rise, a street of antique shops in the south-coast town of Sealock. *The Lady on my Left*

Bachelor, Ben
Smuggler friend of Alex Bluett. *Rory's Fortune*

Badcliff, Noreen
Fiancée of Logan Rossiter. *House of Men*

Baggy Betty
Down-and-out Jarrow woman. *Fanny McBride*

Bailey, Father
South Shields parish priest. *Kate Hannigan & Colour Blind*

Bailey, Mr
Father of William Bailey. *Bill Bailey*

Bailey, Angela
Down's Syndrome daughter of William and Fiona Bailey and half-sister of Mark, Katie and Willie Nelson and the Bailey's adopted daughter Mamie Bailey. *Bill Bailey's Daughter*

Bailey, Arthur
Refined husband of Mona Bailey and son of Gerald and Gwen Bailey and brother to David and Olive Bailey. Wartime homosexual lover of George McCabe; an artificial leg forces him to walk with a limp. *The Invisible Cord*

Bailey, David
Son of Gerald and Gwen Bailey and brother to Arthur and Olive Bailey. *The Invisible Cord*

Bailey, Fiona
(née Nelson) Daughter of Mrs Vidler and the fifth wife of builder William Bailey; mother of Mark, Katie and Willie Nelson and Angela Bailey and adoptive mother of Mamie Bailey. Lives at No 16 Woodland Avenue, Fellburn (Tel: Fellburn 7843) and later Burnstead Mere, Durham. *Bill Bailey, Bill Bailey's Lot, Bill Bailey's Daughter & The Bondage of Love*

Bailey, George
Manager employed by Joe Remington at the Remington Wood Works; known as "Geordie". *Justice is a Woman*

Bailey, Gerald
Husband of Gwen Bailey and father of Arthur, Olive and David Bailey. *The Invisible Cord*

Bailey, Gwen
Wife of Gerald Bailey and mother of Arthur, Olive and David Bailey. *The Invisible Cord*

Bailey, Mamie
Orphan adopted by William and Fiona Bailey. *Bill Bailey, Bill Bailey's Lot, Bill Bailey's Daughter & The Bondage of Love*

Bailey, Mona
(née Broadbent) Wife of Arthur Bailey. Life-long friend of Annie McCabe; lives first at No 114 Weldon Street, South Shields, and then at Hereford. Disfigured and partly blinded during a Second World War air raid. *The Invisible Cord*

Bailey, William
Brash Liverpudlian building contractor and husband of Fiona Bailey; step-father to Mark, Katie and Willie Nelson and adoptive father of Mamie

Bill Bailey

Bailey. Father of Angela Bailey. Lives at No 16 Woodland Avenue, Fellburn, later Burnstead Mere, Durham. *Bill Bailey, Bill Bailey's Lot, Bill Bailey's Daughter* & *The Bondage of Love*

Bailey-Crawford, Mrs
Down-on-his-luck and bedraggled owner of Honeycroft, a large house in Westoe, South Shields. *Rooney*

Baily, Father
Junior priest to Father O'Malley. *The Fifteen Streets*

Bainbridge, James
Metropolitan Police detective sergeant, undercover name John Drake. Nicknamed "The Mohican" because of his hair style and Indian clothing. *Harold*

Baker, Sgt
Fellburn police sergeant. *The Upstart*

Balfour, Mrs
Domineering mother of Tommy Balfour; lives at No 17 The Crescent, London. *Goodbye Hamilton*

Balfour, Tommy
Best friend of Leonard Leviston and director in the London publishing house of Houseman and Rington; lives at No 17 The Crescent, London. *Goodbye Hamilton* & *Harold*

Bannaman, Dan
Murderous and scheming Northumberland father of Mary Bannaman and smuggler, horse dealer and farmer. *A Dinner of Herbs*

Bannaman, Mary
Vindictive and scheming daughter of Dan Bannaman. *A Dinner of Herbs*

Banner
Butler employed at the Hebburn house of Sir William Combe Stockwell, owner of the local coal mine. *The Nipper*

Barker, Nancy
Librarian at Fellburn Public Library and friend of Janet Fairbrother. *The Upstart*

Barnes, Frank
Resident of Ramsay Court in London's East End. *The Branded Man*

Barnes, Mrs
Wife of Frank Barnes and resident of Ramsay Court in London's East End. *The Branded Man*

Barney
Assistant at Paddy's Emporium, a three storey junk shop, owned by Paddy O'Connell. *The Branded Man*

Barrington, Herbert
Soppish lover of Stella Prince. *Kate Hannigan*

Barrington, Miss
Elderly owner of a Fellburn High Street flower shop. *The Menagerie*

Barrington, Timothy
Epileptic half-brother of Penella Brodrick; lives first at The Manor before setting up his own establishment at Briar Close, Fellburn. *The Gillyvors*

Bateman, Marie
Executive secretary at Fellburn wholesale chemist Peamarsh's. *The Nice Bloke*

Batley, Gran
Mother of Ralph Batley; lives at Fowler Hall Farm, Northumberland. *Heritage of Folly*

Batley, Maggie
Wife of farmer Ralph Batley; lives at Fowler Hall Farm, Northumberland. *Heritage of Folly*

Batley, Ralph
Irascible sculptor-turned-farmer and husband of Maggie Batley; employs Linda Metcalfe on Fowler Hall Farm, Northumberland. *Heritage of Folly*

Baxton-Powell, Gregory
Father of May and Richard Baxton-Powell; lives at Towbridge House. *The Tinker's Girl*

Baxton-Powell, May
Daughter of Gregory Baxton-Powell and sister of Richard Baxton-Powell and neighbour of the Shalemans family; lives at Towbridge House. *The Tinker's Girl*

Baxton-Powell, Richard
Charitable son of Gregory Baxton-Powell and brother of May Baxton-Powell. Neighbour and friend of the Shalemans family; lives at Towbridge House. *The Tinker's Girl*

Beardsley, Fred
Outsized, grey-haired husband of Louise Beardsley. Senior science master at Giles Mentor School, Hastings. Nicknamed "Grizzly Beardsley" because of his gruff, quick-tempered behaviour. *Riley*

Beardsley, Louise
(née Barrington) Science teacher at Giles Mentor School, Hastings; marries the school's head of science, Fred Beardsley. *Riley*

Beatrice
School friend of Mary Ann Shaughnessy while at the Convent of the Holy Child of Bethlehem, St Leonard's on Sea. *The Devil and Mary Ann*

Beck
Housekeeper to the Gordon-Platts. *The Lady on my Left*

Beckingtree-Holland, Captain
Husband of Mrs Beckingtree-Holland and tenant of Maisie Leviston. *Harold*

Beckingtree-Holland, Mrs
Doll-like wife of Captain Beckingtree-Holland and tenant of Maisie Leviston. *Harold*

Beeney, Emily
Owner of Wind Fell house-window-shop. *Rory's Fortune*

Bell, Dr
London general practitioner. *Goodbye Hamilton*

Bell, Sister
Ward sister in a Newcastle hospital. *The Year of the Virgins*

Bella
Live-in companion to Mrs Balfour at No 17 The Crescent, London. *Goodbye Hamilton*

Bellingham, Hugh
Autocratic neighbour of Lord Fischel. *The Dwelling Place*

Ben
Butler-cum-handyman employed by Peter Lord. *The Lord and Mary Ann, The Devil and Mary Ann, Love and Mary Ann, Life and Mary Ann, Marriage and Mary Ann, Mary Ann's Angels* & *Mary Ann and Bill*

Benbow, Andrew
Boatman and poacher. *Go Tell It To Mrs Golightly*

Benfield, Kate
First assistant teacher at Miss Benfield's Academy for Young Ladies, Fellburn. *The Gillyvors*

Benfield, Miss
Large-chested proprietor of Miss Benfield's Academy for Young Ladies, Fellburn, and cousin of Kate Benfield. *The Gillyvors*

Bennett, Alicia
Snobbish friend of Matthew Sopwith. *Tilly Trotter Wed*

Bennett, Samuel
Thin-faced property magnate and friend of Reginald and Kate Thorman. *The Moth*

Bensham, Anna
(née Brigmore) Prim governess to Constance and Barbara Farrington and Thomas Mallen's lover. Second wife of Harry Bensham. *The Mallen Streak, The Mallen Girl* & *The Mallen Litter*

Bensham, Barbara
(née Farrington) Tempestuous illegitimate daughter of Thomas Mallen and wife of Daniel Bensham; lives at rue

Nicholas Charles, Paris, and then Brook House, Morpeth. Mother of triplets Ben, Jonathan and Harry Bensham. Michael Radlet's lover. *The Mallen Streak, The Mallen Girl & The Mallen Litter*

Bensham, Ben
Scheming son of Daniel and Barbara Bensham and brother to Jonathan and Harry Bensham; lives at Brook House, Morpeth. *The Mallen Litter*

Bensham, Daniel
Son of Harry and Matilda Bensham and brother of John Bensham and Katie Ferrier. Husband of Barbara Bensham; lives first at High Banks Hall, then rue Nicholas Charles, Paris and finally Brook House, Morpeth. Father of triplets Ben, Jonathan and Harry Bensham. Lover of Ruth Foggety. *The Mallen Girl & The Mallen Litter*

Bensham, Harry
Bullet-headed Manchester mill owner and husband of Matilda Bensham and father of John and Daniel Bensham and Katie Ferrier; master of High Banks Hall. Later marries Anna Brigmore. *The Mallen Girl & The Mallen Litter*

Bensham, John
Son of Harry and Matilda Bensham and brother of Daniel Bensham and Katie Ferrier; lives at High Banks Hall and then Manchester. *The Mallen Girl*

Bensham, Jonathan
Son of Daniel and Barbara Bensham and brother to Ben and Harry Bensham; lives at Brook House, Morpeth. *The Mallen Litter*

Bensham, Matilda
Sickly wife of Harry Bensham and mother of Daniel and John Bensham and Katie Ferrier; lives at High Banks Hall. *The Mallen Girl*

Benton, Arthur
Vindictive and cruel farmhand son of Jim and Polly Benton and elder brother of Polly, Peter and Maggie Benton; employed by Edward MacFell and lives in a workers cottage at Moor Burn Farm, near Kirkwhelpington, Northumberland. Serves with the Durham Light Infantry in the Great War. *The Cinder Path*

Benton, Jim
Invalid husband of Polly Benton and father of Maggie, Polly, Peter and Arthur Benton; lives in a workers cottage at Moor Burn Farm, Northumberland. *The Cinder Path*

Benton, Maggie
Daughter of Jim and Polly Benton, sister of Polly, Peter and Arthur Benton. Housemaid to Edward and Mary MacFell; lives in a workers' cottage at Moor Burn Farm, near Kirkwhelpington, Northumberland. *The Cinder Path*

Benton, Peter
Son of Jim and Polly Benton and brother of Maggie, Polly and Arthur Benton. Outside hand employed by Edward MacFell; lives in a worker's cottage at Moor Burn Farm, near Kirkwhelpington, Northumberland. *The Cinder Path*

Benton, Polly
Daughter of Jim and Polly Benton and sister of Arthur, Maggie and Peter Benton. Childhood friend of Charles MacFell; lives in a workers' cottage at Moor Burn Farm, near Kirkwhelpington, Northumberland. Known as "Young Polly". *The Cinder Path*

Benton, Polly
Wife of Jim and mother of Polly, Maggie, Peter and Arthur Benton; lives in a workers' cottage at Moor Burn Farm, Northumberland. Known as "Big Polly". *The Cinder Path*

Bentwood, Lucy
Second wife of Simon Bentwood and step-mother to Noreen Bentwood. *Tilly Trotter Widowed*

Bentwood, Mary
Ill-tempered, ill-trusting flouncing first wife of farmer Simon Bentwood, mother of Noreen Bentwood. *Tilly Trotter*

Bentwood, Noreen
Hazel-eyed daughter of Simon and Mary Bentwood and friend of William Sopwith and Josefina Cardenas. *Tilly Trotter Widowed*

Bentwood, Simon
Husband first of Mary Bentwood and then Lucy Bentwood and father to Noreen Bentwood; tenant farmer of Mark Sopwith. Lover of Lady Agnes Myton. *Tilly Trotter, Tilly Trotter Wed & Tilly Trotter Widowed*

Beresford, Dr George
Fellburn general practitioner; lives in Melbourne Road, Fellburn. *The Long Corridor*

Beresford, Mrs
Wife of Dr George Beresford; lives in Melbourne Road, Fellburn. *The Long Corridor*

Bernice, David
Owner-manger of The Little Palace Theatre in Fellburn Market Place. *Riley*

Betty
Inmate of Mary Ping's Home for Distressed Women. *The Branded Man*

Big Ned
Allendale blacksmith. *The Mallen Girl*

Biggs, Mr
Veterinary surgeon with a practice in Roland Street, Fellburn. *Hamilton*

Billings, Anna
Daughter of South Shields vet. *Joe and the Gladiator*

Billings, Lucy
Wife of South Shields vet and mother of Anna Billings. *Joe and the Gladiator*

Billings, Mr
South Shields vet and husband of Louise Billings. Father to Anna Billings. *Joe and the Gladiator*

Binn, Mr
Lay preacher and headmaster at Harold Stoddart's school. *Harold*

Birkett, Sister
Ward sister at Fellburn General Hospital. *The Upstart*

Blenheim, Esther
Wife of Harry Blenheim and mother of Gail, John and Terry Blenheim; lives at Hollytree House, Holt Avenue, Fellburn. *The Nice Bloke*

Blenheim, Gail
Daughter of Harry and Esther Blenheim and sister of John and Terry Blenheim; lives at Hollytree House, Holt Avenue, Fellburn. Girlfriend of Robbie Dunn. *The Nice Bloke*

Blenheim, Harry
Husband of Esther Blenheim and father of Gail, John and Terry Blenheim; lives first at Hollytree House, Holt Avenue, Fellburn, and then Scarfield Mill on Fell Rise. Employed by Fellburn wholesale chemist Peamarsh's before becoming a partner in Robbie Dunn's antique business. *The Nice Bloke*

Blenheim, John
Son of Harry and Esther Blenheim and brother of Gail and Terry Blenheim; lives at Hollytree House, Holt Avenue, Fellburn. *The Nice Bloke*

Blenheim, Terry
Youngest son of Harry and Esther Blenheim and brother of Gail and John Blenheim; lives at Hollytree House, Holt Avenue, Fellburn. *The Nice Bloke*

Blenkinsop, Dan
Husband of Ida Blenkinsop and father of Diana, Roland and Jimmy Blenkinsop; lives near Doncaster. *Mary Ann and Bill*

Blenkinsop, Diana
Secretary daughter of Dan and Ida Blenkinsop and sister

of Roland and Jimmy Blenkinsop; lives near Doncaster. *Mary Ann and Bill*

Blenkinsop, Ida
Wife of Dan Blenkinsop and mother of Diana, Roland and Jimmy Blenkinsop; lives near Doncaster. *Mary Ann and Bill*

Blenkinsop, Jimmy
Son of Dan and Ida Blenkinsop and brother of Diana and Roland Blenkinsop; lives near Doncaster. *Mary Ann and Bill*

Blenkinsop, Rodney
An American businessman and cousin of Dan Blenkinsop. *Mary Ann's Angels*

Blenkinsop, Roland
Son of Dan and Ida Blenkinsop and brother of Diana and Jimmy Blenkinsop; lives near Doncaster. *Mary Ann and Bill*

Bluett, Alex
Bearded brother of May Bluett; lives at St Helier's House, near Yarcombe, Devon. *Rory's Fortune*

Bluett, May
Sister of Alex Bluett; lives at St Helier's House, near Yarcombe, Devon. *Rory's Fortune*

Blyth, Farmer
Farmer father of Katie Blyth. Although in his forties has the appearance of a much older man; employed Sandy Gillespie after his father's death until the Gillespies move to Hebburn. *The Nipper*

Blyth, Katie
Silver-haired and grey-eyed daughter of Farmer Blyth. *The Nipper*

Blyth, Mrs
Wife of Farmer Blyth and mother of Katie Blyth. *The Nipper*

Bob
A pawnbroker. *The Fifteen Streets*

Bolton, Brian
Engineering student son of Harry Bolton and boyfriend of

Lorna Higgins. *The Long Corridor*

Bolton, Dr John Howard
Life-long friend and physician to the Knutsson family. *The Slow Awakening*

Bolton, Harry
Conservative mayor of Fellburn. (The author later inadvertently changes his name to "Arthur") and father of Brian Bolton. *The Long Corridor*

Bolton, Mrs
Wife of Harry Bolton and mother of Brian Bolton. *The Long Corridor*

Bolton, Ned
Jarrow police constable. *Fanny McBride*

Booth, Katie
Wife of Stan Booth and landlady of The Hart, Battenbun's public house. *Slinky Jane*

Booth, Stan
Husband of Katie Booth and landlord of The Hart, Battenbun's public house. *Slinky Jane*

Borley, Mr
Village school teacher. *Matty Doolin*

Boucher, Emma
Neighbour of Jessie Honeysett and Bog's End savings club organiser. *The Menagerie*

Bowbent, Harry
Weakly but thoughtful friend of Daniel and Winifred Coulson. *The Year of the Virgins*

Bowman, Ralph
Painter and lover of Lizzie Crawshaw; hires a cottage from Jake Yorkless at Boulder Hill Farm, near Fellburn. Hires Lizzie Crawshaw as his daily help. *The Whip*

Bowmer, Paul
Twelve year old 'miner' working in a Hebburn pit. *The Nipper*

Boyle, Arthur
One-time fiancé of Kate Mitchell. *House of Men*

Boyle, David
Son of Frederick and Mary Ann Boyle and twin brother of Rose Mary Boyle. *Mary Ann's Angels* & *Mary Ann and Bill*

Boyle, Frederick Richard Cornelius
Gangly, ill-dressed mechanic grandson of Fanny McBride. Husband of Mary Ann Boyle and father of twins Rose Mary and David Boyle. Proprietor of Fell Garage. Known as "Corny". *Fanny McBride, Love and Mary Ann, Life and Mary Ann, Marriage and Mary Ann, Mary Ann's Angels* & *Mary Ann and Bill*

Boyle, Hannah
Daughter of Nancy Boyle and bastard child of Matthew Thornton. *The Girl*

Boyle, Mary Ann
(née Shaugnessy) Daughter of Mike and Elizabeth Shaughnessy and sister of Michael Shaughnessy; lives first in the 'attics' at Mulhattan's Hall, No 16 Burton Street, Jarrow, and then Coffin's Farm, Fellhurst, (later changed to Moor Farm). Wife of Frederick Boyle and mother of twins Rose Mary and David Boyle. *A Grand Man, The Lord and Mary Ann, The Devil and Mary Ann, Love and Mary Ann, Life and Mary Ann, Marriage and Mary Ann, Mary Ann's Angels* & *Mary Ann and Bill*

Boyle, Nancy
Mother of Hannah Boyle and lover of Matthew Thornton. . *The Girl*

Boyle, Rose Mary
Daughter of Cornelius and Mary Ann Boyle and twin sister of David Boyle. *Mary Ann's Angels* & *Mary Ann and Bill*

Mary Anne Boyle

Boyle, Tilly
Mother of Tony Boyle. *Slinky Jane*

Boyle, Tony
Dim-witted son of Tilly Boyle. *Slinky Jane*

Bracken, Christine
Granddaughter of Peter Bracken and sister of David Bracken. Shares her grandfather's healing powers; lives next door to the O'Briens in Fadden Street. Dies in a Jarrow Slake boating accident. *The Fifteen Streets*

Bracken, David
Grandson of Peter Bracken and brother of Christine Bracken; lives next door to the O'Briens in Fadden Street. *The Fifteen Streets*

Bracken, Peter
Eighty-six year old Jarrow cobbler and Fadden Street neighbour of the O'Brien family; lives with his grandchildren Christine and David Bracken. A Spiritualist and psychic healer he is nicknamed "The Spook". *The Fifteen Streets*

Brackett, Bella
House-parlourmaid employed by the Bensham family at No 27 The Drive, Manchester. *The Mallen Litter*

Brackett, Jane
Short and overweight cook employed by Mark Sopwith at Highfield Manor. *Tilly Trotter*

Bradley, Alice
Wife of John Bradley and mother of Carrie Bradley; lives near the County Durham village of Lamesley. *The Moth*

Bradley, Bella
Gossip and neighbour of the O'Briens. *The Fifteen Streets*

Bradley, Carrie
Daughter of John and Alice Bradley; lives near the County Durham village of Lamesley. *The Moth*

Bradley, John
Domineering and teetotal husband of Alice Bradley and

doting father to Carrie Bradley. Uncle of Robert Bradley. Lives near the County Durham village of Lamesley where he runs a long-established carpentry business. *The Moth*

Bradley, Kit
Manager of the Duck and Drake public house on the River Estate at Bog's End, Fellburn. *Bill Bailey's Lot*

Bradley, Ma
Midwife and layer-out paid by the workhouse to 'adopt' Kirsten MacGregor. *The Slow Awakening*

Bradley, Robert
Carpenter employed by his uncle John Bradley; lives first at No 122 Upper Fox Glove Road, only yards from where he works at Palmer's shipyard, Jarrow, before living in the wood loft of his uncle's workshop. Employed as a gardener and outside hand by Reginald Thorman at Foreshaw House. *The Moth*

Bradshaw, Bessie
Drunken, foul-mouthed mother of Connie Bradshaw. *Tilly Trotter Widowed*

Bradshaw, Connie
Cruel and thieving daughter of Bessie Bradshaw; nurse-maid employed by Matilda Sopwith at Highfield Manor. *Tilly Trotter Widowed*

Bradshaw, Lieutenant John
Fellow Durham Light Infantry officer of Charles MacFell. *The Cinder Path*

Bradshaw, Michael
Square-jawed, arrogant father of Susan Bradshaw and owner of Thornby House, near Ely, East Anglia. *The Fen Tiger*

Bradshaw, Susan
Down's Syndrome daughter of Michael Bradshaw; lives at Thornby House, near Ely, East Anglia. *The Fen Tiger*

Brian
Friend of Peter Puddleton. *Slinky Jane*

Braintree, Mr
Friend of pit owner Sir William Combe Stockwell. *The Nipper*

Braithwaite, Miss
Blind school teacher in charge of Bella Dodd. *Go Tell It To Mrs Golightly*

Breezy
Fellburn thief. *The Bondage of Love*

Breton-Weir, Carl
Friend of Dick Mallen. *The Mallen Streak*

Brett, Arthur
Husband of Irene Brett and neighbour of Jonathan Ratcliffe; employed as a manager at Affleck & Tate's Engineering Works, Fellburn, a business once owned by his grandmother. *The Round Tower*

Brett, Irene
Civic-minded wife of Arthur Brett; Fellburn councillor and magistrate. *The Round Tower*

Briggs, Fanny
One-time housekeeper employed by Percival Miller at Moor House, Fuller's Moor, County Durham. *The Black Velvet Gown*

Briston, Annie
Over-protective sister of Tol Briston; lives at The Dip, Fuller's Dip, County Durham. *The Black Velvet Gown*

Briston, Maria
(née Millican) Upright and proud wife of Tol Briston and mother to Bridget, Johnny, Maggie and Davey Millican; lives first in a two-roomed earth-floored house in Primrose Row, South Shields, and then employed as a housekeeper by Percival Miller at Moor House. Known to the family as 'Riah'. *The Black Velvet Gown*

Briston, Tol
Husband of Maria Briston and step-father to Bridget, Johnny, Maggie and Davey Millican and brother to Annie

Briston. Carter and outdoor servant employed at The Heights; lives at The Dip, Fuller's Dip, County Durham. *The Black Velvet Gown*

Broadhurst, Frank
Pitman husband of Jinny Broadhurst and father of Jack and Larry Broadhurst and Florence Quigley. *The Menagerie*

Broadhurst, Jack
Short and square-jawed husband of Lena Broadhurst and youngest son of Frank and Jinny Broadhurst and brother of Larry Broadhurst and Florence Quigley. *The Menagerie*

Broadhurst, Jinny
Rotund wife of Frank Broadhurst and mother of Jack and Larry Broadhurst and Florence Quigley. *The Menagerie*

Broadhurst, Larry
Priggish son of Frank and Jinny Broadhurst and brother of Jack Broadhurst and Florence Quigley; works underground in a Fellburn coal mine. *The Menagerie*

Broadhurst, Lena
Fat and bitchy wife of Jack Broadhurst. *The Menagerie*

Broadhurst, Lottie
Simple-minded sister of Jinny Broadhurst. *The Menagerie*

Brodie, Bella
Sister of Cecilia, Charlotte, William, Mary and Jimmy Brodie; lives first at Heatherbrook, County Durham, and then at Pinewood House, Westoe, South Shields, where she works as a maid. *The Dwelling Place*

Brodie, Cecilia
Brown-eyed mother of Richard Fischel. Sister of Charlotte, Bella, William, Mary and Jimmy Brodie; lives first in the County Durham hamlet of Heatherbrook, and then in a rough dwelling on the nearby fells, the 'dwelling place' of the book's title. Known to her family as "Cissie". *The Dwelling Place*

Brodie, Charlotte
Sister of Cecilia, Bella, William, Mary and Jimmy Brodie; lives first at Heatherbrook, County Durham, and then in a rough dwelling on the nearby fells, the 'dwelling place' of the book's title. *The Dwelling Place*

Brodie, Jimmy
Brother of Cecilia, Mary, Bella, William and Charlotte Brodie; lives first in the County Durham hamlet of Heatherbrook, and then in a rough dwelling on the nearby fells, the 'dwelling place' of the book's title. Employed as an apprentice to Jess Watson. *The Dwelling Place*

Brodie, Mary
House servant sister of Cecilia, Bella, Charlotte, William and Jimmy Brodie; lives in Heatherbrook, County Durham. *The Dwelling Place*

Brodie, William
Fair-haired brother of Cecilia, Mary, Bella, Charlotte and Jimmy Brodie; lives first in the County Durham hamlet of Heatherbrook, then a rough dwelling on the nearby fells, the 'dwelling place' of the books title. Works as an apprentice to wheelwright Matthew Turnbull. *The Dwelling Place*

Brodrick, Andrew
Son of Penella Brodrick and her brother-in-law lover Raymond Brodrick. *The Gillyvors*

Brodrick, Penella
Snobby, violent wife of Simon Brodrick and mother of Andrew Brodrick; lives at The Manor. Half-sister to Timothy Barrington, lover of Raymond Brodrick. *The Gillyvors*

Brodrick, Raymond
Brother of Simon Brodrick and lover of his sister-in-law, Penella Brodrick. Father of Andrew Brodrick; lives at The Manor. *The Gillyvors*

Brodrick, Simon
Husband of Penella Brodrick and acquaintance of Miss Netherton and friend of Anna Dagshaw. *The Gillyvors*

Brooker, Henry
Second husband of Lizzie Brooker; works manager at Funnell Cars, Fellburn. *The House of Women*

Brooker, Lizzie
(née Hammond) Hypochondriac wife of Henry Brooker. Widow of Leonard Hammond and mother of Peggy Jones; lives at Bramble House, Bramble Lane, Fellburn. *The House of Women*

Brooks
Butler at High Banks Hall. *The Mallen Girl*

Brooks, David
Half-caste illegitimate son of Mike Remington. A chauffeur-gardener employed by Joe and Elaine Remington at Fell Rise, near Fellburn, and husband of Hazel Egan. Lives at The Cottage beside the entrance to his employer's house. *Justice is a Woman*

Brooks, Florence
Snobbish daughter of Bob and Alicia Henderson and sister to Glen and John Henderson. *The Cultured Handmaiden*

Brooks, Willy
Arrogant, mill worker son of Brooks the High Banks butler. *The Mallen Girl & The Mallen Litter*

Brother Bernard
Member of an East End Benedictine priory and teacher at its adjoining private school. *The Branded Man*

Brother John
Member of an East End Benedictine priory and teacher at its adjoining private school. *The Branded Man*

Brother Peter
Member of an East End Benedictine priory and teacher at its adjoining private school. *The Branded Man*

Brown, Anita
Petite French teacher, engaged to Patrick Lawson. *The Branded Man*

Brown, Claire
Wife of Mick Brown and friend of Peter and Nyrene Riley. *Riley*

Brown, Eva
Debonair but scheming wife of James Brown and mother of Rowland Brown; god-daughter of Sir Charles Kingdom. *Bill Bailey*

Brown, James
Alcoholic business husband of Eva Brown and father of Rowland Brown. *Bill Bailey & Bill Bailey's Lot*

Brown, Mick
Wife of Claire Brown and friend of Peter and Nyrene Riley. *Riley*

Brown jnr, Mr
Policeman son of Mr Brown snr. *Harold*

Brown snr, Mr
Caretaker living in the basement flat of Maisie Leviston's London apartment block. *Harold*

Brown, Mrs
Wife of caretaker in Maisie Leviston's apartment. *Harold*

Brown, Rowland
Son of James and Eva Brown and Swandale class mate of Mark Nelson. *Bill Bailey*

Brown, Tony
Agricultural student employed by Peter Lord at Coffin's Farm, Fellhurst, (later changed to Moor Farm). *The Devil and Mary Ann*

Brownlow, Jinny
Employed in the typing pool by Henderson & Garbrook Engineers at its Fellburn works; girlfriend of Hal Campbell. *The Cultured Handmaiden*

Brownlow, Kate
Housemaid employed by the Overmeers at Balderstone House, County Durham. *The Blind Years*

Brydon, Mrs
Housekeeper employed by Richard Mallen at High Banks Hall. *The Mallen Streak*

Buckham, Alicia
Wife of Charles Buckham and mother of three children, David, Margaret and Victoria Buckham. Employs Janie Waggett as nursemaid. *The Gambling Man*

Buckham, Charles
Husband of Alicia Buckham and father of David, Margaret and Victoria Buckham. *The Gambling Man*

Buckham, David
Son of Charles and Alicia Buckham and brother to Margaret and Victoria Buckham. *The Gambling Man*

Buckham, Margaret
Daughter of Charles and Alicia Buckham and sister to Victoria and David Buckham. *The Gambling Man*

Buckham, Victoria
Daughter of Charles and Alicia Buckham and sister to Margaret and David Buckham. *The Gambling Man*

Buckman, Mrs
Elmholm blacksmith's wife. *The Girl*

Bunting, Mark
Autocratic and violent husband of Katie Fraenkel and step-father of Sarah Rosier. Master weighman employed by George Rosier at his County Durham pit. *Katie Mulholland*

Burgess, Herbert Vincent
Tutor employed to teach the Sopwith children at Highfield Manor. *Tilly Trotter* & *Tilly Trotter Wed*

Burke, Charlie
Crewman on the River Tyne coal boats and husband of Nellie Burke. *The Gambling Man*

Burke, Nellie
Wife of Charlie Burke, daughter of Paddy and Ruth Connor and sister of Jimmy and Rory Connor. *The Gambling Man*

Burrows, PC
Fellburn police officer. *Bill Bailey's Lot*

Cadwell, Edith
One-time fiancée of Ralph Batley. *Heritage of Folly*

Cadwell, Jane
Head of the typing pool at Henderson & Garbrook engineers, Bog's End. *The Cultured Handmaiden*

Cadwell, John
Farmer father of Rouse Cadwell; lives at Crag End Farm. *Heritage of Folly*

Cadwell, Michael
Nephew of Ralph Batley; lives at Fowler Hall Farm, Northumberland. *Heritage of Folly*

Cadwell, Rouse
Son of John Cadwell and employed on the family-owned Crag End Farm. *Heritage of Folly*

Callacter, Thomas
Labourer employed by William Bailey. *Bill Bailey*

Campbell, Arthur
Son of Hal Campbell and brother of Rosie Campbell and step-brother of Michael Morton. *The Cultured Handmaiden*

Campbell, Cissie
Childhood friend and neighbour of the Winter family; lives at No 2 Fenwick Houses, Bog's End, Fellburn. *Fenwick Houses*

Campbell, Dr
Fellburn general practitioner. *The Upstart*

Campbell, Esther
Mother of Bella Dodd and daughter-in-law to Joseph Dodd. *Go Tell It To Mrs Golightly*

Campbell, Hal
Father of Rosie and Arthur Campbell and step-father to Michael Morton. Actor-manager of The Fellburn Players and boyfriend of Jinny Brownlow. *The Cultured Handmaiden*

Campbell, Mr
Friend of pit owner Sir William Combe Stockwell. *The Nipper*

Campbell, Rosie
Only daughter of Hal Campbell and sister of Arthur Campbell and step-sister to Michael Morton. *The Cultured Handmaiden*

Canner, Roddy
Obese South Shields shipyard apprentice; nicknamed "Fattie". *Joe and the Gladiator*

Caplin, Jane
Workhouse seamstress and admissions officer; niece of Isabel and Connie Duckworth. *The Tinker's Girl*

Cardenas, Josefina
Illegitimate Mexican Indian daughter of Matthew Sopwith and adopted daughter of Matilda Sopwith; half-sister to William Trotter. *Tilly Trotter Wed & Tilly Trotter Widowed*

Carey, Father
Catholic priest at a Felling parish. *Mary Ann's Angels & Mary Ann and Bill*

Carr, Winnie
Landlady of Maria Briston and her four children. *The Black Velvet Gown*

Carrie
A woman Bog's End resident. *The Bondage of Love*

Carrington, Phoebe
Librarian at Fellburn Public Library. *The Upstart*

Carrington-Barrett, Florence
Slim, attractive daughter of Major Carrington-Barrett; lives at The Little Manor a little way outside Battenbun. *Slinky Jane*

Carrington-Barrett, Major
Father of Florence Carrington-Barrett; lives at The Little Manor just outside Battenbun. *Slinky Jane*

Carrington-Barrett, Mrs
Wife of Major Carrington-Barrett and mother of Florence; Carrington-Barrett; lives at The Little Manor, just outside Battenbun. *Slinky Jane*

Carter, Betty
Step-daughter of George Carter and sister to Gordon and John Carter and Maisie Leviston; lives at No 7 Wellenmore Terrace, Fellburn. *Goodbye Hamilton*

Carter, Dr
Fellburn general practitioner. *Riley*

Carter, Fanny
Second housemaid at The Manor. *The Branded Man*

Carter, George Michael
Bear-like estranged step-father of Betty, John and Gordon Carter and Maisie Leviston; lives at No 7 Wellenmore Terrace, Fellburn. (Tel: Fellburn 29476). *Hamilton, Goodbye Hamilton & Harold*

Carter, Gordon
Step-son of George Carter and brother to Betty and John Carter and Maisie Leviston; lives at No 7 Wellenmore Terrace, Fellburn. *Goodbye Hamilton*

Carter, Hannah
Mother of George Carter, "Gran" to Maisie Leviston; lives in Fellburn's Bog's End. *Hamilton, Goodbye Hamilton & Harold*

Carter, John
Step-son of George Carter, brother to Betty and Gordon Carter and Maisie Leviston; lives at No 7 Wellenmore Terrace, Fellburn. *Goodbye Hamilton*

Carter, Leoline
Blonde, smart and sophisticated visitor to Battenbun and friend of Peter Puddleton. *Slinky Jane*

Carter, Mary
Wife of George Carter and mother of Betty,

Leoline Carter

116

John and Gordon Carter; lives at No 7 Wellenmore Terrace, Fellburn. *Goodbye Hamilton*

Carter, Mrs
Violent mother of Maisie Leviston, estranged wife of George Carter; lives at No 7 Wellenmore Terrace, Fellburn. *Hamilton*

Cartnell, Ann
Typing-pool secretary employed by Henderson & Garbrook Engineers and workmate of Jinny Brownlow. *The Cultured Handmaiden*

Cartwright, Bella Selton
Frigid, man-hating second cousin of Florence Knutsson. *The Slow Awakening*

Cartwright, Bill
Miner employed at the High Main pit. *Our John Willie*

Cartwright, Jessie Ann
(née Sopwith) Only daughter of Mark and Eileen Sopwith and sister of John, Matthew and Luke Sopwith and half-brother of Harry Sopwith and William Trotter; lives at Highfield Manor. *Tilly Trotter & Tilly Trotter Wed*

Carver, Alice
Wife of Stan Carver; looks more like Stan Carver's sister than his wife. *My Beloved Son*

Carver, Stan
Quiet-spoken husband of Alice Carver and has an uncanny resemblance to his wife. *My Beloved Son*

Casson, Betty
Wife of Johnny Casson. Daughter of Grace Howlett and elder sister to Doreen Howlett. *Rooney*

Casson, Johnny
Diminutive Tyne docker husband of Betty Casson. *Rooney*

Catherine, Sister
Teacher at Mitchell Road Convent School. *Bill Bailey's Lot*

Catherine, Sister
Nun and teacher at the Convent of the Holy Child of Bethlehem, St Leonard's on Sea. *The Devil and Mary Ann*

Catley, Bill
A back overman at the Venus pit, Fellburn. *The Menagerie*

Chapman, Ann
Kindly sister of Rose Chapman; lives at Dower House, near Bishop Auckland. Adoptive 'mother' of Sarah Rosier. *Katie Mulholland*

Chapman, Florence
Large-faced wife of Hal Chapman and mother of Nellie Chapman and Victoria MacFell; lives at Brooklands Farm, Northumberland. *The Cinder Path*

Chapman, Hal
Farmer husband of Florence Chapman and father to Nellie Chapman and Victoria MacFell; lives at Brooklands Farm, Northumberland. *The Cinder Path*

Chapman, Nellie
Daughter of Hal and Florence Chapman and sister of Victoria MacFell; lives at Brooklands Farm, Northumberland. *The Cinder Path*

Chapman, Rose
Sister of Ann; lives at Dower House, near Bishop Auckland. Adoptive 'mother' of Sarah Rosier. *Katie Mulholland*

Charlie
Derelict man living rough on the Northumberland fells. *The Mallen Streak*

Clarke, Angus
Friend of Peter and Nyrene Riley. *Riley*

Clarke, Dorrie
Drunken South Shields midwife. *Kate Hannigan*

Cleverly, Flora
Housekeeper of David McVeigh, lives at Roger's Cross on the Lowtherbeck estate. *The Iron Facade*

Clinton, Daisy
Teenage housemaid to Grannie Flannagan. *Mrs Flannagan's Trumpet*

Coates, Phyllis
First housemaid employed by Mark Sopwith at Highfield Manor. *Tilly Trotter*

Cody, Father
Intimidating Fellside priest. *The Year of the Virgins*

Cole, Ada
Secretary to Harry Blenheim at Peasmarsh's wholesale chemist. *The Nice Bloke*

Collard, Ray
Painter and decorator fiancé of Jinny Brownlow. *The Cultured Handmaiden*

Collington, Dr Stephen
Retired South Shields general practitioner. *Mrs Flannagan's Trumpet*

Collins, Mr
Barrister appearing at Newcastle Assizes. *Hamilton & Goodbye Hamilton*

Collins, Rev. Pollard
Battenbun vicar and brother of Bridget Collins. *Slinky Jane*

Collins, Bridget
Volatile and prissy sister of Battenbun's vicar, Reverend Pollard Collins. *Slinky Jane*

Collins, John
Father of Jane Radlet and cowhand on the High Banks estate. *The Mallen Streak*

Combe Stockwell, Lady Amelia
Wife of pit owner Sir William Combe Stockwell. *The Nipper*

Combe Stockwell, Sir William
Husband of Lady Amelia Combe Stockwell and owner of a Hebburn coal mine; lives in a large house nearby. *The Nipper*

Combo, Billy
Bullying farmhand employed at Bardon Farm by Mary Everton. *Lanky Jones*

Committy, Lady
Wife of Lord Committy; lives at Manor House between Fellburn and the coast. *Go Tell It To Mrs Golightly*

Committy, Lord
Husband of Lady Committy; lives at Manor House between Fellburn and the coast. *Go Tell It To Mrs Golightly*

Conisbie, Mr
Friend of pit owner Sir William Combe Stockwell. *The Nipper*

Connie, Aunt
Keeper of a wayside inn near Allendale; sister of Daisy Loam, the Elmholm butcher's wife. *The Girl*

Connor, Mr
Bailiff employed by the Dulwich Bank. *The Mallen Streak*

Connolly, Lucy
(née Mulholland) Mother of Catherine Connolly. Daughter of Joseph and Mary Mulholland and sister to Bridget and Tommy Mulholland. Lives in Hope Street, Jarrow. *Katie Mulholland*

Connor, Jimmy
Fair-haired, grey-eyed younger son of Paddy and Ruth Connor and brother to Rory Connor and Nellie Burke, known as "Bandy Connor" because of his bowed legs. An apprentice boat builder; lives at No 2 The Cottages. *The Gambling Man*

Connor, Paddy
Husband of Ruth Connor and father to Jimmy and Rory Connor and Nellie Burke. A steelworker in Palmer's Jarrow shipyard where the blast furnaces had turned his face the colour of overcooked beetroot; lives at No 2 The Cottages, a row of houses in the country above East Jarrow. *The Gambling Man*

Connor, Rory
Rent collector employed by the property owner Septimus Kean and eldest son of Paddy and Ruth Connor and brother of Jimmy Connor and Nellie Burke; lives at No 2 The Cottages. He is the addictive gambler of the book's title. *The Gambling Man*

Connor, Ruth
Small, angular-faced wife of Paddy Connor and mother of Rory and Jimmy Connor and Nellie Burke; lives at No 2 The Cottages. *The Gambling Man*

Conway, Charlie
Son of Frank and May Conway; lives in Bramble Lane, Fellburn. *The House of Women*

Conway, Frank
Husband of May Conway and father of Charlie Conway; lives in Bramble Lane, Fellburn. *The House of Women*

Conway, May
Wife of Frank Conway and mother of Charlie Conway; lives in Bramble Lane, Fellburn. *The House of Women*

Rory Connor

Cooper, Bill
School antagonist of Matty Doolin. *Matty Doolin*

Cooper, Dennis
Husband of Mary Cooper and father of Annie McCabe. *The Invisible Cord*

Cooper, Mary
Wife of Dennis Cooper and mother of Annie McCabe. *The Invisible Cord*

Cooper, Sgt
Fellburn police officer. *The Long Corridor*

Corbett, Ted
Devon village blacksmith. *Rory's Fortune*

Cornwallis, Bernie
Son of Morley and Mary Ann Cornwallis, the Wind Fell blacksmith, and brother of Lily Cornwallis; nephew of John and Rose Cornwallis. *Rory's Fortune*

Cornwallis, Dr
Senior partner in the practice of Cornwallis and Falconer with a Fellburn surgery. *The Obsession.*

Cornwallis, John
Honest and upright wheelwright who employs Rory McAlister; lives in the County Durham village of Wind Fell. *Rory's Fortune*

Cornwallis, Lily
Black-haired daughter of Morley and Mary Ann Cornwallis, the Wind Fell blacksmith, and sister of Bernie Cornwallis; niece of John and Rose Cornwallis. *Rory's Fortune*

Cornwallis, Mary Ann
Sharp-tongued wife of Wind Fell blacksmith Morley Cornwallis and mother of Bernie and Rose Cornwallis. *Rory's Fortune*

Cornwallis, Morley
Blustering Wind Fell blacksmith husband of Mary Ann Cornwallis and father of Lily and Bernie Cornwallis and brother of wheelwright John Cornwallis. *Rory's Fortune*

Cornwallis, Rose
Kind-hearted disciplinarian wife of John Cornwallis the Wind Fell wheelwright. *Rory's Fortune*

Cotton, Angus Frederick
Fair-haired husband of Vanessa Cotton. Son of Emily Cotton and brother of Rosie Cotton; lives at No 24 Ryder's Row, Fellburn. One-time foreman at Affleck & Tate's Engineering Works, before becoming a partner in Cotton and Singleton Haulage Contractors. *The Round Tower*

Cotton, Emily
Blunt-speaking mother of Angus and Rosie Cotton and

cleaner employed by Jonathan Ratcliffe at Bower Place. *The Round Tower*

Cotton, Rosie
> Daughter of Emily Cotton and sister of Angus Cotton; lives at No 24 Ryder's Row, Fellburn. *The Round Tower*

Cotton, Vanessa
> (née Ratcliffe) Wife of Angus Cotton and eldest daughter of Jonathan and Jane Ratcliffe, lives first at Bower Place, Fellburn, and then No 24 Ryder's Row. *The Round Tower*

Cotton-Bailey, Sir Geoffrey
> Steel magnate. *Go Tell It To Mrs Golightly*

Coulson, Daniel
> Husband of Winifred Coulson and father of Stephen and Donald and adoptive father of Joe Coulson; lives at Wearcill House, a twenty-eight room mansion on the outskirts of Fellburn. *The Year of the Virgins*

Coulson, Donald
> Youngest son of Daniel and Winifred Coulson and brother of Stephen and Joe Coulson; lives at Wearcill House on the outskirts of Fellburn. *The Year of the Virgins.*

Coulson, Joe
> Accountant and adopted son of Daniel and Winifred Coulson and brother of Stephen and Donald Coulson; lives at Wearcill House on the outskirts of Fellburn. *The Year of the Virgins.*

Coulson, Stephen
> Childish and childlike eldest son of Daniel and Winifred Coulson and brother of Joe and Donald Coulson; lives at Wearcill House on the outskirts of Fellburn. *The Year of the Virgins*

Coulson, Winifred
> Wife of Daniel Coulson and mother of Stephen and Donald and adoptive mother of Joe Coulson; lives at Wearcill House, a twenty-eight room mansion on the outskirts of Fellburn. *The Year of the Virgins*

Cousins
> Farmhand on the High Banks estate. *The Mallen Girl*

Coxon, Arthur
> Miner son of Matthew Coxon and brother of Fred Coxon. *Our John Willie*

Coxon, Fred
> Violent miner son of Matthew Coxon and brother of Arthur Coxon. *Our John Willie*

Coxon, Matthew
> Bullying miner and father of Arthur and Fred Coxon. *Our John Willie*

Cranford, Roger
> Cousin of Mrs Cranford; lives at The Grange. *The Branded Man*

Crawford, Donald
> Elderly Newcastle hotel owner and friend of Roger Maitland. *The Upstart*

Crawford, John
> Charming but unreliable father of Mildred, Martha Mary, Nancy and Roland Crawford; lives at Morland House, The Habitation, a large and decaying riverside house near Riding Mill, Northumberland. Lover of Angela Mear. *Miss Martha Mary Crawford*

Crawford, Martha Mary
> Eldest daughter of John Crawford and sister to Mildred, Nancy and Roland Crawford; lives at Morland House, The Habitation, a large and decaying riverside house near Riding Mill, Northumberland. Fiancée of Dr Harry Fuller. *Miss Martha Mary Crawford*

Crawford, Mildred
> Snobbish daughter of John Crawford and sister to Martha Mary, Nancy and Roland Crawford; lives at Morland House, The Habitation, near Riding Mill, Northumberland. *Miss Martha Mary Crawford*

Crawford, Roland
Self-centred student son of John Crawford and brother to Martha Mary, Nancy and Mildred Crawford; lives at Morland House, The Habitation, near Riding Mill. *Miss Martha Mary Crawford*

Crawford, Sophie
Epileptic sister of John Crawford; lives at Morland House, The Habitation, a large and decaying riverside house near Riding Mill, Northumberland. *Miss Martha Mary Crawford*

Crawshaw, Lizzie
Sour-mouthed grandmother of Emaralda Yorkless; lives in a cottage at Boulder Hill Farm, near Fellburn. Lover of artist Ralph Bowman. *The Whip*

Crewe, Rev Stanley
Diminutive and inarticulate Elmholm vicar. *The Girl*

Crockford, James
Boyfriend of Agnes Thorman; lives at Haughton Manor, County Durham. *The Moth*

Crofton, Joyce
Pale-skinned, thin-nosed wife of Peter Crofton and neighbour of the Overmeer family; lives at The Hillocks, Mickle Taggart. One-time mistress of Laurence Overmeer. *The Blind Years*

Crofton, Peter
Husband of Joyce Crofton; lives at The Hillocks, Mickle Taggart. *The Blind Years*

Crosbie, Mrs
Housekeeper to Alison Read's uncle Humphrey. *The Lady on my Left*

Cruikshanks, Billy
Merchant seaman lover of Beattie Watson; lives at No 4 Boswell Cottages. *Maggie Rowan*

Culbert, Gilbert
A thin and weedy teacher obsessed with winning the affections of a fellow teacher, Mary Llewellyn. *The Fifteen Streets*

Cullen, Jane
Neighbour of the McQueen family living in the Fifteen Streets, East Jarrow. *Colour Blind*

Culmills, Martha
Bedridden half-sister of Veronica Lawson and aunt of Marie Anne Lawson; lives at No 17 Blake Terrace, London. *The Branded Man*

Cummings, Jackie
Ship's deckhand. *Lanky Jones*

Cunningham, Henry
Valet employed by Lord Fischel at Houghton Hall, County Durham. *The Dwelling Place*

Dagshaw, Anna
Daughter of Nathaniel and Maria Martell and sister to Cherry, Benjamin, Jimmy, Oswald and Olan Dagshaw. Works first as a teacher at Miss Benfield's Academy for Young Ladies, Fellburn then employed as a tutor by Simon Brodrick at The Manor. *The Gillyvors*

Dagshaw, Benjamin
Youngest son of Nathaniel and Maria Martell and brother to Cherry, Anna, Jimmy, Oswald and Olan Dagshaw. *The Gillyvors*

Dagshaw, Cherry
Daughter of Nathaniel and Maria Martell and sister to Anna, Benjamin, Jimmy, Oswald, Olan and Cherry Dagshaw. *The Gillyvors*

Dagshaw, Jimmy
Fair-haired son of Nathaniel and Maria Martell and brother to Anna, Cherry, Benjamin, Olan and Oswald Dagshaw. *The Gillyvors*

Dagshaw, Olan
Son of Nathaniel and Maria Martell, twin brother of Oswald Dagshaw; brother to Anna, Benjamin, Cherry and Jimmy Dagshaw. Travelling salesman for George Green, High Quality Confectionery in Gateshead Fell. *The Gillyvors*

Dagshaw, Oswald
Son of Nathaniel and Maria Martell and twin brother of Olan Dagshaw; brother to Anna, Benjamin, Cherry and Jimmy Dagshaw. Manages the George Green, High Quality Confectionery shop in Gateshead Fell. *The Gillyvors*

Dalton, May
First chambermaid at The Little Manor, Moorstone. *The Branded Man*

Dan
Uncle of Maggie Flannagan. *Mrs Flannagan's Trumpet*

Danish, Peggy
Housemaid at Wearcill House, the Fellburn home of Daniel and Winifred Coulson. *The Year of the Virgins*

Darling, Granny
Mother of Joe Darling senior; lives above the Darling home in Mabel Street, South Shields. *Joe and the Gladiator*

Darling, Mrs
Mother of Joe Darling; lives at No 10 Mabel Street, South Shields. *Joe and the Gladiator*

Darling, Joe
Diminutive South Shields shipyard apprentice, son of Joe Darling; lives with his parents at No 10 Mabel Street, South Shields. School friend of Matty Doolin. *Joe and the Gladiator & Matty Doolin*

Darling snr, Joe
Father of Joe Darling; lives at No 10 Mabel Street, South Shields. *Joe and the Gladiator*

Dave
Musician friend of Jimmy McFarlan. *Mary Ann's Angels*

Joe Darling

Davidson, Peggy
Wife of Dr Peter Davidson. *Kate Hannigan*

Davidson, Dr Peter
Bear-framed but gentle South Shields general practitioner husband of Peggy Davidson. *Kate Hannigan, The Fifteen Streets & Colour Blind*

Davis, Mary
Housekeeper employed by George Rosier at his County Durham home. *Katie Mulholland*

Davison, Archie
Son of Joe Davison. *A Dinner of Herbs*

Davison, Joe
Grizzle-haired Northumberland fell farmer and father to Archie Davison. *A Dinner of Herbs.*

Davison, Lennie
Farmhand grandson of Joe Davison. *A Dinner of Herbs.*

Davison, Mrs
Wife of farmer Joe Davison and 'adoptive' mother of Mary Ellen Lee. *A Dinner of Herbs.*

Dawson, Sylvia
Girlfriend of Philip McBride. *Fanny McBride*

Deebar, Mrs
Patient at the County Mental Hospital. *The Year of the Virgins*

de Ferrier, Rosamund
Well connected lover of Rodney Gallacher; lives at Brixton Manor (Tel: Fellburn 27789). *The Invitation*

Delahunty, Patrick
Dim-witted Irish docker and boyfriend of Kate Hannigan. *Kate Hannigan*

Denvers, Nicholas
Schoolfriend of Howard Fairbrother. *The Upstart*

Dickenson, Bruce
Sandy-haired friend of Bridget Gether. *The Blind Years*

Dickenson, Mr
Dignified and honest father of Bruce Dickenson and County Durham farmer. *The Blind Years*

Dickinson, Nell
Elmholm village wife; one of Ned Riley's lovers. *The Girl*

Dickinson, Nellie
Housekeeper to Alison Read and Paul Aylmer. *The Lady on my Left*

Dimple, Fanny
Elderly cook employed by Edward and Mary MacFell at Moor Burn Farm, Northumberland. *The Cinder Path*

Dixon, Art
Elderly first coachman employed at Faircox Priory by the Knutsson family. *The Slow Awakening*

Dixon, John
Gardener/handyman employed by Daniel and Winifred Coulson at Wearcill House, Fellburn. *The Year of the Virgins*

Dobett, Mr
Passenger on the London to Devon train. *Rory's Fortune*

Dodd, Bella
Blind daughter of Esther Campbell and grand-daughter of Joseph Dodd. *Go Tell It To Mrs Golightly*

Dodd, Joseph
White-haired, woman-hating grandfather of Bella Dodd. *Go Tell It To Mrs Golightly*

Doherty, Maggie
Cook at Wearcill House, the Fellburn home of Daniel and Winifred Coulson. *The Year of the Virgins*

Donnelly, Florrie
Sensual and sophisticated daughter of Fred Donnelly and half-sister of Hilda Maxwell; works as a secretary-typist and lives in the Garden Flat at No 46 Brampton Hill, Fellburn. Mistress of "Abel Gray". *The Man Who Cried*

Donnelly, Fred
Undersized, loud-mouthed father of Florrie Donnelly and Hilda Maxwell; lives at No 109 Temple Street, Bog's End, Fellburn. *The Man Who Cried*

Doolin, Jean
Mother of Matty Doolin; lives in Brinkburn Street, South Shields. *Matty Doolin*

Doolin, Matty
Son of Jean Doolin and schoolboy friend of Joe Darling and Willie Styles; lives in Brinkburn Street, South Shields. *Joe and the Gladiator* & *Matty Doolin*

Doolin, Mr
Thick-set shipyard worker husband of Jean Doolin and father of Matty Doolin; lives in Brinkburn Street, South Shields. *Matty Doolin*

Doulton
Clerk employed by John Stokes, editor of the *Daily Reporter* printing works. *The Branded Man*

Dowell, Evelyn
Young actress. *Riley*

Dowling, Don
Vicious and psychotic pitman son of Phyllis Dowling and brother to Sam Dowling. Childhood friend of Christine and Ronnie Winter; lives at No 8 Fenwick Houses, Bog's End, Fellburn. *Fenwick Houses*

Dowling, Sam
Youngest son of Phyllis Dowling and brother of Don Dowling; lives at No 8 Fenwick Houses, Bog's End, Fellburn. Childhood friend of Christine and Ronnie Winter. *Fenwick Houses*

Dowling, Phyllis
Mother of Don and Sam Dowling; lives at No 8 Fenwick Houses, Bog's End, Fellburn. Sister and next door neighbour of Bill Winter. *Fenwick Houses*

Drew, Arthur
Son of Biddy Drew and brother of Katie, Jimmy and Sam Drew; employed by Mark Sopwith on the outside staff at Highfield Manor. *Tilly Trotter* & *Tilly Trotter Wed*

Drew, Biddy
Mother of Katie, Arthur, Jimmy and Sam Drew; lives at Rosier's Village before becoming the cook at Highfield Manor. *Tilly Trotter, Tilly Trotter Wed* & *Tilly Trotter Widowed*

Drew, Jimmy
Son of Biddy Drew and brother of Katie, Sam and Arthur Drew, employed by Mark Sopwith on the outside staff at Highfield Manor. *Tilly Trotter, Tilly Trotter Wed* & *Tilly Trotter Widowed*

Drew, Katie
Daughter of Biddy Drew and child-miner sister of Sam, Arthur and Jimmy Drew and friend of Matilda Sopwith; lives at Rosier's Village and later at Highfield Manor. *Tilly Trotter* & *Tilly Trotter Wed*

Drew, Sam
Pitman son of Biddy Drew and brother of Katie, Arthur, and Jimmy Drew and friend of Matilda Sopwith; lives at Rosier's Village and later at Highfield Manor. *Tilly Trotter* & *Tilly Trotter Wed*

Dring, Jenny
Upper housemaid employed by Harry Bensham at High Banks Hall. *The Mallen Girl*

Dryden, Mr
Book-keeper and one-time solicitor's clerk employed to instruct Rory Connor accountancy and business management. *The Gambling Man*

Ducat, Lawrence
Manager employed by John Crawford to run his Hexham bookshop. Boyfriend of Miss Streaton. *Miss Martha Mary Crawford*

Duckworth, Connie
Sister of Isabel and aunt of Jane Caplin; lives in a cottage near Tollet's Ridge. *The Tinker's Girl*

Duckworth, Isabel
Sister of Connie Duckworth and aunt of Jane Caplin; lives in a cottage near Tollet's Ridge. *The Tinker's Girl*

Dudley, Nell
Cousin of Jinny Brownlow and wife of Peter Dudley; lives in Sunderland Road, South Shields. *The Cultured Handmaiden*

Dudley, Peter
Husband of Nell Dudley; lives in Sunderland Road, South Shields. *The Cultured Handmaiden*

Dudley, Prudence
Novelist and niece of Maggie Fuller. *The Iron Facade*

Duffy, Jimmy
Husband of Mary Duffy and uncle to Ella, the housemaid at Fell Rise. *Justice is a Woman*

Duffy, Mary
Elderly housekeeper employed by Joe and Elaine Remington at Fell Rise, near Fellburn. *Justice is a Woman*

Duke
Musician friend of Jimmy McFarlan. *Mary Ann's Angels*

Dunn, Mr
Butler to the Mallen family at High Banks Hall near Allendale on the Northumberland fells. *The Mallen Streak*

Dunn, Alice
Daughter of Mr Dunn, the former High Banks butler. Employed as the third housemaid at the hall. *The Mallen Girl*

Dunn, Janet
Mother of Robbie Dunn; lives first at No 23 Baker Street, Bog's End, and the Scarfield Millon, Fell Rise. Cleaner employed by the Blenheim family at Hollytree House, Holt

Avenue. *The Nice Bloke*

Dunn, Robbie
Jewish son of Janet Dunn; owns antique shop in Pine Street, Fellburn, with his business partner Harry Blenheim. Lives first at No 23 Baker Street, Bog's End, and the Scarfield Millon, Fell Rise. Boyfriend of Gail Blenheim. *The Nice Bloke*

Dyke, Peter
Hastings resident. *Harold*

Egan, Dan
Firebrand miners' leader and father of Hazel Egan and father-in-law to David Brooks. *Justice is a Woman*

Egan, Hazel
Daughter of Dan Egan and wife of David Brooks; lives at The Cottage beside the entrance to Fell Rise. *Justice is a Woman*

Egan, Mrs
Wife of Dan Egan and mother of Hazel Egan. *Justice is a Woman*

Ella
Housemaid employed by Joe and Elaine Remington at Fell Rise; niece of housekeeper Mary Duffy. Her employer, Elaine Remington, insists on calling her "Jane". *Justice is a Woman*

Ellis, Father
Kind and soft-spoken Bog's End parish priest. *Fenwick Houses*

Emerson
Second footman employed by Harry Bensham at High Banks Hall. *The Mallen Girl*

Emery, Clara
Maid employed at No 17 Blake Terrace, London, the home of Martha Culmills. *The Branded Man*

Eva
Cook-housekeeper employed by Peter Lord. *Marriage and Mary Ann*

Everton, Mrs
Wife of Ernie Everton, proprietor of Ernie Everton's Eating House. *The Branded Man*

Everton, Ernie
Overweight proprietor of Ernie Everton's Eating House, an East End restaurant-cum-bar. *The Branded Man*

Everton, Mary
Mother of Sally Everton and her adopted son Michael Everton; lives at Hillburn Farm, near Bardon Mill, Northumberland. *Lanky Jones*

Everton, Michael
Adopted son of farmer's wife Mary Everton and elder brother of Sally Everton; lives at Hillburn Farm, near Bardon Mill, Northumberland. *Lanky Jones*

Everton, Sally
Daughter of farmer's wife Mary Everton and sister of Michael Everton; lives at Hillburn Farm, near Bardon Mill. *Lanky Jones*

Fairbrother, Alice
Wife of Samuel Fairbrother and mother of Howard, Janet, Edward, Alicia and Jessie Fairbrother. *The Upstart*

Fairbrother, Alicia
Youngest daughter of Samuel and Alice Fairbrother and sister of Janet, Howard, Edward and Jessie Fairbrother. *The Upstart*

Fairbrother, Edward
Youngest son of Samuel and Alice Fairbrother and brother of Janet, Howard, Alicia and Jessie Fairbrother. *The Upstart*

Fairbrother, Howard
Quick-tempered and violent eldest son of Samuel and Alice Fairbrother and brother of Janet, Edward, Alicia and Jessie Fairbrother. *The Upstart*

Fairbrother, Janet
Outspoken and self-confident eldest daughter of Samuel and Alice Fairbrother and sister to Howard, Edward, Alicia and Jessie Fairbrother. *The Upstart*

Fairbrother, Samuel
Ambitious and overbearing boot and shoe manufacturer, husband of Alice Fairbrother and father of Howard, Janet, Edward, Alicia and Jessie Fairbrother. *The Upstart*

Falconer, Beatrice
(née Penrose-Steel) Obsessive and scheming wife of John Falconer and elder daughter of Simon Penrose-Steel and sister to Rosie MacIntosh, Helen Morton Spears and Marion Penrose-Steel; self-appointed 'housekeeper' at the family home, Pine Hurst, near Fellburn. *The Obsession*

Falconer, Catherine
Elderly doting mother of Dr John Falconer; lives in the annexe of Pine Hurst, near Fellburn. *The Obsession*

Falconer, Dr John
General practitioner husband of Beatrice Falconer and son of Catherine Falconer; lives at Pine Hurst, near Fellburn. Partner to Dr Cornwallis with a surgery in the centre of Fellburn. *The Obsession*

Fallenbor, Rev.
Retired cleric and friend of Maurice Rossiter. *House of Men*

Farrel, Ted
War-time boyfriend of Christine Winter. *Fenwick Houses*

Farrington, Mr
Friend of pit owner Sir William Combe Stockwell. *The Nipper*

Farthing, Harry
Bullying South Shields shipyard apprentice. *Joe and the Gladiator*

Fawcett, Annie
Life-long friend of Maggie Gallacher; lives at Savile House, The Rise, Fellburn. *The Invitation*

Fawcett, Maggie
Girlfriend and common-law-wife of Alex Riley; known to everyone as "Nurse". *Riley*

Fawcett, Mrs
Tenant of Pilbey Street, Jarrow, and from whom Rory Connor collects rent. *The Gambling Man*

Featherstone, Roland
School friend of Mark Nelson. *Bill Bailey's Lot*

Feeler, Patrick
Woodman and thief employed on Dan Bannaman's farm. *A Dinner of Herbs*

Fellmore, Arthur
Justice sitting at Fellburn magistrates court. *Bill Bailey's Daughter*

Felton, John
Hebburn miner. *The Nipper*

Fenton, John
Cousin of Arlette Gallacher. *The Invitation*

Fenwick, Charlie
Fellburn coal merchant. *The Obsession*

Fenwick, Morris
Labourer employed by William Bailey. *Bill Bailey's Lot*

Fenwick, Mr
Proprietor of W. Fenwick & Son, Confectioners & Tobacconist (1899) and secondhand bookshop, Fellburn. *The Bondage of Love*

Ferndale, Elsa
Tall, elegant wife of barrister George Ferndale and mother of Roland Ferndale; lives at Willow House, Lime Avenue, Fellburn. *The Bondage of Love*

Ferndale, George
Out-spoken barrister and businessman husband of Elsa Ferndale and father of Roland Ferndale; lives at Willow House, Lime Avenue, Fellburn. *The Bondage of Love*

Ferndale, Roland
Spoilt, blonde-haired son of George and Elsa Ferndale; lives at Willow House, Lime Avenue, Fellburn. *The Bondage of Love*

Ferrier, Katie
(née Bensham) Wife of Pat Ferrier and mother of Lawrence Patrick Charles Ferrier. Daughter of Harry and Matilda Bensham and sister of Daniel and John Bensham.; lives at Burndale Manor. *The Mallen Girl* & *The Mallen Litter*

Ferrier, Lawrence Patrick Charles
Handicapped son of Pat and Katie Ferrier; lives at Burndale Manor. *The Mallen Litter*

Ferrier, Pat
Husband of Katie Ferrier and father of Lawrence Patrick Charles Ferrier; lives at Burndale Manor. *The Mallen Girl* & *The Mallen Litter*

Fielding, Vera
Actress employed by The Little Palace Theatre company. *Riley*

Fieldman, Larry
Repertory company director at The Little Palace and later the New Palace theatres, Fellburn. *Riley*

Findlay, Colonel
Magistrate and uncle of Martin Fonyere-Belling; lives at Brampton Hill, Fellburn. *Fenwick Houses*

Finlay, Alec
Bricklayer employed by William Bailey; speaks with a stammer. *Bill Bailey's Lot*

Finley, William
Crippled father of Catherine Mulholland and grandfather to Joseph and Lizzie Mulholland and Katie Fraenkel; lives at No 3 The Row, off Walter Street, Jarrow. *Katie Mulholland*

Fischel, Clive John James Rembrandt
Artist and elder son of Lord Fischel and brother of Isabelle Fischel; lives at Houghton Hall on the family's 300-acre County Durham estate. Father of Richard Fischel. *The Dwelling Place*

Fischel, Isabelle
Malicious and snobbish daughter of Lord Fischel and younger sister of Clive Fischel; lives at Houghton Hall on the family's 300-acre County Durham estate. *The Dwelling Place*

Fischel, Lord John Horatio James
Religious and embittered father of Clive and Isabelle Fischel; lives at Houghton Hall on his 300-acre County Durham estate. *The Dwelling Place*

Fischel, Richard John Horatio
Illegitimate son of Clive Fischel and Cecilia Brodie; brought up at Houghton Hall as a member of the Fischel family. *The Dwelling Place*

Fisher, Mrs
Midwife and layer-out to the residents of Heatherbrook, County Durham. *The Dwelling Place*

Fitzsimmons, Ronnie
Friend of Joe Lloyd. *The Bonny Dawn*

Fitzsimmons, Tom
Coal face worker in a Hebburn pit and leader of the one of the mine's 'union' factions. *The Nipper*

Flaherty, Peggy
Widow and upstairs neighbour to the O'Brien family in Fadden Street. A semi-educated gossip and 'penny lawyer' who would charge a penny to write a letter or proffer legal advice. *The Fifteen Streets*

Flannagan, Davy
Sea captain husband of Maggie Flannagan and father of Lilian Morley and grandfather to Eddie and Penny Morley; lives at Rock End on the clifftop at South Shields. *Mrs Flannagan's Trumpet*

Flannagan, Harry
Small-framed husband of Nellie Flannagan and father of Sarah Shaughnessy; lives in Burton Street, Jarrow. *A Grand Man, Life and Mary Ann & Marriage and Mary Ann*

Flannagan, Maggie
Waspish, houseproud wife of Davy Flannagan and mother of Lilian Morley and grandmother of Eddie and Penny Morley; lives at Rock End on the clifftop at South Shields. *Mrs Flannagan's Trumpet*

Flannagan, Nellie
Self-righteous and finicky wife of Harry Flannagan and mother of Sarah Shaughnessy; lives in Burton Street, Jarrow. *A Grand Man, Fanny McBride, Life and Mary Ann & Marriage and Mary Ann*

Flood, Hilda
Bejewelled and multi-coloured haired daughter of Max and Janet Flood and sister of May, Rodney and Joseph Flood. *Harold*

Flood, Janet
Wife of Max Flood and mother of Hilda, May, Rodney and Joseph Flood. Housekeeper to publisher Leonard and Maisie Leviston. *Hamilton, Goodbye Hamilton & Harold*

Flood, Joseph
Son of Max and Janet Flood and brother of Hilda, May and Rodney Flood. *Harold*

Flood, Max
Husband of Janet Flood and father to Hilda, May, Rodney and Joseph Flood. *Harold*

Flood, May
Youngest daughter of Max and Janet Flood and sister of Hilda, Rodney and Joseph Flood. *Harold*

Flood, Rodney
Son of Max and Janet Flood and brother of Hilda, May and Joseph Flood; uncle of Harold Stoddart. *Goodbye Hamilton & Harold*

Flynn, Barny
Son of Daniel and Elizabeth Flynn and brother of Colum and Michael Flynn; lives at Tar Abode between Corbridge and Newcastle. *The Slow Awakening*

Flynn, Colum
Son of Daniel and Elizabeth Flynn and brother to Barny and Michael Flynn; lives at Tar Abode, a miniature hilltop castle overlooking the River Tyne between Corbridge and Newcastle. *The Slow Awakening*

Flynn, Daniel
Short, black-haired rope-maker husband of Elizabeth Flynn and father of Colum, Barny and Michael Flynn; lives at Tar Abode overlooking the River Tyne. *The Slow Awakening*

Flynn, Elizabeth
Tall and handsome wife of Daniel Flynn and mother to Colum, Barny and Michael Flynn; lives at Tar Abode, a miniature hilltop castle overlooking the River Tyne. *The Slow Awakening*

Flynn, Michael
Youngest son of Daniel and Elizabeth Flynn and brother to Colum and Barny Flynn; lives at Tar Abode overlooking the River Tyne. *The Slow Awakening*

Foggety, Ruth
Nursery maid employed by Daniel and Barbara Bensham at Brook House, near Morpeth. Lover of Daniel Bensham. Later lives in Linton Street, Jesmond Dene, Newcastle. *The Mallen Litter*

Foggerty, Sarah
Nurse-cum-secretary to the bedridden Martha Culmills; lives at No 17 Blake Terrace, London. Sister of Annie Pollack. *The Branded Man*

Fonyer, Madame
Marseilles-born Newcastle dress shop proprietress and friend of Jessie Honeysett. *The Menagerie*

Fonyere-Belling, Flight-Lieutenant Martin
Married Free French airforce pilot, father of Christine Winter's illegitimate daughter, Constance; stationed at Littleborough air base, County Durham. *Fenwick Houses*

Forbes, Bella
Scullery maid to Samuel and Alice Fairbrother. *The Upstart*

Forbister, Leonard
Wartime friend of Joseph Jebeau; is also an Aircraftsman First Class, Wireless Mechanic Acting Corporal Instructor stationed at RAF Madley, near Hereford. *My Beloved Son*

Forefoot-Meadows, Lady Jane
Possessive mother of Eileen Sopwith; lives at Waterford Place, near Scarborough. *Tilly Trotter*

Fossett, Septimus
Draper and church warden at Rosier's Village, County Durham. *Tilly Trotter*

Fountain, Bill
Portly butcher with a shop near Battenbun's The Hart public house. *Slinky Jane*

Fowler, Andrew
Fellburn architect and businessman and friend of Angus and Vanessa Cotton. *The Round Tower*

Fowler, Miss
Battenbun resident. *Slinky Jane*

Fox, Dr
Fellburn general practitioner. *Riley*

Fraenkel, Andree
Swedish-born husband of Katie Fraenkel and father of Nils Fraenkel. Sea captain and master of the freighter Orn. Lives first at No 14 Crane Street, Temple Town, and then Ogle Terrace, South Shields. Known as "Andy" to his family and friends. *Katie Mulholland*

Fraenkel, Jon
Brother of Andree Fraenkel. *Katie Mulholland*

Fraenkel, Katie
(née Mulholland, née Bunting) Wife of Andree Fraenkel and widow of Mark Bunting. Mother to Sarah Rosier and Nils Fraenkel. Daughter of Rodney and Catherine Mulholland and sister of Joseph Mulholland. Employed as a shilling-a-week scullery-maid by George Rosier prior to her marriage. Rents Putman's Cottage from Ann and Rose Chapman before owning Nos 12, 13 and 14 Crane Street, Temple Town and moving to Ogle Terrace, South Shields. *Katie Mulholland*

Fraenkel, Nils
Spiteful son of Andree and Karie Fraenkel and half-brother to Sarah Rosier. *Katie Mulholland*

Frank
Waiter in a Newcastle hotel. *The Upstart*

Frank, Uncle
Peter Riley's uncle. *Riley*

Frannie
Teenage neighbour of David McVeigh and Flora Cleverly at Roger's Cross, Lowtherbeck. *The Iron Facade*

Fraser, Mr
Verger to the Rev. Pollard Collins in the village of Battenbun. *Slinky Jane*

Fred
Porter employed at the Claremont Auction Rooms, Hastings. *The Lady on my Left*

Katie Mulholland

Freeman Wheatland, Daisy
Life-long friend of Sir Leonard Morton Spears. *The Obsession*

Fuller, Beattie
(née Watson) One-time girlfriend of Tom Rowan and lover of Billy Cruikshanks; lives at No 4 Boswell Cottages. Finally lover of David Taggart. *Maggie Rowan*

Fuller, Danny
Toolmaker employed at Affleck & Tate's Engineering Works, Fellburn. *The Round Tower*

Fuller, Dr Harry
Conscientious sandy-haired and blunt featured assistant general practitioner to Dr Pippin; lives above the surgery in Beaumont Street, opposite Hexham Abbey. Fiancé of Martha Mary Crawford. *Miss Martha Mary Crawford*

Fuller, Hop
Cruel and violent traveller who buys Kirsten MacGregor from Ma Bradley. *The Slow Awakening*

Fuller, Hugo
Swandale class mate of Mark Nelson. *Bill Bailey*

Fuller, Maggie
Aunt of novelist Prudence Dudley; lives in Eastbourne. *The Iron Facade*

Funnell, Emma
Elderly matriarch of Bramble House and mother of Victoria Pollock. *The House of Women*

Funnell, Stanley
Kindly careers master at Matty Doolin's school. *Matty Doolin*

Furness, Florence
Chambermaid to Samuel and Alice Fairbrother. *The Upstart*

Gallacher, Arlette
French-born wife of Samuel Gallacher. *The Invitation*

Gallacher, Elizabeth
Grey-eyed lanky daughter of Rodney and Maggie Gallacher and sister of Paul, Samuel and Willie Gallacher and Frances Walton; lives at Savile House, The Rise, Fellburn. Enters a Fellburn convent to become a novice. *The Invitation*

Gallacher, Margaret
Snobbish wife of Rodney Gallacher and mother of Paul, Samuel, Willie and Elizabeth Gallacher and Frances Walton; known to her family as "Maggie". Lives first at Savile House, The Rise, and then at a bungalow in The Crest, Balham Road, Fellburn. *The Invitation*

Gallacher, Nancy
Wife of Willie Gallacher. *The Invitation*

Gallacher, Nurse
Nurse employed to look after Emanuel Latvig Lawson. *The Branded Man*

Gallacher, Paul
Teacher son of Rodney and Maggie Gallacher and brother of Samuel, Willie, and Elizabeth Gallacher and Frances Walton; lives at Flat 4, Marsh House, Talford Road, (Tel:. Fellburn 1212). *The Invitation*

Gallacher, Rodney
Husband of Maggie Gallacher and father of Paul, Samuel, Willie, and Elizabeth Gallacher and Frances Walton; lives at Savile House, The Rise, Fellburn. Managing director of Gallacher & Sons, Builders and Contractors with offices in Collingswood Mews, Fellburn. Lover of Rosamund de Ferrier. *The Invitation*

Gallacher, Samuel
Masochistic husband of Arlette Gallacher and eldest son of Rodney and Maggie Gallacher and brother of Paul, Willie and Elizabeth Gallacher and Frances Walton. Works in the family building and contracting firm of Gallacher & Sons. *The Invitation*

Gallacher, Willie
Petty thief and husband of Nancy Gallacher. Son of Rodney

and Maggie Gallacher and brother of Paul, Samuel and Elizabeth Gallacher and Frances Walton. *The Invitation*

Gallagher, Annie
Small, auburn-haired wife of Len Gallagher and mother of Daisy, Sep, Frank and Jean and twins Mike and Danny Gallagher; lives at No 45 Brompton Grove West, Bog's End, Fellburn. *The Bondage of Love*

Gallagher, Daisy
Firebrand girlfriend of Jimmy Redding. Youngest daughter of Len and Annie Gallagher, sister of Frank, Sep, Jean and Mike and Danny Gallagher; lives at No 45 Brompton Grove West, Bog's End, Fellburn. *The Bondage of Love*

Gallagher, Danny
Son of Len and Annie Gallagher and brother of Daisy, Jean, Frank and Sep and twin brother of Mike Gallagher; lives at No 45 Brompton Grove West, Bog's End, Fellburn. *The Bondage of Love*

Gallagher, Frank
Son of Len and Annie Gallagher and brother of Daisy, Sep, Jean and twins Mike and Danny Gallagher; lives at No 45 Brompton Grove West, Bog's End, Fellburn. *The Bondage of Love*

Gallagher, Len
Unemployed alcoholic husband of Annie Gallagher and father of Daisy, Sep, Frank, Jean and twins Mike and Jean Gallagher; lives at No 45 Brompton Grove West, Bog's End, Fellburn. *The Bondage of Love*

Gallagher, Mike
Hot-tempered son of Len and Annie Gallagher and brother of Daisy, Sep, Frank and Jean and twin brother of Danny Gallagher; lives at No 45 Brompton Grove West, Bog's End, Fellburn. *The Bondage of Love*

Gallagher, Mirabelle
Adulterous wife of Roderick Gallagher and mother to Mirabelle Hewitt; live at The Towers, South Shields. *The Harrogate Secret*

Gallagher, Roderick
Smuggler husband of Mirabelle Gallagher and father to Mirabelle Hewitt; lives at The Towers, South Shields. *The Harrogate Secret*

Gallagher, Sep
Son of Len and Annie Gallagher and brother of Daisy, Mike, Frank, Jean and twins Mike and Danny Gallagher; employed as an apprentice by William Bailey. Lives at No 45 Brompton Grove West, Bog's End, Fellburn. *The Bondage of Love*

Geary, Hughie
Orphan, taken in by Broderick and Hannah Massey. Lives at No 49 Grosvenor Road, Fellburn, and owns a small cobblers in the centre of Fellburn. Father of Karen Massey. *Hannah Massey*

Gether, Bridget
War orphan adopted by Vance and Sarah Overmeer; lives on the Balderstone Estate in County Durham. *The Blind Years*

Gether, Hester
Step-mother of Sarah Overmeer. *The Blind Years*

Gibbs, Patricia
Classmate of Rose Mary Boyle. *Mary Ann's Angels & Mary Ann and Bill*

Gibson, Gerald
Friend of Michael Bradshaw. *The Fen Tiger*

Gillespie, Helen
Wife of Trevor Gillespie. *The Invitation*

Gillespie, Norah
Thirty-two year old mother of Sandy Gillespie; widowed when her husband died from the cholera. *The Nipper*

Gillespie, Sandy
Teenage son of Norah Gillespie; worked for Farmer Blyth since his father died from the cholera. *The Nipper*

Gillespie, Trevor
Tailor husband of Helen Gillespie. *The Invitation*

Golding, Edward
One-time suitor of Rosie Penrose-Steel; employed in the Diplomatic Service. *The Obsession*

Golightly, Mrs
Large, bright-faced friend of Esther Campbell and Bella Dodd. *Go Tell It To Mrs Golightly*

Gordon-Platt, Charles
Husband of Florence Gordon-Platt and father to Roy and Margaret Gordon-Platt; lives on the Beacon Rise estate with his mother Mrs Freda Gordon-Platt. *The Lady on my Left*

Gordon-Platt, Florence
Wife of Charles Gordon-Platt and mother to Roy and Margaret Gordon-Platt. Daughter-in-law to Mrs Freda Gordon-Platt; lives on the Beacon Rise estate. *The Lady on my Left*

Gordon-Platt, Freda
Eccentric and overweight mother of Charles Gordon-Platt; lives on the Beacon Rise estate. *The Lady on my Left*

Gordon-Platt, Margaret
Daughter of Charles and Florence Gordon-Platt and sister to Roy Gordon-Platt; lives on the Beacon Rise estate. *The Lady on my Left*

Gordon-Platt, Roy
Son of Charles and Florence Gordon-Platt and brother to Margaret Gordon-Platt; lives on the Beacon Rise estate. *The Lady on my Left*

Grainger, Henry
Parson and friend of Ralph Bowman and whose parish extends across the fells south of Fellburn. *The Whip*

Grant, Bessie
Cheating former housemaid to painter Michael Stanhope; lives in the Fifteen Streets. *Colour Blind*

Grant, Sam
Farm worker and driver employed on the Walsh's Northumberland farm. *Joe and the Gladiator*

Gray, Harold
Patient of Dr Paul Higgins. *The Long Corridor*

Gray, Hilda
(née Maxwell) Unlawful wife of "Abel Gray" and step-mother of "Dick Gray". Young wife of Peter Maxwell and daughter of Fred Donnelly and half-sister to Florrie Donnelly; lives at No 3 Newton Road, Brampton Hill, Fellburn. *The Man Who Cried*

Green, Florrie
Head chambermaid employed by George Rosier at his County Durham home. *Katie Mulholland*

Green, Robert
Footman-cum-valet at The Manor. *The Branded Man*

Green, Sgt
Officer at Fellburn police station. *Goodbye Hamilton*

Greenbank, Peter
Sailor father of Rodney Percival Greenbank. *A Dinner of Herbs*

Greenbank, Rodney Percival
Orphaned son of Peter Greenbank. Adopted by Kate Makepeace and becomes a mill smelter; lives at Langley Top on the Northumberland fells. Childhood friend and teenage lover of Mary Ellen Lee. *A Dinner of Herbs*

Guest, Mr
Engineering tutor at South Shields Technical College. *Joe and the Gladiator*

Gullmington, Anthony
Husband of Diana Gullmington and father of Lucy and

Paul Gullmington; lives at The Heights, near Fuller's Moor, County Durham. *The Black Velvet Gown*

Gullmington, Diana
Matriarch of the Gullmington family and grande dame at The Heights, near Fuller's Moor, County Durham. *The Black Velvet Gown*

Gullmington, Grace
Wife of Stephen Gullmington; lives at The Heights, County Durham. *The Black Velvet Gown*

Gullmington, Laurence
Nephew of Anthony and Diana Gullmington; lives at The Heights, near Fuller's Moor, County Durham. Fiancé of Bridget Millican. *The Black Velvet Gown*

Gullmington, Lucille Beatrice
Vicious and spiteful daughter of Anthony and Diana Gullmington and sister to Paul Gullmington; lives at The Heights, County Durham. *The Black Velvet Gown*

Gullmington, Paul
Snobbish and condescending son of Anthony and Diana Gullmington and brother to Lucy Gullmington; lives at The Heights near Fuller's Moor, County Durham. *The Black Velvet Gown*

Gullmington, Stephen
Husband of Grace Gullmington; lives at The Heights, near Fuller's Moor, County Durham. *The Black Velvet Gown*

Gunthorpe, Fitty
Tall, and gangling epileptic son of John Gunthorpe, lives in a caravan on a patch of Bog's End waste ground. *Fenwick Houses*

Gunthorpe, John
Gypsy father of Fitty Gunthorpe; lives in a caravan on a patch of Bog's End wasteground. *Fenwick Houses*

Hall, Dr Davey
Fellburn general practitioner. *Bill Bailey*

Halladay, Davy
Illiterate skeletal-framed child miner and brother of John Willie Halladay. *Our John Willie*

Halladay, John Willie
Deaf and dumb brother of Davy Halladay able to make just one sound "Huh". *Our John Willie*

Hallberry, Geraldine
Samuel Fairbrother's mistress; lives at Dale Cottage, Brandon Park, Fellburn. *The Upstart*

Hamilton

Black-bodied, white maned horse and 'friend' of Maisie Leviston. *Hamilton*

In August, 1983, Catherine Cookson published her sixtieth novel, Hamilton. It was written in the style she had experimented with in the early 1930s. "I intended this book to be a funny book," she admitted. "A one-off."

Her publishers, Heinemann, were hesitant. They believed her reputation as a chronicler of the 19th century was so entrenched that a tragi-comedy about a modern, lonely young woman who talks to an imaginary horse might well be rejected by loyal Cookson fans.

It was hinted that Hamilton should be shelved. Catherine dug in her heels, convinced she knew what her readers wanted.

Hamilton is still her only book to go through three impressions in six weeks and Hamilton her only "talking" animal character.

Hammond
Chauffeur employed by Lord and Lady Menton. *Justice is a Woman*

Hammond, Leonard
Quick tempered and violent husband of Lizzie Jones and father of Peggy Hammond; lives at Bramble House,

Bramble Lane, Fellburn. *The House of Women*

Hankin, Father
Open-minded Fellburn Catholic priest. *Bill Bailey's Daughter*

Hannigan, Annie
Daughter of Kate Hannigan and grand-daughter of Tim and Sarah Hannigan; lives at No 16 Whitley Street, Tyne Dock. *Kate Hannigan.*

Hannigan, Kate
Blue-eyed daughter of Tim and Sarah Hannigan; mother of Annie Hannigan. Lives at No 16 Whitley Street, Tyne Dock. *Kate Hannigan*

Hannigan, Sarah
Wife of Tim Hannigan and mother of Kate Hannigan; lives at No 16 Whitley Street, Tyne Dock. *Kate Hannigan*

Hannigan, Tim
Obstreperous and violent husband of Sarah Hannigan and father of Kate Hannigan; lives at No 16 Whitley Street, Tyne Dock. *Kate Hannigan*

Harding, John
Moorstone farmer husband of Sally Harding. (The author mistakenly calls him "Fred" part way through the book). *The Branded Man*

Harding, Sally
Wife of John Harding, a Moorstone farmer. *The Branded Man.*

Kate Hannigan

Harper, Miss
Gossip and first floor resident of Mulhattan's Hall, No 16 Burton Street, Jarrow. *Fanny McBride* & *A Grand Man*

Harper, Jimmy
Father of May and Mick Harper; works as a River Tyne keelman. *The Harrogate Secret*

Harper, May
Daughter of Jimmy Harper and sister to Mick Harper; works as a shop assistant in Dixon's fruiterers in Union Street, South Shields. *The Harrogate Secret*

Harper, Mick
Stubby-built, loud-mouthed keelman son of Jimmy Harper and sister of May Harper. *The Harrogate Secret*

Harris, Mr
Porter at Fellburn railway station. *The Long Corridor*

Hassan, Ali
Arab friend of James Paterson and Mill Dam, South Shields, eating house owner. *Colour Blind*

Hatter, Johnny
Former mechanic employed at the Bailey's Kingsley's Garage. *The Bondage of Love*

Hatton, Rev
Unitarian minister. *The Upstart*

Hedley, Parson
Soporific-voiced cleric to the County Durham village of Heatherbrook. *The Dwelling Place*

Henderson, Alicia
Wife of Bob Henderson and mother of John and Glen Henderson and Florence Brooks. *The Cultured Handmaiden*

Henderson, Bob
Irascible co-owner of Henderson & Garbrook Engineers overlooking the waterfront at Bog's End. Husband of Alicia Henderson and father to John and Glen Henderson and Florence Brooks. *The Cultured Handmaiden*

Henderson, Glen
Husband of Yvonne Henderson. Son of Bob and Alicia Henderson and brother to John Henderson and Florence Brooks. *The Cultured Handmaiden*

Henderson, John
Stubborn and independent son of Bob and Alicia Henderson and brother to Glen Henderson and Florence Brooks. *The Cultured Handmaiden*

Henderson, Yvonne
Petite, French-born wife of Glen Henderson. *The Cultured Handmaiden*

Heslop, Jack
Miner employed in Matthew Thornton's pit. *The Girl*

Hetherington, Farmer
Heavy-set Heatherbrook farmer. *The Dwelling Place*

Hetherington, Mr
Father of Mary Mulholland and boilershop supervisor in Palmer's shipyard, Jarrow. *Katie Mulholland*

Hewitt, Arnold
Solicitor and partner in the firm Chapel & Hewitt, Solicitors, of Kings Street, South Shields. *Katie Mulholland*

Hewitt, Fred
"Muck Pusher" employed by South Shields Corporation and workmate of Joseph Smith. *Rooney*

Hewitt, Margaret
South Shields money lender and money changer; adoptive 'aunt' of Mirabelle Hewitt. Employs Frederick Musgrave as an assistant and book-keeper. *The Harrogate Secret*

Hewitt, Mirabelle
Daughter of the Roderick and Mirabelle Gallagher; adopted and brought up as a 'niece' by Margaret Hewitt. *The Harrogate Secret*

Higgins, Beatrice
Attractive, hot tempered wife of Dr Paul Higgins and mother of Lorna Higgins; lives at Romfield House, Romfield Square, Bog's End. Known as "Bett" to her family and friends. *The Long Corridor*

Higgins, Dr Paul Hugh
Barrel-chested, second generation doctor husband of Beatrice Higgins and father of Lorna Higgins; lives at Romfield House, Romfield Square, Bog's End. *The Long Corridor*

Higgins, Lorna
Boyish, slightly-built daughter of Dr Paul and Beatrice Higgins; lives at Romfield House, Romfield Square, Bog's End. Girlfriend of Brian Bolton. *The Long Corridor*

Hobson, Rev
Fellburn clergyman. *Goodbye Hamilton*

Hoffman, Jenny
(née Chilmaid) Nurse and cousin of Beatrice Higgins. *The Long Corridor*

Holland, Ralphy
Friend and former business partner of Rodney Gallacher. *The Invitation*

Hollings
Butler employed by the Rossiter family at Tor-Fret House, near Long Framlington, Northumberland. *House of Men*

Honeysett, Jessie
Daughter of Mildred Honeysett and one-time girlfriend of Larry Broadhurst; rises to partner in Miss Barrington's High Street, Fellburn, flower shop. *The Menagerie*

Honeysett, Joe
Drinker at the Duck and Drake public house, Bog's End, Fellburn. *Bill Bailey's Lot*

Honeysett, Mildred
Proud and snobbish mother of Jessie Honeysett. *The Menagerie*

Honeysett, Miss
Presbytery housekeeper to Father Owen at St Peter's Church, Jarrow. *Fanny McBride*

Honnington, Peter
Site foreman employed by William Bailey. *Bill Bailey's Daughter*

Houseman, Bernard
Partner in the London publishing house of Houseman and Rington with offices at No 42 Chapman's Yard. *Hamilton*

Howard, Dr
Plastic surgeon at East Grinstead's Queen Victoria Hospital. *The Lady on my Left*

Howard, Mr
Swandale Preparatory School teacher of Mark Nelson. *Bill Bailey*

Howlett, Doreen
Snobbish daughter of Grace Howlett and younger sister of Betty Casson; lives at No 71 Filbert Terrace, South Shields. *Rooney*

Howlett, Grace
Tarty, carrot-headed mother of Doreen Howlett and Betty Casson and landlady to Joseph Smith; lives in a seven-room house 71 Filbert Terrace, South Shields. *Rooney*

Howlett, Jinnie
Workhouse orphan and shilling-a-week skivvy employed by the Shaleman family at Tollet's Ridge Farm, an isolated and run-down sheep farm near Allendale and towards the Cumbrian border. *The Tinker's Girl*

Hughes-Burton, Beatrice
Gauche, dark-haired sister of Elaine Remington; known as "Betty". *Justice is a Woman*

Inness, John
Librarian at Fellburn Public Library. *The Upstart*

Isaac
Porter at Axminster railway station. *Rory's Fortune*

Isherwood, Caroline
Librarian neighbour of William and Fiona Bailey at Burnstead Mere House. *Bill Bailey's Daughter*

Ivy
Wife of Ken and friend of Peter and Nyrene Riley. *Riley*

Jebeau, Ellen
Strong-willed widowed sister-in-law of Sir Arthur Jebeau and mother of Joseph Jebeau; lives at Screehaugh, on the County Durham-Northumberland border. *My Beloved Son*

Jebeau, Harry
Son of Sir Arthur Jebeau and younger brother of Martin Jebeau; lives at Screehaugh. *My Beloved Son*

Jebeau, Joseph
Only son of Ellen Jebeau; lives at Screehaugh. Joins the Royal Air Force and qualifies as a Aircraftsman First Class, Wireless Mechanic Acting Corporal Instructor stationed at RAF Madley, near Hereford. Lover of Maggie Le Man. *My Beloved Son*

Jebeau, Martin
Son of Sir Arthur Jebeau and elder brother of Harry Jebeau; lives at Screehaugh. *My Beloved Son*

Jebeau, Sir Arthur James
Father of Harry and Martin Jebeau and brother-in-law of Ellen Jebeau. Lives at Screehaugh, the Jebeau family seat on the County Durham-Northumberland border. *My Beloved Son*

Jackson, Flo
Sister of Winifred Coulson; known as "Aunt Flo". *The Year of the Virgins*

Jackson, Frank
Widowed Wind Fell carter. *Rory's Fortune*

Jessie
Housekeeper employed by Mr and Mrs Bluett at St Helier House. *Rory's Fortune*

Jessie
Housemaid employed by Sir and Lady Kingdom at Brookley Manor. *Bill Bailey's Lot*

Jessie
Maid who works for Charlotte Kean. *The Gambling Man*

Jimmy
South Shields coastguard officer. *Mrs Flannagan's Trumpet*

Johnson, Dr
Scottish general practitioner. *Riley*

Johnson, Henry
Labourer employed by Peter Lord on Coffin's Farm, Fellhurst, (later Moor Farm). *Love and Mary Ann*

Johnson, Sarah
Parlourmaid employed by Samuel and Alice Fairbrother. *The Upstart*

Jones, Andrew
Husband of Peggy Jones, son of James and Carrie Jones, brother of Minnie Jones; Showroom manager at Funnell Cars, Fellburn. Lover of Rosie Milburn. *The House of Women*

Jones, Carrie
Wife of James Jones and mother of Andrew and Minnie Jones. *The House of Women*

Jones, Carrie
First housemaid at The Manor. *The Branded Man*

Jones, Daniel
Son of Peter Jones and Clare Ancliff; his height has earned him the nickname "Lanky". Lives at No 22 Baker Avenue, Newcastle. *Lanky Jones*

Jones, Emma
Daughter of Andrew and Peggy Jones and fiancée of Dr Richard Langton. *The House of Women*

Jones, James
Husband of Carrie Jones and father of Andrew and Minnie Jones. *The House of Women*

Jones, Minnie
Daughter of James and Carrie Jones and sister of Andrew Jones. *The House of Women*

Jones, Mr
Farmhand employed by Peter Lord on Coffin's Farm, Fellhurst, (later Moor Farm). *The Lord and Mary Ann* & *Life and Mary Ann*

Jones, Peggy
(née Hammond) Wife of Andrew Jones and daughter of Leonard and Lizzie Hammond; lives at Bramble House, Bramble Lane, Fellburn. *The House of Women*

Jones, Peter
Gardener father of Daniel Jones; lives at No 22 Baker Avenue, Newcastle. *Lanky Jones*

Kane, Dr Mike
Bearded Fellburn general practitioner and friend of Maisie Leviston. *Hamilton* & *Goodbye Hamilton*

Kate
Devon shopkeeper. *Rory's Fortune*

Kate
Housemaid employed by Mrs Mason at No 19 Sweetbanks Gardens. *The Upstart*

Kean, Charlotte
Masculine and unattractive only daughter of the landlord Septimus Kean. *The Gambling Man*

Kean, Septimus
Property owner who employs Rory Connor as a rent collector. *The Gambling Man*

Kelly, Annie
Daughter of Joe and Hannah Kelly and sister to Nancy Kelly. Friend of Molly O'Brien in the Fifteen Streets. *The Fifteen Streets*

Kelly, Hannah
Wife of Joe Kelly and mother of Nancy and Annie Kelly; a neighbour of the O'Brien family. *The Fifteen Streets*

Kelly, Joe
Tyne Dock labourer husband of Hannah Kelly and father of Annie and Nancy Kelly; the Kelly family live opposite the O'Briens in Fadden Street. *The Fifteen Streets*

Kelly, Nancy
Simple-minded teenage daughter of Joe and Hannah Kelly and sister of Annie Kelly, works as a domestic servant for the Fitzsimmons family. *The Fifteen Streets*

Kemp, Hal
South Shields carter, nephew of Davy and Maggie Flannagan; known as "Uncle Hal". *Mrs Flannagan's Trumpet*

Ken
Husband of Ivy and friend of Peter and Nyrene Riley. *Riley*

Kenley, Mrs
Housekeeper employed by Harry Bensham at High Banks Hall. *The Mallen Girl* & *The Mallen Litter*

Kerry, Dorry
Plump distant relative of Daniel Flynn; lives at Tar Abode between Corbridge and Newcastle. *The Slow Awakening*

Kerry, Hannah
Cousin of Sean O'Connor and surrogate mother of Vincent, Moira and Kathy O'Connor; lives at Wheatleys Wall farm, near Hexham. *The Solace of Sin*

Kingdom, Lady Bertha
Overweight and jovial wife of Sir Charles Kingdom; lives at Brookley Manor in the country beyond Fellburn. *Bill Bailey's Lot*

Kingdom, Sir Charles
Elderly Scottish property magnate and business associate of William Bailey; lives at Brookley Manor in the country beyond Fellburn. Godfather to Eva Brown. *Bill Bailey* & *Bill Bailey's Lot*

Kingston, Charles
Lover of Nyrene Forbes-Mason. *Riley*

Knowles
Stableboy employed by Harry Bensham at High Banks Hall. *The Mallen Girl*

Knowles, James
Friend of Dr Paul and Beatrice Higgins. *The Long Corridor*

Knutsson, Florence
Doll-like third wife of Konrad Knutsson and 'adoptive' mother of Oscar Knutsson; lives at Faircox Priory on the banks of the River Tyne. Second cousin of Bella Cartwright. *The Slow Awakening*

Knutsson, Konrad
Blustering husband of Florence Knutsson and 'adoptive' father of Oscar Knutsson; lives at Faircox Priory. Lover of Kirsten MacGregor. *The Slow Awakening*

Knutsson, Oscar Eric Karl
Illegitimate son of Kirsten MacGregor sold at birth to Florence Knutsson and raised as her own son; lives at Faircox Priory. *The Slow Awakening*

Kramer, Mr
Outsized, soft-spoken Scottish paediatrician. *Riley*

Lafflin, Father
Kind and jolly priest; lives at St Vincent's presbytery. *Hannah Massey*

Lang, Ada
London prostitute, friend of Rose Massey. *Hannah Massey*

Langton, Dr Richard
Fellburn general practitioner and fiancé of Emma Jones. *The House of Women*

Laton, Benny
Simple-minded but gifted bicycle mechanic employed by Peter Maxwell. *The Man Who Cried*

Lavey, Sam
Resident of Mulhattan's Hall, off Burton Street, Jarrow. *Fanny McBride*

Lawson, Emanuel Latvig
Shipowning patriarch of the Lawson family and the father of James Lawson; lives at The Little Manor at the far end of The Manor grounds at Moorstone, near Chester-le-Street. *The Branded Man*

Lawson, Evelyn
Daughter of James and Veronica Lawson and sister of Marie Anne, Vincent and Patrick Lawson; lives at The Manor at Moorstone, near Chester-le-Street. *The Branded Man*

Lawson, James
Shipowner son of Emanuel Latvig Lawson and husband of Veronica Lawson and father of Marie Anne, Evelyn, Vincent and Patrick Lawson; lives at The Manor at Moorstone, near Chester-le-Street. *The Branded Man*

Lawson, Marie Anne
Headstrong and independent daughter of James and Veronica Lawson and sister of Patrick, Vincent and Evelyn Lawson; lives at The Manor at Moorstone, near Chester-le-Street. *The Branded Man*

Lawson, Patrick
Self-important second son of James and Veronica Lawson and brother to Marie Anne, Vincent and Evelyn Lawson; lives at the Manor, Moorstone, near Chester-le-Street, and works in the family ship-owning business. Fiancé of Anita Brown. *The Branded Man*

Lawson, Veronica
Wife of James Lawson and mother of Marie Anne, Vincent, Evelyn and Patrick Lawson; lives at The Manor at Moorstone, near Chester-le-Street. *The Branded Man*

Lawson, Vincent
Son of James and Veronica Lawson and brother to Patrick, Marie Anne and Evelyn Lawson; lives at the Manor and works in the family ship owning business. *The Branded Man*

Leary, Collum
Irish-born miner and husband of Kathleen Leary and father to nine surviving children. Prematurely aged, his face is coloured blue by forty-one years of coal dust; lives at No 3 The Cottages, a row of houses in the country above East Jarrow. *The Gambling Man*

Leary, Kathleen
Wife of Collum Leary and mother of sixteen children, of which only nine had survived; lives at No 3 The Cottages. *The Gambling Man*

Leary, Pat
Son of Collum and Kathleen Leary; lives at No 3 The Cottages. *The Gambling Man*

Lee, Bill
Work-worn smelting millhand husband of Jane Lee and father to Mary Ellen Lee. *A Dinner of Herbs*

Lee, Captain Edward
Master of the Spring Fever, a motor yacht owned by Tommy Balfour. *Harold*

Lee, Jane
Wife of Bill Lee and mother of Mary Ellen Lee. *A Dinner of Herbs*

Lee, Mary Ellen
Daughter of Bill and Jane Lee; teenage lover of Rodney Greenbank. Employed as a maid at the Davison's Northumberland fell farm. *A Dinner of Herbs*

Leigh-Petty, Alice
Alcoholic guardian of Margaret, Marian and Tony; lives in the 'attics' of Mulhattan's Hall, off Burton Street, Jarrow. *Fanny McBride*

Leonard, Mr
House master at Swandale Preparatory School. *Bill Bailey*

Leonard, Arthur
Fashion photographer specialising in mature models. *The Invitation*

LeMan, Maggie
NAAFI manageress at RAF Madley, near Hereford and amateur singer and entertainer; just five feet tall and with a full and round figure. Lover of Joseph Jebeau. *My Beloved Son*

Len
Dim-witted cowman employed by Peter Lord. *Life and Mary Ann*

Lennox, William
Friend of Dick Mallen. *The Mallen Streak*

Lesauteur, Lawrence
Thick set French smuggler. *Rory's Fortune*

Levey, Dr
German-born hypnotherapist with a surgery in Newcastle. *Justice is a Woman*

Leviston, Leonard Murray
Husband of Maisie Leviston and editor and partner in the London publishing house of Houseman and Rington with offices at No 42 Chapman's Yard. Nicknamed "Nardy". *Hamilton & Goodbye Hamilton*

Leviston, Maisie
(née Rochester, née Stickle) Author wife of Howard Stickle and daughter of Mrs Carter and step-daughter of George Carter and sister of Betty, John and Gordon Carter; lives at No 7 Wellenmore Terrace. Wife of Leonard Leviston; lives in London. Pen name "Miriam Carter". *Hamilton, Goodbye Hamilton & Harold*

Leyburn, Fred
Coachman-cum-groom employed by the Sopwith's at Highfield Manor and friend of Matilda Sopwith. *Tilly Trotter Wed*

Lily
Housemaid at Wearcill House, the Fellburn home of Daniel and Winifred Coulson. *The Year of the Virgins*

Little Joe
Bookies' runner. *The Gambling Man*

Llewellyn, Beatrice
Wife of James Llewellyn and mother of school teacher, Mary Llewellyn. The family's boat building business allows them to live in a select part of Jarrow and employ two female servants. *The Fifteen Streets*

Llewellyn, James
Prosperous Tyne boat builder and owner of Haggart's Yard. Married to Beatrice Llewellyn and the father of Mary Llewellyn. The family live at Cumberland Villa, Jarrow. *The Fifteen Streets*

Llewellyn, Mary
Well-educated and beautiful teacher at St Jude's Primary School, Simonside. The daughter of Llewellyn the Boatbuilder, who owns and runs Haggart's Yard. *The Fifteen Streets*

Lloyd, Annie
Mother of Joe and Harry Lloyd. (The author mistakenly gives her the Christian name "Mary" in the final pages of the book). *The Bonny Dawn*

Lloyd, Harry
Son of Annie Lloyd and brother of Joe Lloyd. *The Bonny Dawn*

Lloyd, Joe
Pitman son of Annie Lloyd and brother to Harry Lloyd. Half-brother of Bridget Stevens. *The Bonny Dawn*

Mary Llewellyn

Loam, Daisy
Wife of Ted Loam and mother of Fred Loam. *The Girl*

Loam, Fred
Flushed-faced, barrel-chested butcher husband to Daisy Loam; inherited his Elmholm shop from his father. *The Girl*

Loam, Ted
Butcher who lives above his Elmholm shop. *The Girl*

Lord, Lettice
(née Schoffield) Attractive, whimsical mother of Janice Schoffield; lives at The Burrows, Woodlea End, Newcastle. Wife of Tony Lord. *Love and Mary Ann, Life and Mary Ann & Marriage and Mary Ann*

Lord, Peter
Elderly shipyard owner and part-time farmer, employs Mike Shaughnessy on Coffin's Farm, Fellhurst, (later changed to Moor Farm). Grandfather of Tony Lord. *A Grand Man, The Lord and Mary Ann, The Devil and Mary Ann, Love and Mary Ann, Life and Mary Ann & Mary Ann and Bill*

Lord, Peter
Son of Tony and Lettice Lord; named after his grandfather, landowner Peter Lord. *Mary Ann's Angels & Mary Ann and Bill*

Lord, Tony
Tall, handsome grandson of Peter Lord. Second husband of Lettice Lord. *Love and Mary Ann, Life and Mary Ann & Marriage and Mary Ann*

Love, Davey
Irish-born father of Samuel Love and labourer employed by William Bailey. Lived at No 14 Rosedale House, River Estate, Bog's End, before moving to Primrose Crescent, Fellburn. *Bill Bailey's Lot, Bill Bailey's Daughter & The Bondage of Love*

Love, Samuel
Precocious friend of Willie Nelson. Lived at No 14 Rosedale House, River Estate, Bog's End, before moving to Primrose Crescent, Fellburn. *Bill Bailey's Lot, Bill Bailey's Daughter & The Bondage of Love*

Catherine Cookson and one of her characters share the same mentor—Lord Chesterfield.

Sammy Love, the orphan from the dog-end of Fellburn, adopted by Bill Bailey in The Bondage of Love, discovers a copy of Lord Chesterfield's Letters to His Son in Fenwick's Bookshop and—like his creator—decides to use the earl's advice to his illegitimate son, Philip Stanhope, as his life-long guide. This includes: "Disguise your real sentiments, but do not falsify them"; "Go through the world with your eyes and ears open and your mouth mostly shut"; "He that is gentil doeth gentil deeds."

Lovina, Alice
Mother of Florrie Lovina and mistress of Abel Mason. *The Man Who Cried*

Lovina, Florrie
Daughter of Alice Lovina. *The Man Who Cried*

Lucas, Mrs
Thin-lipped and sarcastic housekeeper at Highfield Manor. *Tilly Trotter*

Luckin, Mr
Head porter employed at the Claremont Auction Rooms, Hastings. *The Lady on my Left*

Macallistair, Danny
"Muck Pusher" and dustbin gang foreman employed by South Shields Corporation. Workmate of Joseph Smith. *Rooney*

MacDonald, Dr John
Large-boned physician with a practice in the East End of London and friend of the Overmeer family. *The Blind Years*

MacFarlane, Jessie
Mother of Ronnie MacFarlane and neighbour of the Massey family; lives at No 47 Grosvenor Road, Fellburn. *Hannah Massey*

MacFarlane, Ronnie
Son of Jessie MacFarlane and former boyfriend of Rose Massey. *Hannah Massey*

MacFell, Betty
Brown-eyed daughter of Edward and Mary MacFell and sister of Charles MacFell; lives at Moor Burn Farm, near Kirkwhelpington, Northumberland. *The Cinder Path*

MacFell, Charles
Sensitive and kindly husband of Victoria MacFell. Son of Edward and Mary MacFell and brother of Betty MacFell; lives at Moor Burn Farm, near Kirkwhelpington, Northumberland. Conscripted into the Durham Light Infantry and serves in Flanders in the Great War rising to a major. *The Cinder Path*

MacFell, Edward
Lecherous quick-tempered religious fanatic and husband of Mary MacFell. Father to Betty and Charles MacFell; lives and works on his 50-acre Moor Burn Farm, near Kirkwhelpington, Northumberland. *The Cinder Path*

MacFell, Mary
Surgeon's daughter and wife of Edward MacFell and mother to Betty and Charles MacFell; lives at Moor Burn Farm, near Kirkwhelpington, Northumberland. *The Cinder Path*

MacFell, Victoria
(née Chapman) Promiscuous wife of Charles MacFell and daughter of Hal and Florence Chapman and sister of Nellie Chapman; lives first at Brooklands Farm, Northumberland and then in Newcastle. *The Cinder Path*

MacGregor, Kirsten
Cross-eyed mother of Oscar Knutsson. Orphan 'adopted' by Ma Bradley and sold on to travelling pimp Hop Fuller; employed as a wet-nurse by Florence Knutsson to serve her own son and used as a mistress by Konrad Knutsson. *The Slow Awakening*

MacIntosh, Annie
Mother of Robbie MacIntosh; lives on a 10-acre farmstead adjacent to Pine Hurst. *The Obsession*

MacIntosh, Robbie
Farmer husband of Rosie MacIntosh and son of Annie MacIntosh; lives on a 10-acre farmstead adjacent to Pine Hurst. *The Obsession*

MacIntosh, Rosie
(née Penrose-Steel) Impish wife of Robbie MacIntosh and daughter of Simon Penrose-Steel and sister to Beatrice Falconer, Helen Morton Spears and Marion Penrose-Steel; lives at Pine Hurst, near Fellburn. *The Obsession*

MacIntyre, Justice
Fellburn magistrate. *Our John Willie*

Macintyre, Mrs
Mother of Willy Macintyre. *The Menagerie*

Macintyre, Willie
Workmate and pitman friend of Larry Broadhurst. *The Menagerie*

MacKay, Bill
Irascible Fellburn stationmaster. *Go Tell It To Mrs Golightly*

Mackenzie, Davy
Businessman brother of Mavis Mackenzie. *Slinky Jane*

Mackenzie, Mavis
Teetotal sister of Davy Mackenzie and girlfriend of Peter Puddleton. *Slinky Jane*

Mackenzie, Mr
Haulier father of Davy and Mavis Mackenzie. *Slinky Jane*

Mackin, Father
Chirpy Fellburn priest. *Hamilton & Goodbye Hamilton*

Mackintosh, Ian
Scottish-born Texas trading post owner and friend of Matthew Sopwith. *Tilly Trotter Wed*

MacNally, Shane

Grey-haired, elderly uncle of Ralph Batley. Works as a labourer at Fowler Hall Farm, Northumberland. *Heritage of Folly*

McAlister, Benjamin
Eighteenth-century ancestor of Maggie Flannagan. *Mrs Flannagan's Trumpet*

McAlister, Don
Sculptor, disfigured since birth and forced to wear a mask across half his face, hence he is known as "The Branded Man" of the book's title. Lives in a small rural cottage beside the River Wear at Chester-le-Street. *The Branded Man*

McAlister, Edna
Daughter of Peter and Jane McAlister and sister Rory and Sammy McAlister; lives at Kelly's Row, Hebburn. *Rory's Fortune*

McAlister, Jane
Wife of Peter McAlister and mother of Rory, Sammy and Edna McAlister; lives at Kelly's Row, Hebburn. *Rory's Fortune*

Don McAlister

McAlister, Peter
Invalid husband of Jane McAlister and father of Rory, Sammy and Edna McAlister; lives at Kelly's Row, Hebburn. *Rory's Fortune*

McAlister, Rory
Teenage apprentice employed by wheelwright John Cornwallis; lives in the County Durham village of Wind Fell. Son of Peter and Jane McAlister and brother of Sammy and Edna McAlister. Real name Rodney Thomas McAlister. *Rory's Fortune*

McAlister, Sammy
Son of Peter and Jane McAlister and brother of Rory and Edna McAlister; lives at Kelly's Row, Hebburn. *Rory's Fortune*

McBride, Fanny
Blunt-speaking mother of Jack and Philip McBride and grandmother of Cornelius Boyle; lives in Mulhattan's Hall, No 16 Burton Street, Jarrow. *Fanny McBride, A Grand Man, The Lord and Mary Ann, The Devil and Mary Ann, Love and Mary Ann, Life and Mary Ann, Marriage and Mary Ann & Mary Ann and Bill*

McBride, Jack
Son of Fanny McBride and brother to Philip McBride; lives in Mulhattan's Hall, off Burton Street, Jarrow. *Fanny McBride*

McBride, Philip
Civil servant son of Fanny McBride and brother to Jack McBride; lives in Mulhattan's Hall, off Burton Street, Jarrow. *Fanny McBride*

McCabe, Anastasia
Teacher daughter of George and Annie McCabe and sister of Terence, Kathy and Bill McCabe; lives first in Thornton Avenue, near Mill Dam docks and then at No 17 Bewlar Terrace, South Shields. The family shorten her name to "Tisha". One-time fiancée to Percy Rinkton. *The Invisible Cord*

Rory McAlister

McCabe, Annie
(née Cooper) Wife of George McCabe and mother of Terence, Bill, Kathy and Anastasia McCabe. Daughter of Dennis and Mary Cooper; lives first in Thornton Avenue, near the Mill Dam docks, and then at No 17 Bewlar Terrace, South Shields. Childhood and life-long friend of Mona Broadbent. *The Invisible Cord*

McCabe, Bill
Youngest son of George and Annie McCabe and brother of Terence, Kathy and Anastasia McCabe; lives first in Thornton Avenue, near the Mill Dam docks, and then at No 17 Bewlar Terrace, South Shields. *The Invisible Cord*

McCabe, George
Foul-mouthed husband of Annie McCabe and father of Terence, Bill, Kathy and Anastasia McCabe. Son of Mollie McCabe. Owns and runs his own coal yard before buying a lock-up garage. Lives first in Thornton Avenue, near the Mill Dam docks, and then at No 17 Bewlar Terrace, South Shields. Wartime homosexual lover of Arthur Bailey. *The Invisible Cord*

McCabe, Kathy
Beautiful daughter of George and Annie McCabe and youngest sister of Terence, Bill and Anastasia McCabe; lives at No 17 Bewlar Terrace, South Shields. *The Invisible Cord*

McCabe, Mollie
Rumbustious mother of George McCabe; lives at Armada Street, South Shields. *The Invisible Cord*

McCabe, Terence
Cruel, thieving, drug-pushing son of George and Annie McCabe and older brother to Anastasia, Kathy and Bill McCabe. Nicknamed "Rance" by his family; lives first in Thornton Avenue, near Mill Dam docks, and then at No 17 Bewlar Terrace, South Shields. Works as a mechanic at the family's garage. *The Invisible Cord*

McFarlan, Jimmy
Mechanic employed at Fell Garage by Frederick Boyle. *Mary Ann's Angels* & *Mary Ann and Bill*

McGrath, Hal
Vicious brother of Steve McGrath. *Tilly Trotter*

McGrath, Mrs
Vindictive and vengeful mother of Hal and Steve McGrath. *Tilly Trotter Wed*

McGrath, Steve
Farm labourer brother of Hal McGrath employed by Annie Trotter at Rosier's Village; becomes under-manager at the Sopwith and Rosier mine. *Tilly Trotter, Tilly Trotter Wed* & *Tilly Trotter Widowed*

McGuire, Barney
Building site foreman employed by William Bailey. *Bill Bailey* & *Bill Bailey's Lot*

McIntyre, Hamish
Scottish gardener-cum-handyman to Peter and Nyrene Riley. *Riley*

McMullen, Mrs
Irascible mother of Elizabeth Shaughnessy and grandmother of Mary Ann and Michael Shaughnessy. *A Grand Man, The Lord and Mary Ann, The Devil and Mary Ann, Love and Mary Ann, Life and Mary Ann, Marriage and Mary Ann, Mary Ann's Angels* & *Mary Ann and Bill*

McQueen, Cavan
Boom-voiced docker husband of Kathie McQueen and father of Matt McQueen and Bridget Paterson; lives at No 42 Powell Street, one of East Jarrow's Fifteen Streets. *Colour Blind*

McQueen, Kathie
Rotund wife of Cavan McQueen and mother of Matt McQueen and Bridget Paterson; lives at No 42 Powell Street, one of East Jarrow's Fifteen Streets. *Colour Blind*

McQueen, Matt
Diminutive, vindictive youngest son of Cavan and Kathie McQueen, brother of Bridget Paterson; lives at No 42 Powell Street, one of East Jarrow's Fifteen Streets. *Colour Blind*

McRae, Dave
Tiler employed by William Bailey. *Bill Bailey's Lot*

McVeigh, David Bernard Michael
White-haired, ruddy-skinned brother of Roy McVeigh and farmer-owner of the Lowtherbeck estate. Employer of Flora Cleverly. *The Iron Facade*

McVeigh, Roy
Feuding brother of David McVeigh. *The Iron Facade*

Mad Mark
Elderly Irish cripple with a hook for one hand and with

one leg amputated below the knee; lives in an abandoned coal mine near Hebburn. *The Nipper*

Maddison, Peg
Owner of two Fellburn dress shops. *Hamilton*

Maggie
Elderly Irish housekeeper employed by Michael Bradshaw at Thornby House. *The Fen Tiger*

Maine, Arthur
Friend of Peter and Nyrene Riley. *Riley*

Maitland, Roger
Straight-backed butler to Samuel Fairbrother. *The Upstart*

Makepeace, Barney
Husband of Maggie Makepeace and butler at The Little Manor, home of Emanuel Latvig Lawson. *The Branded Man*

Makepeace, Kate
Elderly witch-like herbalist friend of Peter Greenbank; lives at Langley Top—in the Barony of Langley—on the Northumberland fells. *A Dinner of Herbs*

Makepeace, Maggie
Irish wife of Barney Makepeace and housekeeper-cum-cook at The Little Manor, home of Emanuel Latvig Lawson. *The Branded Man*

Mallen, Dick
Vengeful and cruel son of Thomas Richard Mallen; lives at High Banks Hall, near Allendale on the Northumberland fells. Takes the name of "Monsieur le Brett" while living in France. *The Mallen Streak*

Mallen, Thomas Richard
Womanising but kindly father of Dick Mallen; nicknamed "Turk". Lives at High Banks Hall, near Allendale on the Northumberland

Thomas Richard Mallen

fells. Father of Donald Radlet and Barbara Bensham. Lover of Anna Bensham. *The Mallen Streak*

Margaret
Sister of Marian and Tony; lives in the 'attics' of Mulhattan's Hall, off Burton Street, Jarrow, with their guardian Alice Leigh-Petty. *Fanny McBride*

Marian
Sister of Margaret and Tony; lives in the 'attics' of Mulhattan's Hall, off Burton Street, Jarrow, with their guardian Alice Leigh-Petty. *Fanny McBride*

Martell, Maria
(née Dagshaw) Wife of Nathaniel Martell and mother of twins Oswald and Olan Dagshaw and Anna, Benjamin, Cherry and Jimmy Dagshaw; lives at Heap Hollow Cottage, near Fellburn, County Durham. *The Gillyvors*

Martell, Nathaniel
Schoolmaster husband of Maria Martell and father of twins Oswald and Olan Dagshaw and Anna, Cherry, Benjamin and Jimmy Dagshaw; lives at Heap Hollow Cottage, near Fellburn, County Durham. *The Gillyvors*

Mary Ellen
Elderly woman drunk. *Hamilton*

Mason, Abel
Bigamist husband of Hilda Gray and lawful husband of Lena Mason; father of Dick Mason. Calls himself "Abel Gray" on his return to the north and works as a mechanic-manager for Peter Maxwell; lives first in an attic flat above Maxwell's Fellburn garage before moving into the main house. Lover of Florrie Donnelly. *The Man Who Cried*

Mason, Dick
Son of Abel and Lena Mason; lives at No 3 Newton Road, Brampton Hill, Fellburn. Takes the name "Dick Gray" when he and his father return to the north of England. *The Man Who Cried*

Mason, Insp
Fellburn CID officer. *The Bondage of Love*

Mason, Lena
Shrewish wife of Abel Mason and mother of Dick Mason; lives in a cottage near Hastings, Sussex. *The Man Who Cried*

Mason, Mrs
Mother of Alice Fairbrother; lives at No 19 Sweetbanks Gardens. *The Upstart*

Massey, Arthur
Ginger-haired son of Broderick and Hannah Massey and brother to Rose, Dennis, Jimmy, Shane and Barny Massey; lives at No 49 Grosvenor Road, Fellburn. *Hannah Massey*

Massey, Barny
Youngest son of Broderick and Hannah Massey and brother to Rose, Dennis, Arthur, Shane and Jimmy Massey; lives at No 49 Grosvenor Road, Fellburn. *Hannah Massey*

Massey, Broderick
Irish-born husband of Hannah Massey and father of Rose, Jimmy, Dennis, Arthur, Shane and Barny Massey; lives at No 49 Grosvenor Road, Fellburn. *Hannah Massey*

Massey, Dennis
Tall, lean son of Broderick and Hannah Massey; brother to Rose, Jimmy, Arthur, Shane and Barny. *Hannah Massey*

Massey, Florence
Wife of Dennis Massey and daughter-in-law to Broderick and Hannah Massey. *Hannah Massey*

Massey, Hannah
Formidable and fleshy wife of Broderick Massey and mother of Rose, Arthur, Dennis, Jimmy, Shane and Barny Massey; lives at No 49 Grosvenor Road, Fellburn. *Hannah Massey*

Massey, Jimmy
Handsome son of Broderick and Hannah Massey and brother to Rose, Arthur, Shane, Dennis and Barny Massey; lives at No 49 Grosvenor Road, Fellburn. *Hannah Massey*

Massey, Karen
Daughter of Hughie Geary and bitchy grand-daughter of Broderick and Hannah Massey; lives at No 49 Grosvenor Road, Fellburn. *Hannah Massey*

Massey, Rose
Auburn-haired daughter of Broderick and Hannah Massey and sister of Jimmy, Dennis, Arthur, Shane and Barny Massey; lives at No 49 Grosvenor Road, Fellburn. Secretary at Bunting's Wholesale in Newcastle. *Hannah Massey*

Massey, Shane
Tall and painfully thin son of Broderick and Hannah Massey and brother to Rose, Arthur, Dennis, Jimmy and Barny Massey; lives at No 49 Grosvenor Road, Fellburn, and works at Teefields wireless factory. *Hannah Massey*

Matilda
Demented pig farmer and half-cousin to Dr Armstrong; lives near Leeds. Known locally as "Tilly-the-touched". *The Man Who Cried*

Maudie
Maid employed by the Rev. Stanley Crewe in the village of Elmholm. *The Girl*

Max
Doctor and friend of Leoline Carter. *Slinky Jane*

Max
Workhouse-born simpleton and friend of Jinnie Howlett. *The Tinker's Girl*

Maxwell, Peter
Tee-total husband of Hilda Maxwell and proprietor of a Fellburn bicycle sales, hire and repair business at No 3 Newton Road, Brampton Hill, Fellburn. *The Man Who Cried*

Maybright, John
Stage manager at Fellburn's Little Palace Theatre. *Riley*

Meadows, Mr
Manager of the coal mine jointly owned by the Sopwith and Rosier families. *Tilly Trotter Widowed*

Mear, Angela
Plump, white-faced mistress of John Crawford; lives at No 7 Court Terrace, Newcastle. *Miss Martha Mary Crawford*

Mears, Arthur
Chauffeur and odd-job man employed by Samuel Fairbrother. *The Upstart*

Menton, Lady Sarah
Wife of a Fellburn lord; lives at The Hall, near Fellburn. *Justice is a Woman*

Meredith, Rupert
Distant relative and business secretary to Sir Charles Kingdom; lives at Brookley Manor. *Bill Bailey's Lot & Bill Bailey's Daughter*

Metcalf, Linda
Agricultural student employed by Ralph Batley on Fowler Hall Farm, Northumberland. *Heritage of Folly*

Meyer, Anna
German-born owner of a Texas homestead. *Tilly Trotter Wed*

Milburn, Arthur
William Bailey's accountant. *Bill Bailey's Daughter*

Milburn, Rosie
Mistress of Andrew Jones and housekeeper and cook at Bramble House, Bramble Lane, Fellburn; lives at No 48 Beaconsfield Avenue, Fellburn. *The House of Women*

Miller, Percival Ringmore
Scrooge-like scholarly recluse; lives at Moor House on Fuller's Moor, County Durham. *The Black Velvet Gown*

Miller, Private
Charles MacFell's Durham Light Infantry batman. *The Cinder Path*

Millican, Bridget
Ambitious daughter of Maria Briston and sister to Davey, Maggie and Johnny Millican. Nicknamed "Biddy"; lives at Moor House, Fuller's Moor, County Durham. Employed as a laundry assistant at The Heights. Fiancée of Laurence Gullmington. *The Black Velvet Gown*

Millican, Davey
Pitboy son of Maria Briston and brother to Bridget, Maggie and Johnny Millican; lives at Moor House, Fuller's Moor, County Durham. *The Black Velvet Gown*

Millican, Johnny
Youngest son of Maria Briston and brother to Bridget, Maggie and Davey Millican; lives at Moor House, Fuller's Moor, County Durham. *The Black Velvet Gown*

Millican, Maggie
Daughter of Maria Briston and sister to Bridget, Davey and Johnny Millican; lives at Moor House, Fuller's Moor, County Durham. *The Black Velvet Gown*

Millican, Ted
Dim-witted brother-in-law to Maria Briston. *The Black Velvet Gown*

Milligan, Nellie
Crow-faced abortionist and fixer. Resident of the Fifteen Streets. *Colour Blind*

Minister
Allendale clergyman. *The Mallen Girl*

Mitchell, Kate
Daughter of Tom Mitchell, part-time secretary to Maurice Rossiter. One-time fiancée of Arthur Boyle. *House of Men*

Mitchell, Mrs
Brusque wife of Tom Mitchell and mother of Kate Mitchell. *House of Men*

Mitchell, Tom
Father of Kate Mitchell. *House of Men*

Molinero, Jose Layaro
Spanish-born Father of Emaralda Yorkless. Circus performer and knife-thrower; known to his companions as "Georgie". *The Whip*

Monkton, Bella
Cook employed by the Thornton family at Elmholm House, Elmholm. *The Girl*

Monkton, Clifford
Friend of Rosamund Morley. *The Fen Tiger*

Moore, Katie
Friend of Maisie Leviston. *Hamilton*

Moorhead, Aggie
Tenant on the High Banks estate and mother of Barney Moorhead; lives at Studdon. *The Mallen Streak*

Moorhead, Barney
Illegitimate son of Aggie Moorhead employed on a Northumberland fell farm; lives at Studdon. *The Mallen Girl*

Moran, Alec
Jarrow agent for The New London Insurance company and one-time fiancé of Kate Hannigan. *Kate Hannigan*

Morgan, Captain
Sea captain friend of Davy Flannagan; lives at The Sea Bream, Ogle Terrace, South Shields. *Mrs Flannagan's Trumpet*

Morgan, Janet
(née Smith) Daughter of Dick and Jessie Smith, sister to Mick, Florrie, Carrie, Charlie and Mary Smith; lives first on the Screehaugh estate, then in Hereford. *My Beloved Son*

Morley, Eddie
Son of Lilian Morley and brother of Penny Morley. *Mrs Flannagan's Trumpet*

Morley, Henry
Alcoholic silversmith father of Rosamund and Jennifer Morley; lives and owns Heron Mill, near Ely, East Anglia. *The Fen Tiger*

Morley, Jennifer
Daughter of Henry Morley and sister of Rosamund

Morley; lives at Heron Mill, near Ely, East Anglia. *The Fen Tiger*

Morley, Lilian
Mother of Eddie and Penny Morley and daughter of Davy and Maggie Flannagan. *Mrs Flannagan's Trumpet*

Morley, Leonard
Scardyke teacher; nicknamed "Farty Morley". *The Bonny Dawn*

Morley, Penny
Daughter of Lilian Morley and sister of Eddie Morley. *Mrs Flannagan's Trumpet*

Morley, Rosamund
Daughter of Henry Morley and sister of Jennifer Morley; lives at Heron Mill, near Ely, East Anglia. *The Fen Tiger*

Morgan, Mr
Cancer specialist at Fellburn General Hospital. *Bill Bailey*

Morgan-Blythe, Dr
London general practitioner. *Goodbye Hamilton*

Morton, Mrs
Office worker employed by builder Bob Quinton. *Mary Ann's Angels*

Morton, Albert
"Muck Pusher" employed by South Shields Corporation and workmate of Joseph Smith. *Rooney*

Morton, Annabel
Classmate of Rose Mary Boyle. *Mary Ann's Angels* & *Mary Ann and Bill*

Morton, Michael
Step-son of Hal Campbell and step-brother of Rosie and Arthur Campbell. *The Cultured Handmaiden*

Morton Spears, Lady Helen
(née Penrose-Steel) Alabaster-skinned wife of Sir Leonard Spears and daughter of Simon Penrose-Steel and sister to Rosie MacIntosh, Beatrice Falconer and Marion Penrose-

Steel. Lives first at Pine Hurst, near Fellburn and then at nearby Col Mount. *The Obsession*

Morton Spears, Major Sir Leonard
Husband of Helen Spears and friend of the Penrose-Steel family; lives at Col Mount, near Fellburn. Retired from the Army after contracting tuberculosis. *The Obsession*

Mowbray, Jack
Labourer employed by William Bailey. *Bill Bailey & Bill Bailey's Lot*

Mulberry, Mr
Assistant editor of the *Daily Reporter*. *The Branded Man*

Mulcaster, James
Overseer at a Langley, Northumberland, mill. *A Dinner of Herbs*

Mulholland, Bridget
Daughter of Joseph and Mary Mulholland and sister to Lucy and Tommy Mulholland. *Katie Mulholland*

Mulholland, Catherine
(née Connolly) Wife of Tom Mulholland and daughter of Lucy Connolly. *Katie Mulholland*

Mulholland, Catherine
Wife of Rodney Mulholland and mother Joseph and Lizzie Mulholland and Katie Fraenkel; lives at No 3 The Row, off Walter Street, Jarrow and then Putman's Cottage, near Bishop Auckland. *Katie Mulholland*

Mulholland, Joseph
Husband of Mary Mulholland and father of Tommy and Bridget Mulholland and Lucy Connolly. Only son of Rodney and Catherine Mulholland and brother to Lizzie Mulholland and Katie Fraenkel. Lives at No 3 The Row, off Walter Street, Jarrow; Putman's Cottage, near Bishop Auckland, and No 14 Crane Street, Temple Town in South Shields. Employed first as a pitman, then a gardener-cum-handyman and then as a boiler man in Palmer's shipyard. *Katie Mulholland*

Mulholland, Lizzie
Downs Syndrome daughter of Rodney and Catherine Mulholland and sister to Joseph Mulholland and Katie Fraenkel; lives at No 3 The Row, off Walter Street, Jarrow and then Putman's Cottage, near Bishop Auckland and then No 14 Crane Street, Temple Town in South Shields. *Katie Mulholland*

Mulholland, Mary
(née Hetherington) Wife of Joseph Mulholland and mother of Tommy and Bridget Mulholland and Lucy Connolly. *Katie Mulholland*

Mulholland, Rodney
Husband of Catherine Mulholland and father of Joseph and Lizzie Mulholland and Katie Fraenkel. Works in Palmer's shipyard and lives at No 3 The Row, off Walter Street, Jarrow. *Katie Mulholland*

Mulholland, Tom
Palmer's shipyard worker husband and cousin of Catherine Mulholland. *Katie Mulholland*

Mulholland, Tommy
Son of Joseph and Mary Mulholland and brother to Bridget Mulholland and Lucy Connolly. *Katie Mulholland*

Mullen, Annie
Elderly charwoman patient of Dr Paul Higgins. *The Long Corridor*

Mullen, Big
Unwashed drunkard father of the three Mullen boys; neighbours of Norah and Sandy Gillespie in Ballast Row, Hebburn. *The Nipper*

Mullen, Bill
Youngest son of Big Mullen; lives in Ballast Row, Hebburn. *The Nipper*

Mullen, Joe
Middle of Big Mullen's three sons; lives in Ballast Row, Hebburn. *The Nipper*

Mullen, Maggie
Dumpy mother of Rosie Mullen and neighbour of the Hannigan family and fellow Fifteen Streets resident; lives at No 14 Whitley Street, East Jarrow. *Kate Hannigan*

Mullen, Mr
Husband of Maggie Mullen and father of Rosie Mullen; lives at No 14 Whitley Street, East Jarrow. *Kate Hannigan*

Mullen, Rosie
Daughter of Maggie Mullen and childhood friend of Annie Hannigan; lives at No 14 Whitley Street, East Jarrow. *Kate Hannigan*

Mullen, Stan
Eldest son of Big Mullen; lives in Ballast Row, Hebburn. *The Nipper*

Murgatroyd, Johnny
Womanising construction site foreman. *Mary Ann and Bill*

Murphy
Workhouse orphan and friend of James Paterson; lives in Mill Dam, South Shields. *Colour Blind*

Murray, Mrs
Wife of Parson Murray. *Our John Willie*

Murray, Parson
Kindly Fellburn minister. *Our John Willie*

Musgrave, Frederick
Tyne river sculler and smuggler's runner; son of Robert and Jinny Musgrave and brother to John and Nancy Musgrave. Employed first as a gardener by Margaret Hewitt and then promoted to assistant and book-keeper in her money-lending office. Lives at Bing Cottage, South Shields. *The Harrogate Secret*

Musgrave, Jinny
Wife of Robert Musgrave and mother of Frederick, John and Nancy Musgrave; works first in a South Shields' rope factory and then employed as housekeeper to Margaret Hewitt; lives at Bing Cottage. *The Harrogate Secret*

Musgrave, John
Pitboy son of Robert and Jinny Musgrave and brother to Frederick and Nancy Musgrave; lives at Bing Cottage, South Shields. *The Harrogate Secret*

Musgrave, Nancy
Blind and beautiful daughter of Robert and Jinny Musgrave and sister to Frederick and John Musgrave; lives at Bing Cottage, South Shields. *The Harrogate Secret*

Musgrave, Robert
Crippled carpenter husband of Jinny Musgrave and father of Frederick, Nancy and John Musgrave; lives at Bing Cottage, South Shields. *The Harrogate Secret*

Myter, Elizabeth
London boutique and dress shop owner. *Harold*

Myton, Lady Agnes
Passionate and man-hungry friend of Mark Sopwith; lives at Dean House. Lover of Simon Bentwood. Nicknamed "Loose Lady Aggie". *Tilly Trotter & Tilly Trotter Widowed*

Myton, Lord
Elderly husband of Agnes Myton; lives at Dean House. *Tilly Trotter Widowed*

Napier, Nathaniel
Moorstone farmer. *The Branded Man*

Nelson
Elderly and hunched friend of antique dealers Alison Read and Paul Aylmer; the patch over one of his eyes had prompted his "Nelson" nickname. *The Lady on my Left*

Nelson, Dr
General practitioner treating John Paget. *Bill Bailey's Lot*

Nelson, Katie
(later Bailey) Daughter of Fiona Bailey and step-daughter of William Bailey; sister of Mark and Willie Nelson and Angela Bailey and her adopted sister Mamie Bailey. Lives at No 16 Woodland Avenue, Fellburn, and later Burnstead Mere, Durham. *Bill Bailey, Bill Bailey's Lot, Bill Bailey's*

Daughter & *The Bondage of Love*

Nelson, Mark
(later Bailey) Son of Fiona Bailey and step-son of William Bailey; brother of Katie and Willie Nelson and Angela Bailey and his adopted sister, Mamie Bailey. Lives at No 16 Woodland Avenue, Fellburn, and later Burnstead Mere, Durham. *Bill Bailey, Bill Bailey's Lot, Bill Bailey's Daughter* & *The Bondage of Love*

Nelson, Mrs
Wellenmore Terrace, Fellburn, neighbour of Maisie and Howard Stickle. *Hamilton*

Nelson, Willie
(later Bailey) Thoughtful youngest son of Fiona Bailey and step-son of William Bailey and brother of Mark and Katie and Angela Bailey and his adopted sister Mamie Bailey. Lives at No 16 Woodland Avenue, Fellburn, and later Burnstead Mere, Durham. *Bill Bailey, Bill Bailey's Lot, Bill Bailey's Daughter* & *The Bondage of Love*

Nesbitt, Willy
Resident of Allendale. *The Mallen Streak*

Netherton, Miss
Philanthropic Fellburn property owner and church elder; lives Brindle House, Fellburn. *The Gillyvors*

Neville, Mike
A long-time friend of Catherine and Tom Cookson, the BBC North-East television presenter Mike Neville is the only 'living' character to appear in a Cookson novel. *Bill Bailey* & *Bill Bailey's Lot*

Newman, Albert
Editor of the *Newcastle Courier. Mary Ann and Bill*

Nicholson, Bill
Miner employed in Matthew Thornton's pit. *The Girl*

Noble, Arnold
Stubble-chinned and balding husband of Theresa Noble. *Katie Mulholland*

Noble, Theresa
Plain but ambitious wife of Arnold Noble and daughter of George and Agnes Rosier and sister to Bernard and Roger Rosier. Owns and runs a Westoe, South Shields, school. Loyal friend of Katie Fraenkel eventually living at her Ogle Terrace home as tutor. *Katie Mulholland*

Nuttal, Mr
Father of Nancy Nuttal. *Nancy Nuttal and the Mongrel*

Nuttal, Mrs
Wife of Mr Nuttal and mother of Nancy Nuttal. *Nancy Nuttal and the Mongrel*

Nuttal, Nancy:
Daughter of Mr and Mrs Nuttal. *Nancy Nuttal and the Mongrel*

Catherine Cookson never forgot the bubbling excitement of reading—of owning—her first book, a copy of Grimm's Fairy Tales. She also remembered herself eagerly studying a picture in a story book her soldier uncle had stolen from his school billet in 1914. It showed a cosy room, warmed by a blazing fire, and lived in by a little girl who had her own cup and saucer, her own tea pot, and her own kitten which sat on the floor beside her.

In 1982 Catherine distilled those childhood memories to create Nancy Nuttall and the Mongrel. Nancy is a child with a houseproud mother and noisy baby brother, who longs for the same picture of privacy as the writer once did. Catherine made one alteration. "I changed the cat to a dog, the mongrel, because I love dogs so much."

O'Brien, Dominic
The oafish and evil second surviving son of Shane and Mary Ellen O'Brien. *The Fifteen Streets*

O'Brien, John
The twenty-two year old eldest son of Shane and Mary Ellen O'Brien's five surviving children and the least handsome of the three boys. *The Fifteen Streets*

O'Brien, Katie
The kind-eyed and considerate youngest surviving daughter of Shane and Mary Ellen O'Brien. *The Fifteen Streets*

O'Brien, Mary Ellen
Wife of Shane O'Brien. During their twenty-six year marriage she gave birth to eleven children, of which only John, Dominic, Mick, Molly and Katie survived. Lives at No 10 Fadden Street. *The Fifteen Streets*

Mary Ellen O'Brien

O'Brien, Mick
The cruel and bigoted third son of Shane and Mary Ellen O'Brien. *The Fifteen Streets*

O'Brien, Molly
The silent and strong-willed oldest surviving daughter of Shane and Mary Ellen O'Brien. *The Fifteen Streets*

O'Brien, Shane
Father of three sons and two daughters, the only survivors of eleven children born through his twenty-six year marriage to Mary Ellen O'Brien. Works as a stevedore at Tyne Dock and lives at No 10 Fadden Street. *The Fifteen Streets*

O'Connell, Paddy
Proprietor of Paddy's Emporium, a three-storey junk shop. *The Branded Man*

O'Connor, Florence
Stately wife of farmer Sean O'Connor and mother of Vincent and Moira O'Connor; lives at Wheatleys Wall farm, near Hexham. *The Solace of Sin*

O'Connor, Kathy
Trainee nurse and daughter of Sean O'Connor and Hannah Kerry; sister of Vincent and Moira O'Connor. *The Solace of Sin*

O'Connor, Moira
Daughter of Sean O'Connor and Hannah Kerry and youngest sister of Vincent and Kathy O'Connor; lives at Wheatleys Wall farm, near Hexham. *The Solace of Sin*

O'Connor, Sean
Rough-spoken Irish farmer husband of Florence O'Connor and father of Vincent and Moira O'Connor; lives at Wheatleys Wall farm, near Hexham. *The Solace of Sin*

O'Connor, Vincent
Tall, angular-faced sculptor son of Sean O'Connor and Hannah Kerry and brother of Moira O'Connor; lives at Wheatleys Wall farm, near Hexham. *The Solace of Sin*

O'Dowd, Lizzie
Brown-eyed, round-bodied Irish half-cousin to Paddy Connor; lives with the Connor family at No 2 The Cottages. *The Gambling Man*

O'Malley, Father
Domineering and stiff-backed priest who fills his parishioners with nightmares of purgatory. *Kate Hannigan, The Fifteen Streets & Colour Blind*

O'Toole, Mary
Grandmother of Harry Blenheim. *The Nice Bloke*

Ord
First footman employed by Richard Mallen at High Banks Hall. *The Mallen Streak*

Ormesby, Bert
Stringy-built Sunday school teacher and electrician husband of Nell Ormesby; employed by William Bailey. *Bill Bailey, Bill Bailey's Lot & The Bondage of Love*

Ormesby, Nell
(née Paget) Wife of Bert Ormesby and one-time neighbour and friend of Fiona and William Bailey; lived at No 14 Woodland Avenue, Fellburn. *Bill Bailey, Bill Bailey's Lot, Bill Bailey's Daughter & The Bondage of Love*

Osborn, Jimmy
School friend of Daniel Jones. *Lanky Jones*

Overmeer, Laurence
Son of Vance and Sarah Overmeer and fiancé of Bridget Gether. *The Blind Years*

Overmeer, Mrs
Housekeeper and cook to Christopher and Maggie Taggart at their Brampton Hill home. *Maggie Rowan*

Overmeer, Sarah
Wife of Vance Overmeer and mother of Laurence Overmeer; lives at Balderstone House, County Durham. Aunt of Bridget Gether. *The Blind Years*

Overmeer, Vance
Husband of Sarah Overmeer and father of Laurence Overmeer; lives at Balderstone House, County Durham. Uncle of Bridget Gether. *The Blind Years*

Owen
Cousin to Mamie Bailey, the Baileys' adopted daughter, and nephew of her Grandfather. *The Bondage of Love*

Owen, Father
White-haired, kindly priest at St Peter's Church, Jarrow. *Fanny McBride, A Grand Man, The Lord and Mary Ann, The Devil and Mary Ann, Love and Mary Ann, Life and Mary Ann & Marriage and Mary Ann*

Paget, Bella
Mother-in-law of Nell Paget; lives at No 14 Woodland Avenue, Fellburn. *Bill Bailey & Bill Bailey's Lot*

Paget, John
Schizophrenic husband of Bella Paget and father-in-law of Nell Paget; lives at No 14 Woodland Avenue, Fellburn. *Bill Bailey's Lot*

Paine, Alfred
Family solicitor employed to manage the estate of John Crawford. *Miss Martha Mary Crawford*

Palmer, John
Quiet-mannered husband of Olive Palmer. *The Bonny Dawn*

Palmer, Olive
Hypochondriac and snobbish wife of John Palmer and neighbour of the Talbot family. *The Bonny Dawn*

Parkin, Nancy
Lamesley neighbour of the Bradley family. *The Moth*

Parkins, Roy
Friend of Dr Paul Higgins and member of Fellburn's Conservative Club. *The Long Corridor*

Partridge, Alan
Son of Olive Partridge. *The Invisible Cord*

Partridge, Olive
Married mother of Alan Partridge and daughter of Gerald and Gwen Bailey and sister to Arthur and David Bailey. *The Invisible Cord*

Paterson, Bridget
Wife of James Paterson and mother to Rose Angela Paterson; daughter of Cavan and Kathie McQueen and sister to Matt McQueen. Nicknamed "Rose" by her husband. *Colour Blind*

Paterson, James
Bell-voiced black seaman husband of Bridget Paterson and father to Rose Angela Paterson. *Colour Blind*

Bridget Patterson

Paterson, Rose Angela
Half-caste daughter of James and Bridget Paterson, employed as a daily maid by painter Michael Stanhope. *Colour Blind*

Paterson, Dr Roger
Doctor and friend of Leoline Carter. *Slinky Jane*

Peabody, Christine
Daughter of Francis Peabody and nursemaid employed by Matilda Sopwith at Highfield Manor. *Tilly Trotter Widowed*

Peabody, Francis
Father of Christine Peabody and butler employed by John and Anna Sopwith at Highfield Manor, County Durham. *Tilly Trotter Widowed*

Peamarsh, Miss
Eccentric yet kindly resident of the near derelict Gorge Manor, south of Fellburn. *Our John Willie*

Pearce, Dr
Fellburn general practitioner. *Justice is a Woman*

Pearson, Bobby
County Durham-born cow-hand son of Tom Pearson; lives in Texas. *Tilly Trotter* & *Tilly Trotter Wed*

Pearson, Jenny
Mill owner's daughter and fiancée of John Bensham. *The Mallen Girl*

Pearson, Mr
Religious grandfather of Mamie Bailey, the Bailey's adopted daughter, and uncle of Owen. *The Bondage of Love*

Pearson, Mr
Fellburn solicitor. *Hamilton*

Pearson, Tom
Painter and odd-job man father to Bobby Pearson; lives at Rosier's Village. *Tilly Trotter* & *Tilly Trotter Wed*

Peeble, Mr
Elderly solicitor, partner to Mr Rice. *Joe and the Gladiator*

Peel, Mary
Nursery attendant to Constance and Barbara Farrington; lives first at High Banks Hall and then in a nearby cottage. *The Mallen Streak* & *The Mallen Girl*

Penrose-Steel, Marion
Mischievous daughter of Simon Penrose-Steel and sister to Rosie MacIntosh, Beatrice Falconer and Helen Morton Spears; lives at Pine Hurst, near Fellburn. *The Obsession*

Penrose-Steel, Simon
Compulsive gambler and father of Marion Penrose-Steel Beatrice Falconer, Helen Morton Spears and Rosie MacIntosh; lives at Pine Hurst, near Fellburn. *The Obsession*

Pete
Half-Russian dwarf and friend of James Paterson; lives in Mill Dam, South Shields. *Colour Blind*

Peters, Dr
Fellside general practitioner. *The Year of the Virgins*

Pettit, Hannah
(née Radlet) Daughter of Michael and Sarah Radlet; lives at Wolfburn Farm. Later works as a nurse at High Banks Hall military hospital. *The Mallen Litter*

Phyllis
Inmate of Mary Ping's Home for Distressed Women. *The Branded Man*

Phyllis
A maid employed by the Llewellyn family at Cumberland Villa, Jarrow. *The Fifteen Streets*

Pickford, Frank
Butler employed by James Lawson at The Manor, Moorstone, near Chester-le-Street. *The Branded Man*

Pickman-Blyth, Constance
Businesswoman friend of Fellburn theatre owner David Bernice. *Riley*

Picton, Gerry
Bullying older brother of Pat Picton. *Go Tell It To Mrs Golightly*

Picton, Pat
Brother of Gerry Picton. *Go Tell It To Mrs Golightly*

Piggott, Lena
Housekeeper to the Lawson family at The Manor. *The Branded Man.*

Pippin, Dr John
Elderly general practitioner with his surgery in Beaumont Street; employs Dr Harry Fuller as his assistant. *Miss Martha Mary Crawford*

Pittie, Dan
Younger brother of Sam Pittie. *The Gambling Man*

Pittie, Sam
Bullet-headed older brother of Dan Pittie. *The Gambling Man*

Plum, Miss
Rose Mary Boyle's teacher. *Mary Ann's Angels*

Polgar, Gertie
Drug-runner; lives at Pembroke Place, Fellburn. *The Bondage of Love*

Polinski, Mrs
Wife of farmhand employed on Coffin's Farm, Fellhurst, (later changed by Moor Farm). *The Devil and Mary Ann*

Pollack, Annie
Wife of Arthur Pollack and mother to Maureen Pollack; sister of Sarah Foggerty. Lives at No 3 Ramsay Court in London's East End. *The Branded Man*

Pollack, Arthur
Husband of Annie Pollack and father to Maureen Pollack; lives at No 3 Ramsay court in London's East End. *The Branded Man*

Pollack, Jack
Farmer with land east of Fellburn. *Go Tell It To Mrs Golightly*

Pollack, Maureen
Daughter of Arthur and Annie Pollack; lives at No 3 Ramsay Court in London's East End. *The Branded Man*

Pollock, Molly
Roly-poly friend of Christine Winter; lives first at Norton Terrace while working as a shop assistant at Turner's Drapery Store and then at No 21B Gordon Street, Fellburn while employed in a munitions factory. *Fenwick Houses*

Pollock, Victoria
Mother of Lizzie Hammond and grandmother to Peggy Hammond; lives at Bramble House, Bramble Lane, Fellburn. *The House of Women*

Polly
Cook to James and Janet Allison. *The Year of the Virgins*

Poodle Patter
Musician friend of Jimmy McFarlan. *Mary Ann and Bill*

Poole, Johnny
Long distance lorry driver husband of Lily Poole. *Riley*

Poole, Lily
Fellburn actress wife of Johnny Poole. *Riley*.

Portes, Alvero
Mexican-born father of Luisa Portes and uncle and business associate of Matthew Sopwith. *Tilly Trotter Wed*

Portes, Luisa
Clip-tongued daughter of Alvero Portes. *Tilly Trotter Wed*

Portman, Peter
Proprietor of Portman's Taxis, office in Fowler Street, Fellburn, a friend of Elizabeth Gallacher. *The Invitation*

Potter, Dan
Former gardener employed by Miss Peamarsh at Gorge Manor; whose sole distinguishing feature was a large mole on the side of his nose. *Our John Willie*

Poulter, Mrs
Housekeeper employed to run Faircox Priory by the Knutsson family. *The Slow Awakening*

Power, Noreen
Typing-pool secretary employed by Henderson & Garbrook Engineers and workmate of Jinny Brownlow. *The Cultured Handmaiden*

Praggett, Howard
Cruel and inflexible manager of the Beulah mine overlooking Fellburn. *The Gillyvors*

Preston, John
Fat, grey-haired friend of Daniel and Winifred Coulson. *The Year of the Virgins*

Price, Dr John
Bog's End general practitioner husband to Muriel Price and friend of Dr Paul Higgins. *The Long Corridor*

Price, Mabel Venner
Companion-cum-maid to Eileen Sopwith at Highfield Manor. *Tilly Trotter*

Price, Miss
Secretary-receptionist to Dr Mike Kane. *Goodbye Hamilton*

Price, Muriel
Wife of Dr John Price. *The Long Corridor*

Prince, Dr Rodney
Kindly Jarrow general practitioner and husband of Stella Prince; lives at Conister House, Harton. *Kate Hannigan*

Prince, Stella
Snobbish and ambitious wife of Dr Rodney Prince; lives at Conister House, Harton. Lover of Dr Swinburn and Herbert Barrington. *Kate Hannigan*

Pringle, Dr
Fellburn general practitioner. *Bill Bailey's Daughter* & *The Bondage of Love*

Pringle, May
Secretary to Joe Remington. *Justice is a Woman*

Pringle, Nurse
Private nurse employed to look after Donald Coulson at Wearcill House, Fellburn. *The Year of the Virgins*

Prior, Father
Prior of an East End Benedictine priory and head of its adjoining private school. *The Branded Man*

Proctor, Billy
Cowman employed by Jake Yorkless at Boulder Hill Farm, near Fellburn. *The Whip*

Proctor, Meggie
Resident of a tenement block in Crane Street, Temple Town, South Shields. Friend to Katie Fraenkel. *Katie Mulholland*

Proctor, Mrs
Public toilet supervisor for Jarrow Town Council. *Fanny McBride*

Prodhurst, Edward
Elderly rag and bone man with a scrap yard at the end of Brick Fields Gate, South Shields; known as "Tangerine Ted". His horse, the Gladiator, is named in the book's title. *Joe and the Gladiator*

Prout, Mary
Burton Street neighbour of Fanny McBride. *Fanny McBride*

Puddleton, Harry
Elderly patriarch of Battenbun's Puddleton clan. Husband of Rosie Puddleton and father to Jimmy, Johnny, Joe and Peter Puddleton; lives in a seven-room house in the Northumberland village of Battenbun. Known as "Grandpop Puddleton". *Slinky Jane*

Puddleton, Jimmy
Son of Harry and Rosie Puddleton and twin brother of Johnny and younger brother of Peter and Joe Puddleton, the Battenbun garage owner. *Slinky Jane*

Puddleton, Joe
Son of Harry and Rosie Puddleton and brother to Johnny, Jimmy and Peter Puddleton and father of Peter Puddleton. *Slinky Jane*

Puddleton, Johnny
Son of Harry and Rosie Puddleton and twin brother of Jimmy and younger of Peter and Joe Puddleton, the Battenbun garage owner. *Slinky Jane*

Puddleton, Peter
Son of Joe Puddleton and great-grandson of Harry and Rosie Puddleton. *Slinky Jane*

Puddleton, Peter
Son of Harry and Rosie Puddleton and brother to Johnny, Jimmy and Joe Puddleton; owner of Battenbun's only garage. *Slinky Jane*

Puddleton, Rosie
Wife of Harry Puddleton, mother of Peter and Joe and twins Jimmy and Johnny Puddleton; lives in a seven-room house in Northumberland village of Battenbun. *Slinky Jane*

Quigley, Amy
Wife of Barry Quigley; lives Mulhatten's Hall, of Burton Street, Jarrow. *Fanny McBride*

Quigley, Barry
Husband of Amy Quigley; lives in Mulhatten's Hall, of Burton Street, Jarrow. *Fanny McBride*

Quigley, Florence
Eldest daughter of Frank and Jinny Broadhurst and sister of Jack and Larry Broadhurst. *The Menagerie*

Quinn, Patricia
Friend of Mrs Vidler and neighbourhood gossip; lives at No 20 Woodland Avenue, Fellburn. *Bill Bailey's Lot*

Quinton, Connie
Waspish wife of Robert Quinton. *Love and Mary Ann*

Quinton, Robert
Jarrow building contractor husband of Connie Quinton. *The Lord and Mary Ann* & *Mary Ann's Angels*

Quinton Burrows, Esther
Snobbish mother of Molly Quinton Burrows. *The Man Who Cried*

Quinton Burrows, Molly
Daughter of Esther Quinton Burrows and friend and neighbour of Dick Mason. *The Man Who Cried*

Radlet, Constance
(née Farrington) Wife of Donald Radlet and mother to Michael Radlet and niece of Thomas Mallen. Friend of Dick Mallen. *The Mallen Streak, The Mallen Girl* & *The Mallen Litter*

Radlet, Donald
Farmer husband of Constance Radlet. Illegitimate son of Thomas Mallen and half-brother of Matthew Radlet; lives at Wolfbur Farm. *The Mallen Streak*

Radlet, Jane
(née Collins) Wife of Michael Radlet and mother of Donald and Matthew Radlet; lives at Wolfbur Farm. *The Mallen Streak* & *The Mallen Girl*

Radlet, Matthew
Son of Jane Radlet and brother to Donald Radlet. *The Mallen Streak*

Radlet, Michael
Morose illegitimate son of Constance Farrington—later Radlet—and Donald Radlett and husband of Sarah Radlet and father of Hannah Pettit; lives at Wolfbur Farm. Lover of Barbara Bensham. *The Mallen Streak, The Mallen Girl* & *The Mallen Litter*

Radlet, Sarah
(née Waite) Wife of Michael Radlet and mother of Hannah Pettit. Niece of Harry Waite; lives at Wolfbur Farm. *The Mallen Girl* & *The Mallen Litter*

Radley, Mrs
Flirty woman friend of Mike Shaughnessy and mother of Yvonne Radley. *Marriage and Mary Ann*

Radley, Yvonne
Simpering daughter of Mrs Radley. *Marriage and Mary Ann*

Ramsey, Alan
Ambitious Fellburn Baptist minister. *The Menagerie*

Ramshaw, Father
Kind and quiet Fellburn priest. *The Year of the Virgins*

Rankin, John
    Classmate of Harold Stoddart. *Harold*

Rankine, Mr
    Asthmatic teacher of Stephen Taggart. *Maggie Rowan*

Ratcliffe, Jane
    Wife of Jonathan Ratcliffe and father of Ray and Susan Ratcliffe and Vanessa Cotton, lives at Bower Place, Fellburn. *The Round Tower*

Ratcliffe, Jonathan
    Husband of Jane Ratcliffe and father of Ray and Susan Ratcliffe and Vanessa Cotton; lives at Bower Place, Fellburn. Works manager at Affleck & Tate's Engineering Works. *The Round Tower*

Ratcliffe, Ray
    Only son of Jonathan and Jane Ratcliffe and brother of Susan Ratcliffe and Vanessa Cotton; lives at Bower Place, Fellburn. *The Round Tower*

Ratcliffe, Susan
    Daughter of Jonathan and Jane Ratcliffe and sister of Ray Ratcliffe and Vanessa Cotton; lives at Bower Place, Fellburn. *The Round Tower*

Ray, Betty
    Typing-pool secretary at Peamarsh's wholesale chemist; lives in Pullman Street, Bog's End. *The Nice Bloke*

Ray, Mrs
    Tarty mother of Betty Ray; lives in Pullman Street, Bog's End. *The Nice Bloke*

Read, Alison
    Antique dealer; works and lives with her guardian uncle Paul Aylmer in the south-coast town of Sealock. *The Lady on my Left*

Reade, Eddie
    Boat owner and smuggler friend of Davy Flannagan. *Mrs Flannagan's Trumpet*

Reade, Mrs
    Wife of Eddie Reade. *Mrs Flannagan's Trumpet*

Redding, Jimmy
    Tall and aggressive Bog's End youth. *The Bondage of Love*

Reilly
    Pupil at Mitchell Road Convent School. *Bill Bailey's Lot*

Remington, Elaine
    Snobbish and proud wife of Joe Remington and mother of Martin Remington; lives at Fell Rise, near Fellburn. Sister to Beatrice Hughes-Burton. *Justice is a Woman*

Remington, Joe
    Third generation owner of Remington Wood Works. Husband of Elaine Remington and father of Martin Remington; lives at Fell Rise, near Fellburn. *Justice is a Woman*

Remington, Martin
    Son of Joe and Elaine Remington; lives at Fell Rise, near Fellburn. *Justice is a Woman*

Remington, Mike
    Invalid, grey-haired father of Joe Remington and David Brooks; lives at Fell Rise, near Fellburn. *Justice is a Woman*

Rice, Dave
    Pit manager employed by Mark Sopwith on his County Durham estate. *Tilly Trotter*

Rice, Mr
    South Shields shipyard worker. *Joe and the Gladiator*

Rice, Mr
    Elderly solicitor and partner to Mr Peeble. *Joe and the Gladiator*

Richards, Clara
    Wife of Dr Joe Richards. *Kate Hannigan*

Richards, Dr Joe
    South Shields general practitioner and husband of Clara Richards. *Kate Hannigan*

Richardson, Mr
Newcastle hospital surgeon treating Donald and Annette Coulson. *The Year of the Virgins*

Rider, Mr
Officer at Fellburn Workhouse. *Our John Willie*

Ridley, Dr John
Moorstone General Practitioner. *The Branded Man*

Ridley, Joe
Skeletal, club-footed mechanic and workmate of Frederick Boyle. *Life and Mary Ann*

Ridley, Maggie
Lover of John George Armstrong. *The Gambling Man*

Ridley, Ned
Black-haired, browned-eyed horse dealer; lives with his grandfather in a Pele tower near Elmholm village. *The Girl*

Ridley, old man
Deaf and almost bald octogenarian grand-father of Ned Ridley; lives in a Pele tower near the Northumberland village of Elmholm. *The Girl*

Riley, Nurse
Irish nurse at East Grinstead's Queen Victoria Hospital. *The Lady on my Left*

Riley, Alex
Work-shy husband of Mona Riley, father to Peter and Betty Riley; lives in Fellburn. *Riley*

Riley, Betty
Daughter of Alex and Mona Riley and sister to Peter Riley; lives in Fellburn. *Riley*

Riley, Charles
Sickly son of Peter and Nyrene Riley. *Riley*

Riley, Dick
Odd job man. *Go Tell It To Mrs Golightly*

Riley, Mona
Small, evil-minded wife of Alex Riley and mother to Peter and Betty Riley. Lives in Fellburn and works as a cleaner to one of the town's professional families. *Riley*

Riley, Nyrene
(née Forbes-Mason) Frosty, enigmatic actress wife of Peter Riley and mother to Charles Riley. Nicknamed "Nonagon" by David Bernice, the owner-manager of the Little Palace Theatre, Fellburn. *Riley*

Riley, Peter
Ambitious and confident actor husband of Nyrene Riley. Son of Alex and Mona Riley and brother to Betty. Lives first in Fellburn and then in a Scottish country house. *Riley*

Riley, Timothy
Man servant employed by Richard Baxton-Powell; lives at the Back Lodge Cottage in the grounds of Towbridge House. *The Tinker's Girl*

Peter Riley

Rington, Tom
Partner in the London publishing house of Houseman and Rington with offices at No 42 Chapman's Yard. *Hamilton*

Rinkton, Percy
Doctor's son and fiancé of Anastasia McCabe. *The Invisible Cord*

Ripley, Jack
South Shields shipyard foreman. *Joe and the Gladiator*

Rippon, David
Athletic father of Esther Blenheim and director of Fellburn's Peamarsh's wholesale chemist. *The Nice Bloke*

Riston, Dilly
Fishwife mother of Maria Briston crippled and stooped with rheumatism. *The Black Velvet Gown*

Robberton, Thomas
Associate of William Smith; nicknamed "Trucker". *Harold*

Roberts, Mrs
Housekeeper to Fred and Louise Beardsley. *Riley*

Robson, Elizabeth
Elderly aunt of Maggie LeMan; and wartime friend of Joseph Jebeau; lives in a cottage just outside Blakemere, near Hereford. *My Beloved Son*

Robson, Joss
Caretaker at Giles Mentor School, Hastings. *Riley*

Robson, Mrs
Wife of Joss Robson, caretaker at Giles Mentor School, Hastings. *Riley*

Robson, Mrs
One-time landlady of No 14 Crane Street, Temple Town in South Shields. *Katie Mulholland*

Robson, Nancy
(née Crawford) Giddy wife of Robert Robson and daughter of John Crawford and sister to Martha Mary, Mildred and Roland Crawford; lives at Morland House, The Habitation, a large and decaying riverside house near Riding Mill, Northumberland. *Miss Martha Mary Crawford*

Robson, Robert
Spirited drover husband of Nancy Robson and son of Samuel Armstrong; lives at Morland House, The Habitation, near Riding Mill, Northumberland. *Miss Martha Mary Crawford*

Rochester, Harvey Clement Lincoln
Handsome coloured barrister and fiancé of Flo Jackson. *The Year of the Virgins*

Rogers
Butler to Lady Menton at The Hall. *Justice is a Woman*

Rosier, Agnes
Wife of George Rosier and mother of Bernard and Roger Rosier and Theresa Noble; lives at Greenwall Manor, County Durham. *Katie Mulholland*

Rosier, Bernard
Arrogant and irascible father of Daniel Rosier. Son of George and Agnes Rosier and brother to Roger Rosier and Theresa Noble. Fiancé of Ann Talford and father of Katie Fraenkels child, Sarah Rosier; lives at Greenwall Manor, County Durham. *Katie Mulholland*

Rosier, Daniel
Husband and half-brother to Sarah Rosier. Son of Bernard Rosier; lives at Greenwall Manor. *Katie Mulholland*

Rosier, Daniel III
American-born great grandson of Katie Fraenkel and grandson of Daniel and Sarah Rosier and heir to Greenwall Manor and the Rosier estate. *Katie Mulholland*

Rosier, George Daniel
Swarthy and grizzle-haired husband of Agnes Rosier and father to Bernard and Roger Rosier and Theresa Noble. County Durham pit owner; the hamlet where his miners live is named Rosier's Village. Lives at Greenwall Manor, County Durham. *Tilly Trotter & Katie Mulholland*

Rosier, Roger Philip
Feminine-featured son of George and Agnes Rosier and brother to Bernard Rosier and Theresa Noble; lives at Greenwall Manor, County Durham. *Katie Mulholland*

Rosier, Sarah
(née Bunting) Wife and half-sister of Daniel Rosier and Nils Fraenkel. Daughter of Katie Fraenkel and Bernard Rossier; step-daughter of Mark Bunting. Adopted by Ann and Rose Chapman and brought up at Dower House, near Bishop Auckland. *Katie Mulholland*

Ross, Ellen
Wife and part-time teacher of County Durham parson George Ross. *Tilly Trotter*

Ross, George
Parson for the County Durham hamlet of Rosier's Village and husband of Ellen Ross. *Tilly Trotter*

Rossiter, Bernard
White-haired uncle to Maurice and Logan Rossiter. *House of Men*

Rossiter, Logan
Solicitor fiancé of Noreen Badcliffe and brother and general factotum to Maurice Rossiter at Tor-Fret House, near Long Framlington, Northumberland. *House of Men*

Rossiter, Maurice Alastair
Embittered polio victim and writer; lives at Tor-Fret House, near Long Framlington, Northumberland. *House of Men*

Rossiter, Stanley
Uncle to Maurice and Logan Rossiter. *House of Men*

Rowan, George
Miner husband of Nellie Rowan and father of Tom Rowan and Maggie and Ann Taggart. *Maggie Rowan*

Rowan, Nellie
Pious Protestant wife of George Rowan and mother of Tom Rowan, Maggie and Ann Taggart. *Maggie Rowan*

Rowan, Tom
Pitman son of George and Nellie Rowan and brother of Ann Taggart and half-brother of Maggie Taggart. Works at the Venus pit, Fellburn. *Maggie Rowan*

Rowland, Lillian
Plump and pretty girlfriend of Richard Baxton-Powell. *The Tinker's Girl*

Rowlandson, Mr
Headmaster of Swandale Preparatory School. *Bill Bailey*

Roystan, Gabriel
Smelting mill clerk father of Hal Roystan. *A Dinner of Herbs*

Roystan, Hal
Son of Gabriel Roystan and childhood friend of Rodney Greenbank. *A Dinner of Herbs*

Ryan, Elsie
Receptionist to Dr Paul Higgins at his Romfield House,
Bog's End, surgery. *The Long Corridor*

Ryan, Peggy
Member of an RAF Gang Show backstage crew. *My Beloved Son*

Ryde-Smithson, Phillipa
Daughter of Steve McGrath. *Tilly Trotter Widowed*

Ryder, Ned
Outside servant employed by Vance and Sarah Overmeer at Balderstone House, County Durham. *The Blind Years*

Sam
Building site labourer. *Mary Ann and Bill*

Samson, Constable
Village policeman. *Go Tell It To Mrs Golightly*

Sandy
An innkeeper. *The Girl*

Sarah
Housemaid employed by James and Janet Allison. *The Year of the Virgins*

Scanlon, Joyce
Salvation Army officer and daughter-in-law of Fanny McBride. *Fanny McBride*

Schoffield, Janice
Daughter of Lettice Lord and schoolfriend of Mary Ann Shaughnessy; lives at The Burrows, Woodlea End, Newcastle. *Life and Mary Ann*

Schoffield, Mr
Bullying and adulterous businessman husband of Lettice Lord and father of Janice Schoffield; lives at The Burrows, Woodlea End, Newcastle. *Life and Mary Ann*

Scott, Doug
Texan ranchhand employed by Matthew Sopwith. *Tilly Trotter Wed*

Seaton, Dave
Village blacksmith. *Go Tell It To Mrs Golightly*

Shaggy
Doctor and friend of Leoline Carter. *Slinky Jane*

Shaleman, Bruce
Son of Pug and Rose Ann Shaleman and brother of Hal Shaleman; lives at Tollet's Ridge Farm beyond Allendale. *The Tinker's Girl*

Shaleman, Hal
Spiteful and vindictive lead miner son of Pug and Rose Ann Shaleman and brother of Bruce Shaleman; lives at Tollet's Ridge Farm, an isolated and run-down sheep farm near the Cumbrian border. *The Tinker's Girl*

Shaleman, Pug
Alcoholic and undersized husband of Rose Ann Shaleman and father to Hal and Bruce Shaleman; lives at Tollet's Ridge Farm, The New Coach Road, Whitfield. *The Tinker's Girl*

Shaleman, Rose Ann
Pinch-nosed bedridden wife of Pug Shaleman and mother of Bruce and Hal Shaleman; lives at Tollet's Ridge Farm, The New Coach Road, Whitfield, an isolated and run-down sheep farm near the Cumbrian border. *The Tinker's Girl*

Shaughnessy, Elizabeth
Dignified wife of Mike Shaughnessy and mother of Mary Ann and Michael Shaugnessy; lives first in the 'attics' at Mulhattan's Hall, No 16 Burton Street, Jarrow, and then on Coffin's Farm, Fellhurst, (later changed to Moor Farm). *A Grand Man, The Lord and Mary Ann, The Devil and Mary Ann, Love and Mary Ann, Life and Mary Ann, Marriage and Mary Ann, Mary Ann's Angels & Mary Ann and Bill*

Shaughnessy, Michael
Only son of Mike and Elizabeth Shaughnessy and younger brother of Mary Ann Shaughnessy. Husband of Sarah Shaughnessy (née Flannagan). *A Grand Man, The Lord and Mary Ann, Love and Mary Ann, Life and Mary Ann & Marriage and Mary Ann*

Shaughnessy, Mike
Alcoholic but jovial husband of Elizabeth Shaughnessy and father of Mary Ann and Michael Shaughnessy; lives first in the 'attics' at Mulhattan's Hall, No 16 Burton Street, Jarrow, and then as a farmhand on Coffin's Farm, Fellhurst, (later changed to Moor Farm). *A Grand Man, The Lord and Mary Ann, The Devil and Mary Ann, Love and Mary Ann, Life and Mary Ann, Marriage and Mary Ann, Mary Ann's Angels & Mary Ann and Bill*

Shaughnessy, Sarah
(née Flannagan) Childhood adversary and later sister-in-law of Mary Ann Shaughnessy; wife of Michael Shaughnessy. *A Grand Man, The Lord and Mary Ann, The Devil and Mary Ann, Love and Mary Ann, Life and Mary Ann & Marriage and Mary Ann*

Shelley, Father Patrick
Catholic priest. *The Solace of Sin*

Shilla, Jane
Sister of Henry Brooker. *The House of Women*

Simpson, Doctor
Small-framed general practitioner with the surgery in Prudhoe Street, near Westoe. *Tilly Trotter Wed*

Singleton, Fred
Business partner of Angus Cotton and co-owner of Cotton and Singleton Haulage Contractors. *The Round Tower*

Skipton, Tessie
Teenager rescued from the workhouse by Matthew Thornton and employed at his Elmholm House as combined housemaid, handmaiden and nursemaid. *The Girl*

Slater, Sidney
Farmhand employed by Edward MacFell at Moor Burn Farm, Northumberland. Served as a sergeant in the Great War with the Durham Light Infantry. Nicknamed "Ginger" because of the colour of his hair. *The Cinder Path*

Smith, Carrie
Daughter of Dick and Jessie Smith and sister to Mick, Florrie, Mary and Charlie Smith and Janet Morgan. *My Beloved Son*

Smith, Charlie
Son of Dick and Jessie Smith and brother to Mick, Florrie, Carrie and Mary Smith and Janet Morgan; employed as a bootblack by Sir Arthur Jebeau. *My Beloved Son*

Smith, Dick
Husband of Jessie Smith and father to Mick, Charlie, Florrie, Carrie and Mary Smith and Janet Morgan; chauffeur and groom employed by Sir Arthur Jebeau at Screehaugh. *My Beloved Son*

Smith, Dr Sheila
Newcastle psychiatrist and hypnotist. *The Bondage of Love*

Smith, Florrie
Promiscuous kitchen maid daughter of Dick and Jessie Smith and sister to Mick, Charlie, and Mary Smith and Janet Morgan. Lover of Martin Jebeau. *My Beloved Son*

Smith, Jessie
Scheming wife of Dick Smith and mother to Mary, Florrie, Carrie, Charlie and Mick Smith and Janet Morgan; employed as a cook by Sir Arthur Jebeau at Screehaugh. *My Beloved Son*

Smith, Joseph Rooney
"Muck Pusher" for South Shields Corporation; lives as a thirty-five shilling a week lodger at No 71 Filbert Terrace, South Shields. Known as "Rooney" to his friends. *Rooney*

Rooney

Smith, Major
Officer commanding Charles MacFell's Durham Light Infantry company. *The Cinder Path*

Smith, Mary
Kitchen maid daughter of Dick and Jessie Smith and sister to Charlie, Florrie, Carrie, Mick Smith and Janet Morgan. *My Beloved Son*

Smith, Mick
Son of Dick and Jessie Smith and brother to Charlie, Mary, Florrie, Carrie Smith and Janet Morgan; employed with the outside staff by Sir Arthur Jebeau at Screehaugh. During the war serves as a flight-sergeant wireless operator with the RAF. *My Beloved Son*

Smith, Rene
School friend of Katie Bailey. *Bill Bailey*

Smith, Sgt
Fellburn police sergeant. *Riley*

Smith, William
Indian-dressed associate of "John Drake"; nicknamed "Bunty". *Harold*

Smollet, Dandy
Workhouse foundling employed as a gardener and stable-lad by the Thornton's at Elmholm House, Elmholm. *The Girl*

Sopwith Anna
(née McGill) Birthmark-disfigured wife of John Sopwith and friend of Matilda Sopwith; lives first at Felton Hall, beyond Fellburn, and then at Highfield Manor, County Durham. *Tilly Trotter Wed & Tilly Trotter Widowed*

Sopwith, Eileen
Hypochondriac, wife of Mark Sopwith. Mother to John, Matthew, and Luke Sopwith and Jessie Ann Cartwright. Harry Sopwith's step-mother. Lives at Highfield Manor at the heart of the Sopwith Estate. *Tilly Trotter*

Sopwith, Harry

Son of Mark Sopwith and step-son of Eileen Sopwith, Half-brother to John, Matthew and Luke Sopwith and Jessie Ann Cartwright; lives at Highfield Manor. Half-brother to William Trotter. *Tilly Trotter*

Sopwith, John

Husband of Anna Sopwith. Youngest son of Mark and Eileen Sopwith and brother of Matthew and Luke Sopwith and Jessie Ann Cartwright and half-brother of Harry Sopwith and William Trotter; lives at Highfield Manor. Speaks with a stutter. *Tilly Trotter, Tilly Trotter Wed & Tilly Trotter Widowed*

Sopwith, Luke

Son of Mark and Eileen Sopwith and brother of John, and Matthew Sopwith and Jessie Ann Cartwright and half-brother of Harry Sopwith and William Trotter; lives at Highfield Manor. *Tilly Trotter & Tilly Trotter Wed*

Sopwith, Mark John Henry

Philanthropic County Durham pit owner and husband of Eileen Sopwith and father to John, Matthew, Harry and Luke Sopwith and Jessie Ann Cartwright and William Trotter; lives at Highfield Manor at the heart of the Sopwith Estate. Lover of Matilda Sopwith. *Tilly Trotter*

Sopwith, Matilda

(née Trotter) Wife of Matthew Sopwith and mother of William Trotter and step-mother to Josefina

Tilly Trotter

Cardenas. One-time housekeeper and mistress of Mark Sopwith. Grand-daughter of William and Annie Trotter. Employed first as nursemaid to Mark and Eileen Sopwith's children at Highfield Manor, then as a miner in the Sopwith pit before returning to the manor as housekeeper. Nicknamed "Tilly". *Tilly Trotter, Tilly Trotter Wed & Tilly Trotter Widowed*

Tilly Trotter—as Mrs Matilda Sopwith—is the only major Catherine Cookson character to cross the Atlantic and live in America.

Tilly Trotter Wed, the second of the trilogy, appeared in January, 1981. Transporting a large part of the action not only out of the North-East of England, but across the Atlantic to 1850s Texas, did give the writer second thoughts.

Catherine studied Sue Flanagan's photographic record Sam Houston's Texas and read T.R. Fehrenbach's Lone Star and Comanches.

In her author's note she confesses: "It wasn't until I was advised to read these books that the audaciousness of my effort opened up before me and I hesitated whether to continue with my story."

Sopwith, Matthew George

Granite-faced husband of Matilda Sopwith and step-father to his half-brother William Trotter; father of Josefina Cardenas. Eldest son of Mark and Eileen Sopwith and brother of John and Luke Sopwith and Jessie Ann Cartwright and half-brother of Harry Sopwith; lives first at Highfield Manor, County Durham, then on a Texan home-stead. *Tilly Trotter & Tilly Trotter Wed*

Spragg, Mamie

Mother of seven children. *Slinky Jane*

St Francis, Mother

Sister of Peter Lord and mother superior of the Convent of the Holy Child of Bethlehem, St Leonard's on Sea. *The Devil and Mary Ann*

Stanford, Arthur
Head librarian at Fellburn Public Library. *The Upstart*

Stanhope, Bert
Short, dumpy mechanic and workmate of Frederick Boyle. *Life and Mary Ann*

Stanhope, Michael
Arrogant painter who employs Rose Angela Paterson as housemaid; lives at Whark House, Cassy's Wharf in South Shields' Mill Dam. *Colour Blind*

Stapleton, Ada
Promiscuous shop assistant daughter of Harry and Millie Stapleton; lives at No 18 Quilter Street, Newcastle. *The Solace of Sin*

Stapleton, Constance
Wife of James Stapleton and mother of Peter Stapleton; lives first in Bickley Street, Newcastle, and then Shekinah Hall, near Hexham. *The Solace of Sin*

Stapleton, Harry
Husband of Millie Stapleton and father of Ada Stapleton. Brother to James Stapleton. *The Solace of Sin*

Stapleton, James
Novelist husband of Constance Stapleton and father of Peter Stapleton; lives in Bickley Street, Newcastle. *The Solace of Sin*

Stapleton, Millie
Wife of Harry Stapleton and mother of Ada Stapleton. *The Solace of Sin*

Stapleton, Peter
Son of James and Constance Stapleton; lives in Bickley Street, Newcastle. *The Solace of Sin*

Steel, Emma
Simpleton employed at Fellburn Workhouse. *Our John Willie*

Stenhouse, Ben
Manager employed at the Bensham & Sons warehouse and wholesale rooms, Newcastle. *The Mallen Litter.*

Stevens, Mr
Chief clerk to Newcastle solicitors Masre, Boulter and Pierce. *The Mallen Streak*

Stevens, Alice
Nagging wife of Tom Stevens and mother of Bridget and Willie Stevens; lives in Cornford Terrace, South Scardyke. *The Bonny Dawn*

Stevens, Bridget
Half-sister to Joe Lloyd; lives with her parents and brother Willie in Cornford Terrace, South Scardyke; known as "Brid" by the family. *The Bonny Dawn*

Stevens, Tom
Lorry driver husband of Alice Stevens and father to Bridget and Willie Stevens; lives in Cornford Terrace, South Scardyke. *The Bonny Dawn*

Stevens, Willie
Son of Tom and Alice Stevens and older brother of Bridget Stevens; lives in the family home in Cornford Terrace, South Scardyke. *The Bonny Dawn*

Stickle, Howard
Pompous and brutal husband of Maisie Leviston and brother of May Stickle; lives in Wellenmore Terrace, Fellburn. Father of Neil Stickle. *Hamilton & Goodbye Hamilton*

Stickle, May
Exuberant neighbour of Maisie Levison and sister of Howard Stickle; lives in Wellenmore Terrace, Fellburn. *Hamilton*

Stickle, Neil
Son of Howard Stickle. *Goodbye Hamilton*

Stillwater, Miss
    Librarian at Fellburn Public Library. *The Upstart*
Stock, Nick
    Above ground horse-keeper at a Hebburn pit; a dour Scot.
    The Nipper
Stoddart, Harold
    Adopted son of Maisie Leviston. Son of James and Maggie
    Stoddart and grandson of Janet Flood. *Goodbye Hamilton* &
    Harold
Stoddart, James
    Husband of Maggie Stoddart and father of Harold
    Stoddart. Nephew of Janet Flood. *Harold*
Stoddart, Maggie
    Blowzy wife of James Stoddart and mother of Harold
    Stoddart. *Harold*
Stoddart, Robert
    Coachman employed by Miss Netherton at Brindle House,
    Fellburn. *The Gillyvors*
Stokes, John
    Editor of the *Daily Reporter*. *The Branded Man*
Streaton, Miss
    Assistant in the Crawford's Hexham bookshop and girl-
    friend of the manager, Lawrence Ducat. *Miss Martha Mary
    Crawford*
Stringer, Rodney
    Baker in the village of Rothcorn, Northumberland. *House
    of Men*
Stubbley, Bill
    "Muck Pusher" for South Shields Corporation and work-
    mate of Joseph Smith. *Rooney*
Styles, Willie
    Teenage friend of Joe Darling and fellow South Shields
    shipyard apprentice. School friend of Matty Doolin. *Joe and
    the Gladiator* & *Matty Doolin*

Summers, Mrs
    Cook employed by Dr Rodney and Stella Prince at Conister
    House, Harton, South Shields. *Kate Hannigan*
Swaine, Lieutenant
    Durham Light Infantry Section commander. *The Cinder
    Path*
Swan, Maggie
    Housekeeper employed by Dr Paul Higgins and Beatrice
    Higgins at Romfield House, Romfield Square, Bog's End.
    The Long Corridor
Swatland, Miss
    Rose Mary and David Boyle's headmistress. *Mary Ann and
    Bill*
Swinburn, Dr John
    Assistant doctor in Dr Rodney Prince's South Shields prac-
    tice; lover of Stella Prince. *Kate Hannigan*
Swinburn, Mr
    Manager of a coal mine near Hebburn. *The Nipper*
Sylvia
    Girlfriend of Philip McBride. *Fanny McBride*
Taggart, Mr
    Prosecution counsel at Newcastle Assizes. *Hamilton*
Taggart, Alan
    Son of Sep and Kitty Taggart and brother of Christopher,
    David, Bert, Fred and twin brother Peter Taggart. *Maggie
    Rowan*
Taggart, Ann
    Wife of David Taggart and daughter of George and Nellie
    Rowan and sister of Tom Rowan and half-sister of Maggie
    Taggart. *Maggie Rowan*
Taggart, Arthur
    Night watchman employed by William Bailey at his
    Brampton Hill, Fellburn, development site. *Bill Bailey*

Taggart, Bert
Son of Sep and Kitty Taggart and brother of Christopher, David, Alan, Fred and Peter Taggart; works at the Venus pit, Fellburn. *Maggie Rowan*

Taggart, Billy
Husband of Mary Taggart and landlord of The Bull inn at Lamesley. *The Moth*

Taggart, Christopher
Hunchbacked husband of Maggie Taggart and father of Stephen Taggart. Son of Sep and Kitty Taggart and brother of David, Bert, Fred, Alan and Peter Taggart. Lives first above his bicycle shop in Bush Street, Fellburn, before becoming a war-time profiteer and moving to Brampton Hill. *Maggie Rowan*

Taggart, David
Husband of Ann Taggart and son of Sep and Kitty Taggart and brother of Christopher, Bert, Fred, Alan and Peter Taggart; works at Fellburn's Venus pit. *Maggie Rowan*

Taggart, Fred
Son of Sep and Kitty Taggart and brother of Christopher, David, Bert, Alan and Peter Taggart. Works as a miner at Fellburn's Phoenix pit. *Maggie Rowan*

Taggart, Jim
Arrogant manual worker employed at Affleck & Tate's Engineering Works, Fellburn. *The Round Tower*

Taggart, Kitty
Jovial and simple wife of Sep Taggart and mother of Christopher, David, Fred, Bert, Alan and Peter Taggart. *Maggie Rowan*

Taggart, Maggie
(née Rowan) Plain-faced and ambitious wife of Christopher Taggart and mother of Stephen Taggart. Daughter of George and Nellie Rowan and half-sister of Tom Rowan and Ann Taggart; works as assistant manageress at Thornton's Laundry, Fellburn. Lives above her husband's bicycle shop in Bush Street, Fellburn, before moving to Brampton Hill. Finally moves to a small house in Pinwinkle Street, near Thornton's Laundry. *Maggie Rowan*

Taggart, Mary
Wife of Billy Taggart and landlady of The Bull inn, Lamesley. *The Moth*

Taggart, Peter
Son of Sep and Kitty Taggart and brother of Christopher, David, Bert, Fred and twin brother Alan. *Maggie Rowan*

Taggart, Sep
Blustering, loud-mouthed pitman husband of Kitty Taggart and father of Christopher, David, Bert, Fred, Alan and Peter Taggart; works at Fellburn's Venus pit. *Maggie Rowan*

Taggert, Ben
Carrier's driver. *The Mallen Streak*

Talbot, Bill
Father of Charlie Talbot. *The Bonny Dawn*

Talbot, Charlie
Son of Bill Talbot and friend of Joe Lloyd. *The Bonny Dawn*

Talbot, Florrie
Blowzy cousin of Harry Bensham. *The Mallen Girl*

Talbot, Mrs
Mother of Charlie Talbot. *The Bonny Dawn*

Talbot, Peter
Quarry worker at Fellburn Workhouse. *Our John Willie*

Talford, Ann
Daughter of James Talford and fiancée of Bernard Rossier. *Katie Mulholland*

Talford, James
Industrialist father of Ann Talford. *Katie Mulholland*

Tallow, Miss
Runs a house-window drapery shop in Battenbun. *Slinky Jane*

Tate, Ivy
Plump, wavy-haired lover of Dr Paul Higgins; lives at Moor Lane, Fellburn. *The Long Corridor*

Taylor, Miss
Secretary to builder Bob Quinton. *Mary Ann's Angels*

Telford, Jeff
A horse drover; a 'decent' man. *The Nipper*

Tellman, Mr
Clerk to Mr Peeble, a South Shields solicitor. *Joe and the Gladiator*

Thompson, Harry
Smallholder and father of John Thompson. *Go Tell It To Mrs Golightly*

Thompson, John
Teenage son of Harry Thompson. *Go Tell It To Mrs Golightly*

Thompson, Lilian
Cook employed by the Crawford family at Morland House, The Habitation, Riding Mill. Known to the household as "Dilly". *Miss Martha Mary Crawford*

Thompson, Miss
Companion to Mrs Ratcliffe. *The Long Corridor*

Thorman, Agnes
Daughter of Reginald and Kate Thorman and sister to Arnold, Roland, and Stanley and half-sister to Millicent Thorman; lives at Foreshaw House on the Thorman estate. Girlfriend of James Crockford. *The Moth*

Thorman, Arnold
Son of Reginald and Kate Thorman and brother to Agnes, Roland and Stanley and half-brother to Millicent Thorman; lives at Foreshaw House on the Thorman estate, near Lamesley. *The Moth*

Thorman, Kate
Wife of Reginald Thorman and mother to Agnes, Arnold, Roland, Millicent and Stanley Thorman; lives at Foreshaw House of the wild and neglected Thorman estate, near Lamesley. *The Moth*

Thorman, Millicent
Simple-minded but harmless illegitimate daughter of Kate Thorman and sister to Agnes, Arnold, Stanley and Roland Thorman; lives at Foreshaw House on the wild and neglected Thorman estate. Known to the family as "Millie". *The Moth*

Thorman, Reginald
Gentleman farmer husband of Kate Thorman and father to Agnes, Arnold, Roland and Stanley Thorman; lives at Forshaw House, on the 2,000-acre Thorman estate, near Lamesley. *The Moth*

Thorman, Roland
Son of Reginald and Kate Thorman and brother to Agnes, Arnold and Stanley and half-brother to Millicent Thorman; lives at Forshaw House, on the wild and neglected Thorman estate. *The Moth*

Thorman, Stanley
Son of Reginald and Kate Thorman and brother to Agnes, Arnold and Roland and half-brother to Millicent Thorman; lives at Forshaw House, on the Thorman estate, near Lamesley. *The Moth*

Thornton, Anne
Tall, pale-skinned wife of Matthew Thornton and mother to four children; lives at Elmholm House, Elmholm, where she employs three servants. *The Girl*

Thornton, Beatrice
Spoilt youngest child of Matthew and Anne Thornton; nicknamed "Betsy" by the family. *The Girl*

Thornton, John
Eldest son of Matthew and Anne Thornton shares his mother's fair hair and round, blue eyes. Takes over as manager of the Elmholm pit after the death of his father. *The Girl*

Thornton, Margaret
Sensitive, grey-eyed and wide-mouthed eldest daughter of Matthew and Anne Thornton. *The Girl*

Thornton, Matthew
Square-faced, grey-eyed lead mine manager; lives at Elmholm House, Elmholm, two-and-a-half miles south of Allendale, Northumberland, with his wife Anne Thornton and their four children. His brief affair with Nancy Boyle produced a daughter, Hannah Boyle. *The Girl*

Thornton, Robert
Stubbornly adventurous second son of Matthew and Anne Thornton. *The Girl*

Thornycroft, Peg
Housemaid and servant employed by the Crawford family at Morland House, The Habitation, Riding Mill, Northumberland. *Miss Martha Mary Crawford*

Threadgill, Ralph
Farmer neighbour of Mary Everton. *Lanky Jones*

Tiffy
Doctor and friend of Leoline Carter. *Slinky Jane*

Tilda
Servant girl employed by Mr and Mrs Bluett at St Helier House. *Rory's Fortune*

Tipple, Insp
Fellburn police inspector. *The Upstart*

Tollett, Maria
Friend of Winifred Coulson. *The Year of the Virgins*

Tollett, Mr
Affluent Brinkburn Street neighbour of the Doolin family. *Matty Doolin*

Tollett, Peter
Septuagenarian wheelwright employed in John Cornwallis's workshop. *Rory's Fortune*

Tollgood
Rustler associate of Billy Combo. *Lanky Jones*

Tony
Brother of Margaret and Marian; lives in the 'attics' of Mulhattan's Hall, off Burton Street, Jarrow, with their guardian Alice Leigh-Petty. *Fanny McBride*

Tony
Teenage lodger living with the McQueen family at No 42 Powell Street, East Jarrow. Works as an assistant in Crawley's grocers shop, Jarrow. *Colour Blind*

Toppin, Maggie
Sparrow-faced Jarrow ladies' toilet attendant. *Fanny McBride*

Trackman, Delia
Wife of the Rev James Trackman. *The Branded Man*

Trackman, Rev James
Minister and husband of Delia Trackman. *The Branded Man*

Travers, Frances
Bulbous circus performer wife of Septimus Travers. *The Whip*

Travers, Septimus
Husband of Frances Travers. Circus owner and proprietor of Travers Travelling Show. *The Whip*

Trenchard, Mrs
Aunt of Lettice Lord. *Life and Mary Ann*

Trotter, Annie
Wife of William Trotter; lives at Rosier's Village, County Durham. *Tilly Trotter*

Trotter, William
Crippled husband of Annie Trotter; lives at Rosier's Village, County Durham. *Tilly Trotter*

Trotter, William
Illegitimate son of Matilda Sopwith and Mark Sopwith and half-brother and step-son to Matthew Sopwith; half-

brother to John, Jessie Ann, Harry, and Luke Sopwith and Josefina Cardenas. *Tilly Trotter Wed & Tilly Trotter Widowed*

Tullett, Johnny
Gateshead-born Army friend of Charles MacFell serving with the Durham Light Infantry. *The Cinder Path*

Tummomd, Annie
Wife of Robert Tummomd; circus fire-eater and a partner in the Flying Tummomds acrobatic act. *The Whip*

Tummomd, Robert
Husband of Annie Tummond and partner in the Flying Tummomds acrobatic act. *The Whip*

Turnbull, James
Invalid wheelwright husband of Nancy Turnbull and father of Matthew Turnbull; lives in the house attached to his Benham, County Durham, workshop. *The Dwelling Place*

Turnbull, Josh
Battenbun farmer. *Slinky Jane*

Turnbull, Matthew
Kindly wheelwright-turned-coffin maker son of James and Nancy Turnbull with a workshop and house in the County Durham village of Benham. *The Dwelling Place*

Turnbull, Nancy
Bitter and scraggy wife of James Turnbull and mother of wheelwright Matthew Turnbull; lives in Benham, County Durham. *The Dwelling Place*

Turnbull, Pamela
Lover and one-time fiancée of Larry Broadhurst. *The Menagerie*

Tyler, Fred
Mechanic digger operator. *Mary Ann and Bill*

Tyler, Mrs
Cook to the Buckham household. *The Gambling Man*

Tyler, Tommy
Fellburn Air Raid Precautions warden and friend of Christine Winter; works as a mechanic. *Fenwick Houses*

Van, Mr
Belgian emigré living in South Shields; nicknamed "Mr Van" because no one could remember his full Flemish name. *Mrs Flannagan's Trumpet*

Vidler, Susan
Acrimonious and overweight mother of Fiona Bailey. *Bill Bailey, Bill Bailey's Lot, Bill Bailey's Daughter & The Bondage of Love*

Wagget, Bill
A widowed Tyne Dock stevedore; lives at No 1 The Cottages, a row of houses in the country above East Jarrow. *The Gambling Man*

Wagget, Gran
Mother of Bill Wagget; lives with her son at No 1 The Cottages. *The Gambling Man*

Wagget, Janie
Seventh and only surviving child of Bill Wagget; lives with her father and grandmother at No 1 The Cottages. Works as nursemaid in the Buckham's household; marries Rory Connor. *The Gambling Man*

Waite, Daisy
Kindly wife of Harry Waite and mother of Jim Waite. *The Mallen Streak*

Waite, Harry
Husband to Daisy Waite and father to Jim Waite. Second footman employed by Richard Mallen at High Banks Hall. Later manager of Wolfbur Farm. *The Mallen Streak*

Waite, Jim
Son of Harry and Daisy Waite; lives at Wolfbur Farm. *The Mallen Girl & The Mallen Litter*

Wallace, Dave
Violent farmer husband of Mollie Wallace and father of Jackie Wallace. *The Obsession*

Wallace, Jackie
Son of Dave and Mollie Wallace. *The Obsession*

Wallace, Mollie
Irritable wife of farmer Dave Wallace and mother of Jackie Wallace. Patient of Dr John Falconer. *The Obsession*

Walsh, Arthur
Brusque farmer and husband of Mona Walsh and father of Jessica Walsh; employs Matty Doolin on his Northumberland farm. *Joe and the Gladiator & Matty Doolin*

Walsh, Jessica
Daughter of Northumberland farmer Arthur and Mona Walsh. *Joe and the Gladiator & Matty Doolin*

Walsh, Mona
Plump, soft-spoken wife of Northumberland farmer Arthur Walsh and mother of Jessica Walsh. *Joe and the Gladiator & Matty Doolin*

Walters, Dr
Newcastle Hospital doctor treating Donald and Annette Coulson. *The Year of the Virgins*

Walton, Dave
Scheming husband of Frances Walton. *The Invitation*

Walton, Frances
Wife of Dave Walton and daughter of Rodney and Maggie Gallacher and sister of Paul, Samuel, Willie and Elizabeth Gallacher. *The Invitation*

Warrington, Bill
Husband of Sally Warrington; lives at Lode Cottage, between Elmholm Creek and Matthew Thornton's mine. *The Girl*

Warrington, Sally
Wife of Bill Warrington; lives at Lode Cottage, between Elmholm Creek and Matthew Thornton's mine. Also one of the pit manager's mistresses. *The Girl*

Waters, Dave
Stableman employed by Reginald Thorman at Forshaw House, near Lamesley. *The Moth*

Watson
Pupil at Mitchell Road Convent School. *Bill Bailey's Lot*

Watson, Jess
Kindly flour mill owner and father of Rose Watson. *The Dwelling Place*

Watson, Rose
Daughter of Jess Watson the Brockdale mill owner. *The Dwelling Place*

Watson, Sep
Cattleman employed by Ralph Batley at Fowler Hall Farm. *Heritage of Folly*

Weaver
Violent enemy of the Rossiter family. *House of Men*

Weeks, Parson
County Durham cleric. *The Black Velvet Gown*

Weir, Mrs
Publican at Surfpoint Bay on the Northumberland coast. *Heritage of Folly*

Wells, Dr
Paediatrician at Fellburn General Hospital. *Bill Bailey's Daughter*

Wentworth, Miss
Inquisitive and snooty southern writer and journalist. *Maggie Rowan*

The majority of Cookson novels contain memories and incidents from her own life. Only once did she base one of her characters on herself.

In 1952 Catherine returned to Tyneside and met her cousins for the first time in almost thirty years. Tempers flared, sparked by a complaint about the high price of coal in the south of England. She did not see why she should have to pay almost £7 a ton for coal in Hastings while those in the North-East were getting it for "next to nothing". Catherine found herself facing four angry miners—and a challenge to descend a pit and discover the real cost of coal.

Her trip down the Betty Pit at Birtley, near Gateshead, lasted three hours. Back in Sussex she abandoned the 40,000 words she had already written of her new novel. She reworked the characters, only this time giving the story a mining background.

In Maggie Rowan, a Miss Wentworth—a "snooty piece" from the south who writes magazine features—arrives in Fellburn and accepts a challenge to descend the Venus Pit. The pages of her underground tour, her questions and the answers she receives are almost a direct transcript of Catherine's own visit. Catherine Cookson is Miss Wentworth.

West, PC
Fellburn police constable. *The Bondage of Love*

Wheatley, Connie
Midwife and herbalist to the gutter-end families of South Shields; mother of Mirabelle Gallagher. Lives at The Towers, South Shields. *The Harrogate Secret*

Wheatley, Mrs
Taunton to London train passenger. *Rory's Fortune*

Whelan, Harry
Estimator and surveyor for Peamarsh's wholesale chemist. *The Nice Bloke*

White, Bill
Gardener employed by Daniel and Winifred Coulson; lives in The Lodge on the Wearcill House estate. *The Year of the Virgins*

White, Miss
Charles Riley's elderly teacher. *Riley*

Wicklow, Peggy
Bog's End hairdresser. *Hamilton*

Wilding, Mrs
Cook to Samuel and Alice Fairbrother. *The Upstart*

Wilkins, Dan
Battenbun baker. *Slinky Jane*

Will
A coachman employed by Charlotte Kean. *The Gambling Man*

Wilson, Jinny
Resident of a tenement block in Crane Street, Temple Town, South Shields, and friend to Katie Fraenkel. *Katie Mulholland*

Wilson, Mr
Assistant manager of a coal mine near Hebburn. *The Nipper*

Wilton, Mr
Assistant general manager at Affleck & Tate's Engineering Works, Fellburn. *The Round Tower*

Winter, Ann
Wife of Bill Winter and mother of Christine and Ronnie Winter; lives at No 6 Fenwick House, Bog's End, Fellburn. *Fenwick Houses*

Winter, Bill
Husband of Ann Winter and father of Christine and Ronnie Winter; lives at No 6 Fenwick Houses, Bog's End, Fellburn. Brother and next door neighbour of Phyllis Dowling. *Fenwick Houses*

Winter, Christine
Mother of Constance Winter. Daughter of Bill and Ann Winter and sister to Ronnie Winter; lives at No 6 Fenwick Houses, Bog's End, Fellburn. Works behind the counter in Turner's Drapery Store, Fellburn. *Fenwick Houses*

Winter, Constance
Illegitimate daughter of Christine Winter and Martin Fonyere; lives at No 6 Fenwick Houses, Bog's End, Fellburn. *Fenwick Houses*

Winter, Jackie
    Stable lad employed by Samuel and Alice Fairbrother. *The Upstart*

Winter, Ronnie
    Pitman son of Bill and Ann Winter and brother to Christine Winter; lives at No 6 Fenwick Houses, Bog's End, Fellburn. *Fenwick Houses*

Winterbottom, Mr
    Pudding-faced, jovial solicitor to Mrs Mason. *The Upstart*

Winters, Jess
    Member of The Fellburn Players. *The Cultured Handmaiden*

Wright, Jos
    Labourer employed by William Bailey. *Bill Bailey's Lot*

Yarrow, Tim
    Workshop assistant and carpenter employed by John Bradley. *The Moth*

Yorkless, Barney
    Husband of Emaralda Yorkless and son of Jake and Dilly Yorkless and brother of Dan and Peter Yorkless and twin brother of Luke Yorkless. *The Whip*

Yorkless, Dan
    Son of Jake and Dilly Yorkless and brother of Pete and twins Luke and Barney Yorkless. *The Whip*

Yorkless, Dilly
    Overbearing wife of Jake Yorkless and mother to Pete and Dan and twins Luke and Barney Yorkless. *The Whip*

Yorkless, Emaralda
    (née Molinero) Wife of Barney Yorkless and daughter of Jose Layaro Molinero. Adopted and brought up as Emma Crawshaw by her grandmother Lizzie Crawshaw in a cottage at Boulder Hill Farm, near Fellburn. *The Whip*

Yorkless, Jake
    Owner of Boulder Hill Farm, near Fellburn, and husband of Dilly Yorkless and father of Pete and Dan Yorkless and twins Barney and Luke Yorkless. *The Whip*

Yorkless, Luke
    Son of Jake and Dilly Yorkless and brother of Dan and Peter Yorkless and twin brother of Barney Yorkless. *The Whip*

Yorkless, Pete
    Son of Jake and Dilly Yorkless and brother of Dan and Peter and twins Barney and Luke Yorkless. *The Whip*

Yvette
    Fred Beardsley's beautiful niece and Peter Riley's lover. *Riley*

"An Out and Out Snob"

THROUGHOUT THE SPRING of 1978 the *Sunday Sun* in Newcastle invited local authors to contribute a short story to its women's page. On 5 March it published an untitled story by Catherine Cookson.

The subject of the story is close to Catherine's heart. Jessica and James McIntyre have been invited to a business party. For fifteen years the Tyneside-born Jessica has struggled to forget her past and lose her Geordie accent. Within minutes of arriving at the party she is recognised by an old friend ... "you haven't changed. I'd have known you anywhere".

The story, little more than a thousand words, was published once. For twenty-one years it remained forgotten until rediscovered in the newspaper archive at Newcastle City Library.

It is reproduced here—with the permission of the Trustees of the Catherine Cookson Charitable Trusts—as a final tribute to one of the world's best loved and best read story tellers.

⋆

"Who's going to be there?"

"I'm not quite sure."

"You're not quite sure? You amaze me. A private dinner party given by the head of your firm and—you're not quite sure."

"Don't keep on, Jessica; I'm worked up enough as it is."

"Here, let me fix that tie. You'd think you were knotting a ship's cable. Are the Remingtons invited?"

"I think so."

"And the Morleys?"

"I don't know. I only know Arnold Talford's coming. He was called in after me. I tell you it came as a surprise; the boss sprung it on us at the last minute."

"The Talfords! Why them? He can't be in the running. And she, talk about until death us do part; you never know what she's coming out with, and you need a brush and shovel to sweep up the h's she drops."

"You know what, Jessica? You're an out-and-out snob, and a bitch into the bargain."

"Put your coat on and straighten your back, you're getting round-shouldered. As for being a snob, my picking and choosing hasn't done you any harm has it? And re the bitch remark. My answer to that is I'm not a hypocrite; lower your standards and where are you? Would you like the Paris office?"

"Would I like it? I don't really know. It means leaving the country. I haven't had time to think about it. I tell you, it was sprung on us, at least on me. Wentworth called me in and in his usual God-like way said "If you're free tonight, McIntyre, I would like you and your wife to come to dinner. That's if you're interested. Monsieur Fonière is here on a brief visit and is looking for a man to take charge of that part of the market. His wife is with him—his second wife, much younger than him I understand, in her late thirties, but I'm told he lays great stock on her judgment.' And he actually smiled at me."

"That seems significant."

"What! Him smiling at me?"

"No. Him saying that about the wife. It was as much to say, if your wife passes, you pass. There was a piece in the paper recently about the importance of executives' wives."

"Executives' wives me foot. He meant nothing of the sort ... it'll have nothing to do with you ..."

"Oh! Nothing to do with me ... Really! Then whatever I say or do doesn't count?"

"I'm not saying that, I'm only saying—warning you, not to play the la ... Aw, forget it."

"That's keeping to the McIntyre pattern, isn't it, forget it? If I'd forgotten it before and hadn't played the lady you'd still be on the shop floor in Shields."

"There're worse places."

"Tell me where?"

"I'd go back the morrow if I could."

"Over my dead body! It's fifteen years since we left and if I live another fifteen it won't see me. Anyway, neither of us has a relative living there now. They all got out an' all—America, Australia, Canada ... Oh if only we could get the chance to go abroad and live among civilised people."

"I thought you considered the South highly civilised. You've almost broken your neck edging your way across the country to get down here ... You're never satisfied."

"No; because what happened? Before the van was hardly unloaded they were at the door. Are you a

Geordie? Which part are you from? Join the Northerners' Club."

"Well, that's what we are, aren't we, Geordies? And I can see nothing to be ashamed of in that. And as I've told you afore ... "

"Before."

"Bloody hell! Before—afore; I'll say it as I've always said it 'cos I was about to inform you yet again you cannot throw off your environment. Those early years stamp you for life. And here's one that's not ashamed of them."

"Well, let me inform you yet again that you can; nobody takes me for a Northerner any more because I've worked at it."

"Aye, time-and-a-half."

"Don't be facetious."

" ... You know something, Jessica? I've been asking meself lately why I've put up with it all these years, being tret like ..."

"Treated ... Now don't you go looking like that ... James, do you hear me? Wait till I get my coat ... James ..."

"Don't call me James, me name's Jimmy."

"You might let me get in before you start the car ... Put your seat belt on."

"To hell's flames with the seat belt!"

"You'll upset me."

"Huh! I'll upset you? That's funny."

"Now don't get into one of those moods."

"Jessica—what say we don't talk for the next half-hour, eh? Just act like we've had a row, eh?"

"Really! ... Turn down here."

"What?"

"I said turn down here."

"Well, there, I've turned. What now?

"Drive to Kathy's."

"Kathy's at this time of the night? She'll be shut. Anyway, what do you want to go to Kathy's for?"

"Not for your favourite point end of brisket; she happens to sell flowers remember? And being Friday night she'll be staying late, getting up orders."

"What do you want flowers for now?"

"Well, just to enlighten you, I was thinking—that was during the time you were brooding on your wrongs—that she has got a passion for flowers, hasn't she, Mrs Wentworth? So it would be a nice gesture and do no harm if I took her some. I don't suppose any of the others will think of it."

"No, I'm sure they won't, Jessica."

"Oh you! Give me some money."

"How much?"

"How do I know how much until I see what I want? I'm not going to take her a bunch of Canterbury bells!"

"What's that?"

"What does it look like? It's a bassket."

"I can see that. Are you taking it to Covent Garden?"

"Why buy a bassket?"

"Because nobody else is likely to think of it."

"You've said it there. How much was it?"

"Seven fifty."

"What! Seven ...?"

"Well, the bassket can be used again, it's got a container inside and a flower holder."

"It should have a bloody seed bed an' all for that."

"There's five cars on the drive—no six, we're late."

"Well, you always like to make an entrance to a full house, don't you? What's the good of looking the part it there's no audience ... Allow me, Madam. What's that you say?"

"I said you were right; there are some people who find it impossible to throw off their environment. the old adage holds, you cannot make a silk purse ..."

"Oh, good evening, Mr Wentworth—Mrs Wentworth."

"How nice to see you, Mrs McIntyre. And this is for me?—No! How beautiful, how unusual."

"Yes, I rather thought so too. It was the bassket that attracted me as much as the flowers."

"Yes, yes, indeed, indeed, most unusual. Come and meet Madam Fonière. Madam, this is ..."

"... No need to tell me, Mrs Wentworth, who this is. Why! I'd've known that voice anywhere. Jessie! Jessie lass, Jessie Suggett. Or what is it now?"

"... M ...McIntyre ... This ... this is my husband ... James."

"How do you do, James. I bet she calls you Jimmy on the quiet, eh? ... Well, fancy meeting you again, Jessie. How many years is it? Eighteen? Nineteen? And you haven't changed I'd've known you anywhere. An' your voice. As soon as you said bassket I knew it was you ...

... Remember when we tried to talk posh? I was always hopeless but you, you were marvellous, except on bassket ... Remember, you could do Newcarstle and boocher, but you could never make it barsket ... Oh Jean, come here; this is a friend of mine from years back, in Shields, you know, the place I've told you about where all the funny things happened. She was right in the thick of it weren't you, Jessie? By! you were a right bassket."

Fellburn

To CATHERINE COOKSON's worldwide readers Fellburn has become more than a fictional Tyneside setting for her latest story. It has become safe and recognisable and familiar. Book by book Catherine Cookson released fascinating pieces of the Fellburn jigsaw. This map attempts to visualise that picture as Catherine imagined it. More than thirty years after she first introduced Fellburn, Catherine admitted the origin of her fictitious North-East town—it was a combination of the Felling area of Gateshead, and Hebburn, west of Jarrow.

Fellburn is a two- sometimes three-dimensional location. Not only is it mentioned in almost thirty of her books, it ranges in timescale from little more than a late 19th century village to a hard-pressed, hard-working 1970s town. And, like the novels in which it features, Fellburn contains every social class and condition from the docks and slums of Bog's End to the rampant snobbery and elitism of Brampton Hill.

A detailed description of the locations appears on the following pages.

1 Christy's all-night café
2 The New Palace Theatre
3 Claremont Terrace
4 No 19 Sweetbank Gardens
5 Prims Restaurant
6 The Little Palace Theatre
7 The Fairbrother House
8 Wearcill House
9 Dale Cottage
10 Assembly Rooms
11 No 24 Ryder's Row
12 Fellburn Central Library
13 Fairbrother's Shoe Shop
14 Fairbrother's Shoe Factory
15 Fellburn Dip Drift
16 Gorge Manor

17 The Cottage
18 Fell Rise
19 The Hall
20 Giles Mentor School
21 No 16 Woodland Avenue
22 The Palace Hotel
23 Mowbray Road Junior School
24 No 14 Rosedale Avenue, River Est.
25 Duck and Drake
26 No 72 Drayburn Avenue
27 Fickleworth Leisure Centre
28 No 45 Brompton Grove West
29 Woodbine Grove
30 Bower Place
31 Pembroke Place
32 Bristol's Club

33 Willow House, Lime Avenue
34 Laburnum Walk
35 Romfield House
36 Farley Court
37 No 7 Wellenmore Terrace
38 Hollytree House, Holt Avenue
39 Peamarsh's Wholesale Chemists
40 No 23 Baker Street
41 Scarfield Mill
42 Venus Pit
43 Bramble House
44 No 48 Beaconsfield Avenue
45 Funnell Cars
46 St Vincent Catholic School
47 No 49 Grosvenor Road

Fellburn Places

1 Christy's all-night café: Situated in the market place a short walk from the Fellburn railway station. *Riley*

2 The New Palace Theatre: In the late 1990s local businesswoman Constance Pickman-Blyth acquired the old town hall buildings and converted part of it to a theatre. *Riley*

3 Claremont Terrace: A street of red-brick, semi-detached houses fronted by a narrow park known as Caymen Gardens. The first choice for Fellburn's professional families. *The Year of the Virgins*

4 No 19 Sweetbanks Gardens: The former Fairbrother home and the house inherited by Janet Fairbrother from her grandmother. *The Upstart*

5 Prims Restaurant: Fellburn's few openly wealthy residents eat and drink at Prims, a smart and expensive town centre restaurant. *Riley*

6 The Little Palace Theatre: Its auditorium lined with mahogany panelling, as was its entrance lobby and stairs, the Little Palace is still family owned and one of Fellburn's oldest institutions. *Riley*

7 The Fairbrother House: With the expansion of Samuel Fairbrother's footwear empire he moved his family out of Sweetbanks Gardens and into a thirty-four-roomed mansion more befitting his new status in life. *The Upstart*

8 Wearcill House: The twenty-eight room mansion stands in six acres of land and is the home of Daniel and Winifred Coulson and their three sons. Behind the main house are stables for eight horses—empty now—and at the bottom of the drive is a lodge where one of the gardeners lives.

9 Dale Cottage: The home of Geraldine Hallberry, boot and shoe magnate Samuel Fairbrother's mistress. *The Upstart*

10 Assembly Rooms: The scene of several dances and celebrations. Mentioned in several books.

11 No 24 Ryder's Row: Surrounded by the incessant clutter and noise of a goods yards, Ryder's Row is the home of Emily Cotton, her daughter Rose and factory worker turned haulage boss son, Angus. *The Round Tower*

12 Fellburn Central Library: The bright and confident Janet Fairbrother works at the Victorian-built library and it is here she rejects a proposal of marriage from head librarian Arthur Stanford. *The Upstart*

13 Fairbrother's Shoe Shop: Samuel Fairbrother's first and still premier shop. It was here he started as a cobbler. *The Upstart*

14 Fairbrother's Shoe Factory: From a single shop Samuel Fairbrother expanded his business to include a factory supplying more than ten outlets across Tyneside and as far south as Middlesbrough. *The Upstart*

15 Fellburn Dip Drift: The abandoned and flooded drift mine from which John Willie Halladay, his brother Davy and miner Bill Cartwright escape after the High Main Pit disaster. *Our John Willie*

16 Gorge Manor: The semi-derelict home of the eccentric but kindly Miss Peamarsh. It is here that Davy Halladay and his deaf and dumb brother, John Willie, find shelter and work and where the body of Richard Peamarsh is found buried in the summer house. *Our John Willie*

17 The Cottage: Built more than two hundred years ago and named Fell Rise after the hill on which it stood, the house was renamed The Cottage by businessman and engineer Mike Remington when he transferred the name to his new home nearby. Now the home of his illegitimate son, David Brooks. *Justice is a Woman*

18 Fell Rise: The hilltop home built for the Remington family in the early 1900s. Now the home of the philanthropic Joe

Remington, the third generation owner of Fellburn's Remington Wood Works. *Justice is a Woman*

19 The Hall: The owner of thousands of Fellburn acres and a no of local pits, Lord Menton is mentioned but never personally appears. His wife Lady Sarah Menton, who lives permanently at The Hall, is a sour-faced and sarcastic woman. *Justice is a Woman*

20 Giles Mentor School: The senior school where Fred and Louise Beardsley are teachers and the school from which Peter Riley leaves to work as an assistant stage manager at The Little Palace Theatre (6). *Riley*

21 No 16 Woodland Avenue: The home of Fiona Nelson and her three children, Mark, Katie and Willie, and where builder Bill Bailey lodges before his marriage to Fiona. *Bill Bailey*

22 The Palace Hotel: Fellburn's only four-star hotel and where Bill and Fiona Bailey held their wedding reception. *Bill Bailey.*

23 Mowbray Road Junior School: The school from which Katie Nelson is kidnapped by a disgruntled labourer employed by her stepfather, Bill Bailey. *Bill Bailey*

24 No 14 Rosedale House, River Estate, Bog's End: Home to Samuel Love and his father. The River Estate replaced many of the Victorian back-to-back terraces built on the banks of the Tyne and the once busy Fellburn docks and shipyards. *Bill Bailey's Lot*

25 Duck and Drake: Named after a farm on which it stands, the Duck and Drake public house is managed by Kit Bradley and is the River Estate local. It is here that Davey Love, one of Bill Bailey's workmen, drinks. *Bill Bailey's Lot*

26 No 72 Drayburn Avenue: The home of vengeful James Brown. *Bill Bailey's Lot*

27 Fickleworth Sports and Leisure Centre, Bog's End: A series of buildings stretching like wings from a central high point and pillared entrance and portico. It is here Willie and

Katie Bailey Nelson and Sammy Love attend weekly sports lessons with Daisy Gallagher. *The Bondage of Love*

28 No 45 Brompton Grove West, Bog's End: Home of Daisy Gallagher and her family. *The Bondage of Love*

29 Woodbine Grove: At the far end of Woodbine Grove and behind Fellburn's Central Library is a woodworking factory. The attached house is where Johnny Hatter and Gertie Polgar run their drug running operation and where Sammy Love is attacked and kidnapped. *The Bondage of Love*

30 Bower Place: In 1949 Jonathan Ratcliffe paid £500 for a two acre plot of land in the better end of Fellburn. He spent another £4,000 building his dream home. By the mid-Sixties Bower Place, where he and his wife Jane lived, was surrounded by sitka trees at the end of a larch lined lane. Petty and jealous, Ratcliffe cannot reconcile himself to the fact that even though he has risen to manage Affleck & Tate's Engineering Works his neighbour, Arthur Brett, who works under him, still owns more land and a bigger house. *The Round Tower*

31 Pembroke Place: Gertie Polgar lived in the respectable Fellburn terrace overlooking Caymen Gardens while running her drug trafficking operation. *The Bondage of Love*

32 Bristol's Club: Fellburn's most exclusive club, complete with a uniformed doorman. *The Bondage of Love*

33 Willow House, Lime Avenue: Ten minutes walk from the centre of Fellburn, and with its gardens backing on to the park is Willow House, the home of barrister George Ferndale and his wife Elsa and their son, Roland. *The Bondage of Love*

34 Laburnum Walk: A dimly lit walk between house gardens where Fellburn barrister's son Roland Ferndale attempts to rape the teenage Katie Bailey. *The Bondage of Love*

35 Romfield House: A Georgian-fronted house overlooking Romfield Square; once on the outskirts of Fellburn, now within Bogs End. The home and surgery of Dr Paul Higgins. *The Long Corridor*

36 Farley Court, Brampton Hill: A one-time gentleman's residence, now converted to four apartments. It is here that Jenny Hoffman lives in a ground floor flat. *The Long Corridor*

37 No 7 Wellenmore Terrace: Birthplace and home of Maisie Rochester before her marriage to the scheming Howard Stickle. When Maisie moves to London to follow her career as a writer and marry Leonard Leviston she allows her stepfather, George Carter, and his new family to move into the house. *Hamilton*

38 Hollytree House, Holt Avenue: The home of Harry and Esther Blenheim. *The Nice Bloke*

39 Peamarsh's Wholesale Chemists: On the first floor, overlooking Broad Street and opposite the chiming clock above Howards the Jewellers, is Harry Blenheim's office. *The Nice Bloke*

40 No 23 Baker Street, Bog's End: The home of Janet Dunn, the Jewish cleaner employed by Harry and Esther Blenheim at Hollytree House in Holt Avenue, and her son Robbie. In just six years Robbie has progressed from a market trader to owning his own antique shop in Fellburn's Pine Street. *The Nice Bloke*

41 Scarfield Mill: In the country three miles beyond Beulah Pit stands Scarfield Mill, a derelict water mill and factory. Robbie Dunn sets about buying and restoring the buildings after moving from his cramped terrace birthplace in Baker Street, Bog's End. It is here he brings Harry Blenheim on his release from prison and where Harry agrees to become a partner in the Dunn's antique business. *The Nice Bloke*

42 Venus Pit: Overlooking Fellburn from the gentle hills each side of the town are two coal mines; the Phoenix mine to the west of the town and the Venus pit to the east. All the men of the Broadhurst family are employed in the Venus pit. It is here that twenty eight face workers including Frank and Jack Broadhurst, are killed by an explosion and Willy Macintyre is injured in a second blast. *The Menagerie*

43 Bramble House: Built in 1913 when Bramble Lane was a country lane, Bramble House was laid out and constructed by Builder Patrick Funnell. His widow Emma Funnell remains the matriarch of the house and the family business which has now diversified into Funnell's garage and showroom (**45**). *The House of Women*

44 No 48 Beaconsfield Avenue: The neat-gardened terraced home of Rosie Milburn, housekeeper and cook at Bramble House, Bramble Lane, Fellburn. *The House of Women*

45 Funnell's Garage and Showroom: The business owned by the Funnell family. *The House of Women*

46 St Vincent Catholic School: On Mitchell Road, opposite Funnell's Garage, is the red brick Victorian convent school attended by Hannah Massey until she was fifteen. In the same enclosure, and backed on the south by Duke's Park, is St Vincent's Catholic Church and Convent. *Hannah Massey*

47 No 49 Grosvenor Road: The houses in Grosvenor Road are large and terraced, old and respectable. Each front garden was enclosed by a wrought iron fence and each front door protected by four stone steps. The steps of No 49, the home of Broderick and Hannah Massey and their eleven children, are made up of red and ochre-coloured tiles. *Hannah Massey*

Mike Ne

A friend v
Catherine
when Cat
friendly w

On the dr
I kept thi
them 'Cat
and arrog

We arrive
ful man w
mine. "M

"Tom!" I

A second

"Catherin
other's ch

In a coup
and "Cath
And there

We had so
with her v
hour and

Tom was
the time,

Mike
chara
Bill B